⟩ 2023 ⟨

HOROSCOPES

365 daily predictions for every zodiac sign

PATSY BENNETT

ROCKPOOL

THE MOON'S PHASES FOR THE YEAR

The moon's phases, including eclipses, new moons and full moons, can all affect your mood. All of these events are explained and listed in the diary, enabling you to plan ahead with the full knowledge you're moving in synchronicity with the sun and the moon. On the following pages are the moon's phases for 2023 both for the southern hemisphere and the northern hemisphere in GMT.

JANUARY

S	M	T	W	T	F	S
1	2	3	4	5	6	7
8	9	10	11	12	13	14
15	16	17	18	19	20	21
22	23	24	25	26	27	28
29	30	31				

FEBRUARY

S	M	T	W	T	F	S
			1	2	3	4
5	6	7	8	9	10	11
12	13	14	15	16	17	18
19	20	21	22	23	24	25
26	27	28				

MARCH

S	M	T	W	T	F	S
			1	2	3	4
5	6	7	8	9	10	11
12	13	14	15	16	17	18
19	20	21	22	23	24	25
26	27	28	29	30	31	

APRIL

S	M	T	W	T	F	S
30						1
2	3	4	5	6	7	8
9	10	11	12	13	14	15
16	17	18	19	20	21	22
23	24	25	26	27	28	29

MAY

S	M	T	W	T	F	S
	1	2	3	4	5	6
7	8	9	10	11	12	13
14	15	16	17	18	19	20
21	22	23	24	25	26	27
28	29	30	31			

JUNE

S	M	T	W	T	F	S
				1	2	3
4	5	6	7	8	9	10
11	12	13	14	15	16	17
18	19	20	21	22	23	24
25	26	27	28	29	30	

2023 SOUTHERN HEMISPHERE MOON PHASES

JULY

S	M	T	W	T	F	S
30	31					1
2	3	4	5	6	7	8
9	10	11	12	13	14	15
16	17	18	19	20	21	22
23	24	25	26	27	28	29

AUGUST

S	M	T	W	T	F	S
		1	2	3	4	5
6	7	8	9	10	11	12
13	14	15	16	17	18	19
20	21	22	23	24	25	26
27	28	29	30	31		

SEPTEMBER

S	M	T	W	T	F	S
					1	2
3	4	5	6	7	8	9
10	11	12	13	14	15	16
17	18	19	20	21	22	23
24	25	26	27	28	29	30

OCTOBER

S	M	T	W	T	F	S
1	2	3	4	5	6	7
8	9	10	11	12	13	14
15	16	17	18	19	20	21
22	23	24	25	26	27	28
29	30	31				

NOVEMBER

S	M	T	W	T	F	S
			1	2	3	4
5	6	7	8	9	10	11
12	13	14	15	16	17	18
19	20	21	22	23	24	25
26	27	28	29	30		

DECEMBER

S	M	T	W	T	F	S
31					1	2
3	4	5	6	7	8	9
10	11	12	13	14	15	16
17	18	19	20	21	22	23
24	25	26	27	28	29	30

○ New moon   ● Full moon

2023 NORTHERN HEMISPHERE MOON PHASES

JANUARY

S	M	T	W	T	F	S
1	2	3	4	5	6	7
●	●	●	●	●	●	●
8	9	10	11	12	13	14
●	●	●	●	◐	◐	◐
15	16	17	18	19	20	21
◐	◐	◐	☽	☽	☽	○
22	23	24	25	26	27	28
☽	☽	☽	☽	☽	◑	◑
29	30	31				
●	●	●				

FEBRUARY

S	M	T	W	T	F	S
			1	2	3	4
			●	●	●	◐
5	6	7	8	9	10	11
●	●	●	●	●	◐	◐
12	13	14	15	16	17	18
◐	◐	◐	☽	☽	☽	☽
19	20	21	22	23	24	25
☽	○	☽	☽	☽	◑	◑
26	27	28				
◑	◑	●				

MARCH

S	M	T	W	T	F	S
			1	2	3	4
			●	●	●	●
5	6	7	8	9	10	11
●	●	●	●	●	●	●
12	13	14	15	16	17	18
◐	◐	◐	☽	☽	☽	☽
19	20	21	22	23	24	25
☽	☽	○	☽	☽	☽	☽
26	27	28	29	30	31	
◑	◑	◑	●	●	●	

APRIL

S	M	T	W	T	F	S
30						1
●						●
2	3	4	5	6	7	8
●	●	●	●	●	●	●
9	10	11	12	13	14	15
●	●	●	◐	◐	◐	☽
16	17	18	19	20	21	22
☽	☽	☽	☽	○	☽	☽
23	24	25	26	27	28	29
☽	☽	◑	◑	◑	●	●

MAY

S	M	T	W	T	F	S
	1	2	3	4	5	6
	●	●	●	●	●	●
7	8	9	10	11	12	13
●	●	●	●	◐	◐	☽
14	15	16	17	18	19	20
☽	☽	☽	☽	☽	○	☽
21	22	23	24	25	26	27
☽	☽	☽	☽	◑	◑	◑
28	29	30	31			
●	●	●	●			

JUNE

S	M	T	W	T	F	S
				1	2	3
				●	●	●
4	5	6	7	8	9	10
●	●	●	●	●	●	◐
11	12	13	14	15	16	17
◐	◐	☽	☽	☽	☽	☽
18	19	20	21	22	23	24
○	☽	☽	☽	☽	☽	◑
25	26	27	28	29	30	
◑	◑	◑	●	●	●	

2023 NORTHERN HEMISPHERE MOON PHASES

JULY

S	M	T	W	T	F	S
30	31					1
2	3	4	5	6	7	8
9	10	11	12	13	14	15
16	17	18	19	20	21	22
23	24	25	26	27	28	29

AUGUST

S	M	T	W	T	F	S
		1	2	3	4	5
6	7	8	9	10	11	12
13	14	15	16	17	18	19
20	21	22	23	24	25	26
27	28	29	30	31		

SEPTEMBER

S	M	T	W	T	F	S
					1	2
3	4	5	6	7	8	9
10	11	12	13	14	15	16
17	18	19	20	21	22	23
24	25	26	27	28	29	30

OCTOBER

S	M	T	W	T	F	S
1	2	3	4	5	6	7
8	9	10	11	12	13	14
15	16	17	18	19	20	21
22	23	24	25	26	27	28
29	30	31				

NOVEMBER

S	M	T	W	T	F	S
			1	2	3	4
5	6	7	8	9	10	11
12	13	14	15	16	17	18
19	20	21	22	23	24	25
26	27	28	29	30		

DECEMBER

S	M	T	W	T	F	S
31					1	2
3	4	5	6	7	8	9
10	11	12	13	14	15	16
17	18	19	20	21	22	23
24	25	26	27	28	29	30

○ New moon ● Full moon

Patsy Bennett is a rare combination of astrooger and psychic medium. She contributes horoscopes to magazines both in Australia and internationally and has appeared on several live daytime TV and radio shows. She is a speaker, provides astrology and psychic consultations and holds astrology and psychic development workshops in Byron Bay, Australia, where she lives.

Patsy runs www.astrocast.com.au, www.patsybennett.com, facebook@patsybennettpsychicastrology and instagram @patsybennettastrology

FURTHER INFORMATION

Find out your moon sign and ascendant sign at www.astrocast.com.au. For an in-depth personal astrology chart reading contact Patsy Bennett at patsybennettastrology@gmail.com
Further astronomical data can be obtained from the following:

- Michelsen, Neil F. and Pottenger, Rique, *The American Ephemeris for the 21st Century 2000–2050 at Midnight*, ACS Publications, 1997.
- The computer program Solar Fire from Esoteric Technologies Pty Ltd.

A Rockpool book
PO Box 252
Summer Hill
NSW 2130
Australia

rockpoolpublishing.com
Follow us! f ⊙ rockpoolpublishing
Tag your images with #rockpoolpublishing

Published in 2022 by Rockpool Publishing
Copyright text © Patsy Bennett 2022
Copyright design © Rockpool Publishing 2022

ISBN 9781922579669

Design by Sara Lindberg, Rockpool Publishing
Edited by Lisa Macken
Illustrations by Shutterstock

Printed and bound in China
10 9 8 7 6 5 4 3 2 1

All dates are set to Greenwich Mean Time (GMT). Astrological interpretations take into account all aspects and the sign the sun and planets are in on each day and are not taken out of context.

CONTENTS

INTRODUCTION

Make 2023 your best year yet! Start the year with clarity, clearly seeing your amazing year ahead for love, luck, loot and lifestyle. We all consult our horoscopes, but what we really want to know is how best to plan ahead for ourselves personally. Astrology is the study of the movement of celestial objects and their impact on us here on earth, but we need to know what that means on an individual level according to our own sun sign.

The key in 2023 is to be innovative and to look outside the box, and above all to be proactive. This guide doesn't just show you when good things will happen to you; it also shows you how to view positive astrological days as opportunities to initiate new ideas, organise wonderful events in your life and see challenging days as days to excel, to draw on your inner reserves and find success by overcoming obstacles. Your greatest achievements will often occur when you overcome hurdles and allow your inner hero to rise to the challenge.

In *2023 Horoscopes* you'll find insight into your own strengths and weaknesses and into your particular way to move ahead throughout the year. Success is all in the timing and in knowing what to do with your own strengths in mind, and there's no better time than the present to consult your individual guide to success in 2023. Embrace your star power, starting now!

Astrology is not a phenomenon that happens to you: you need to take action. For example, when the sun passes through Leo from 22 July to 23 August Leos will tend to feel revitalised, energised and motivated, so this is the time to get things rolling. For Scorpios this phase may not be the same; there will be more focus on career, direction and hard work as opposed to simply feeling energised. *2023 Horoscopes* will provide invaluable direction to help you find your best-case scenario during various phases of the year and know the pitfalls to avoid.

MERCURY AND VENUS RETROGRADE PERIODS IN 2023

The dates listed in this section indicate when both Mercury and Venus will be retrograde in 2023. A planet is termed 'retrograde' when it appears to be going backwards around the sun from our point of view on earth. Of course, no planet actually goes retrograde – it's an optical illusion – but these phases do exhibit certain characteristics.

During the Mercury retrograde phase communications can tend to be a little more difficult than during the direct phase, when the planet has a forward motion. Travel may be delayed or cancelled. However, the Mercury retrograde phase can be an excellent time for reviewing your circumstances, for reassessing where you are in life and for reorganising your various duties. Plan to take a slightly slower line in life such as a holiday, and don't expect communications to be perfect.

During the Venus retrograde phase you might find that relationships are less likely to forge ahead in blue skies, and that when a Venus retrograde phase coincides with a Mercury retrograde phase communications may be complex or easily predisposed to arguments. The plus side is that Venus retrograde phases provide an ideal time to take things a little more slowly, to be less demanding on yourself and others within your relationships and practise compassion and kindness. Patience is truly a virtue during the Mercury and Venus retrograde periods.

Mercury retrograde phases in 2023:
1 January to 18 January
21 April to 15 May
23 August to 15 September
13 December to 31 December

Venus retrograde phase in 2023:
23 July to 4 September

ARIES

20 March – 20 April

FINANCES

Uranus continues to transit your second house of finances in 2023, bringing changes that will on occasion be unexpected and potentially even out of the ordinary. On the plus side, this will offer you the chance to make considerable alterations to your investments and the way you balance the books. Jupiter in your money house from mid-May will also potentially buffer your finances but you may be inclined to overspend and even to lean towards extravagance, so ensure you put in place a foolproof budget in 2023.

HEALTH

Chiron in your sign all year will contribute to the need to look after yourself and avoid overwork, especially in the stressful times during March and October, which are the eclipse seasons that will be particularly potent for you this year. Forgetfulness could be a bit of a bugbear for you in 2023, so it's the perfect time to invest in finding ways to be more focused. You will also be drawn to deepen your spirituality and your understanding of the way gratitude and karma work in your life.

LOVE LIFE

Be prepared for a fresh phase in your personal life. This year's eclipses signal it is all change for you, especially if you were born at the end of March or after mid-April. The full moon on 6 April and the solar eclipse on 20 April will be significant, especially if it's your birthday on or around either date, as a new beginning will appeal. If you're single, this is the year to make a change in your status if you wish. Couples will also find the need, especially after mid-July, to discover more meaning and purpose in life, so if you feel you've grown distant from a partner this may be the year you finally go your separate ways.

CAREER

The end of March to mid-June will bring about the chance to alter your direction career-wise and also your status, bringing additional changes to your financial situation. Look out for wonderful opportunities to develop your career and status, and you may even surprise yourself with the kinds of progress you make and the new avenues you enter. The second quarter of the year will involve the main developments, and in May you mustn't let the chance to revolutionise both your career and finances pass you by. With Jupiter in your sign until May, 2023 really is the year to start something new, so be optimistic and positive.

HOME LIFE

As Pluto brings changes in your status and career so, too, will you experience developments at home. Mars through your fourth house of domesticity from the end of March will bring a need to feather your nest, so you can complete a great deal of work at home through until the end of May. Venus joining Mars there during May will bring the chance to renovate, improve or beautify your home, which you'll enjoy. Changes at home may, however, be bittersweet because you will need to factor in how others feel about the changes you wish to make. Diplomacy will be your key to success.

January

1 JANUARY

You'll enjoy a sociable start to the year, so even if you're missing someone you will not be alone.

2 JANUARY

You'll enjoy a reunion or a return to an old haunt. If you feel vulnerable or tired, ensure you maintain perspective.

3 JANUARY

It's a good day to meet a fresh group of people and try something new.

4 JANUARY

This is another good day for a reunion. It is also a good time for a health or beauty treat.

5 JANUARY

You'll enjoy a fresh environment or unexpectedly hearing from someone whose company you enjoy. Your workplace and your career may entail a surprise.

6 JANUARY

The Cancer full moon falls in your domestic zone, signalling changes at home or with family. Some Aries may turn a corner at work.

7 JANUARY

You may receive important news in relation to your status and plans. Be prepared to be spontaneous and optimistic.

8 JANUARY

This is a good day to take the initiative with work and personal plans. You may be surprised by events.

9 JANUARY

This is a good day for meetings at work and socially. Romance could flourish.

10 JANUARY

The more focused you are at work and regarding health matters the better for you. Just avoid being super critical of yourself and others.

11 JANUARY

This is a good day for a health check and also a good day to take communications carefully to avoid mix-ups. Traffic may be delayed.

12 JANUARY

You may receive significant financial or personal news. It's a good day to plan carefully within these two areas of your life.

13 JANUARY

You may receive good news at work. It's an ideal day for a reunion and a beauty or health check.

14 JANUARY

Your projects and chores are likely to go well. An authority figure or friend could be super helpful, so you should reach out.

15 JANUARY

The more tactful you can be the better, as some plans may alter at short notice. Avoid taking developments personally.

16 JANUARY

You are a passionate person and like to get things done. Someone may feel sensitive, so tread lightly.

17 JANUARY

This is a good day to be careful with communications to avoid hurting someone's feelings. Avoid overspending and impulsiveness.

18 JANUARY

You may receive unexpected or intense news to do with work, finances or your general status. A friend or organisation may be helpful.

19 JANUARY

Be practical, as you could make great strides with your favourite interests and projects.

20 JANUARY

You're likely to feel more outgoing and upbeat about meeting new people and trying new activities. Enjoy.

21 JANUARY

The new moon in Aquarius will present fresh people to meet and places to go. This is a good time to make a wish. You'll enjoy romance.

22 JANUARY

This is a good day to make a commitment to a person or a plan. You'll enjoy a reunion or a return to an old haunt.

23 JANUARY

The Pisces moon will bring out your sense of idealism over the next two days, so be sure to be realistic and also practical.

24 JANUARY

You are inspired and could formulate new and exciting plans. Just avoid allowing your imagination to run away with you.

25 JANUARY

This is a lovely day for get-togethers and meetings, both in your personal life and at work.

26 JANUARY

The moon in Aries will encourage you to be proactive but you must avoid appearing bossy.

27 JANUARY

This is a good day for health and beauty appointments. You must avoid misunderstandings and minor accidents.

28 JANUARY

You'll enjoy a favourite activity or interest and feeling more spontaneous. Just be careful with communications.

29 JANUARY

Take the time to enjoy a lovely venture or meeting, but you must avoid obstinacy either in yourself or others.

30 JANUARY

There is a productive and proactive atmosphere around and you can achieve a great deal. You may receive unexpected news.

31 JANUARY

A reunion or meeting will be enjoyable. This is also a good day for work and improving health.

February

1 FEBRUARY

This is a lovely day to boost your self-worth, health and well-being. You may enjoy a meeting with a teacher or a healer.

2 FEBRUARY

The moon in Cancer is excellent for getting in touch with your true feelings. You may even feel a little bit psychic and will gain insight into a personal matter.

3 FEBRUARY

You have deeper insight than usual but may feel a little more sensitive. Avoid taking people's random comments personally.

4 FEBRUARY

You may experience an unexpected development, so be sure to be spontaneous and avoid taking circumstances personally.

5 FEBRUARY

The full moon in Leo will magnify your feelings, especially concerning an uncertain situation. Avoid being impulsive and find ways to carefully manage your finances.

6 FEBRUARY

There is a romantic aspect to the day. You will enjoy a reunion either at work or socially but must avoid being forgetful and absent-minded.

7 FEBRUARY

Certain matters will deserve careful attention to detail such as work and finances. Just avoid being hypercritical of yourself and others.

8 FEBRUARY

You may hear unexpected news. This is a good day to be inspired at work. You will enjoy a reunion.

9 FEBRUARY

This is a good day for being practical and down to earth, especially at work and with groups, friends and organisations. You could make a valid commitment.

10 FEBRUARY

Meetings and discussions will be intense but you could bring about a positive development at work or regarding your status.

11 FEBRUARY

You'll enjoy a change of pace and socialising will appeal. Just avoid being at loggerheads with someone you find difficult.

12 FEBRUARY

This is another lovely day for socialising and reunions. However, the moon in Scorpio will bring out strong emotions so be careful.

13 FEBRUARY

You have a natural empathy with people at the moment so be guided by your intuition. Just avoid conflict with those you disagree with. Be practical.

14 FEBRUARY

Happy St Valentine's Day! Today and tomorrow are ideal for romance, so go ahead and make some plans.

15 FEBRUARY

You'll enjoy indulging in the arts and a little luxury but you must avoid overindulgence in bad habits. You may be a little forgetful, so avoid mishaps.

16 FEBRUARY

It's a good day to get work done and for clearing chores. You may need to be a little tactful with some conversations, however, to avoid hurt feelings.

17 FEBRUARY

Today's moon in Capricorn is ideal for getting things done so be proactive. If you have been feeling vulnerable, find ways to boost your self-esteem.

18 FEBRUARY

This is an excellent day for housework and gardening and also for focusing on your self-development. Exercise, romance and the arts will appeal.

19 FEBRUARY

You will appreciate the opportunity to meet someone in a position of authority or power and to improve your relationship. It's a good day for romance, music and the arts.

20 FEBRUARY

The new moon in Pisces will inspire you to bring more romance, beauty and love into your life. You may be drawn to a reunion; just avoid misunderstandings.

21 FEBRUARY

Be prepared to look at circumstances from a fresh perspective. Avoid mix-ups and traffic delays.

22 FEBRUARY

This is a better day for communication. Be prepared to take the initiative with a financial or social situation.

23 FEBRUARY

The moon in Aries will help you to get things done, so be positive and take the initiative both at work and with your health and personal life.

24 FEBRUARY

You'll enjoy meeting someone close. You may meet someone new who seems strangely familiar. This is a good day for a reunion.

25 FEBRUARY

You may find yourself in a new or different circumstance. This is a good day to be practical. Romance could blossom.

26 FEBRUARY

As the day goes by you'll feel a little more communicative and that people understand you better as a result.

27 FEBRUARY

This is a good day for meetings and discussions. It's also a good day for health and beauty appointments.

28 FEBRUARY

You'll enjoy being upbeat and initiating get-togethers. However, there may be some delays and misunderstandings so take things one step at a time.

March

1 MARCH

This is a good time for self-development and for boosting your health. Trust your intuition.

2 MARCH

You are likely to meet someone special; this may be related to health, well-being or work. Avoid overspending.

3 MARCH

This is another good day for a health consultation and for self-improvement. You may hear important work or health news and will enjoy a reunion.

4 MARCH

The Leo moon will contribute to an upbeat feeling and you'll enjoy meeting family and friends. Romance could flourish.

5 MARCH

You will enjoy an unexpected meeting or event – that is, unless you dislike surprises!

6 MARCH

News from your past or to do with work will be encouraging. Be prepared to be spontaneous but avoid making rash decisions.

7 MARCH

The full moon in Virgo signifies a fresh chapter either at work or in your health and daily routine, so be prepared for something new.

8 MARCH

Attention to detail is required, so be prepared to work hard to achieve your goals. You may be required to be a peacemaker later in the day.

9 MARCH

This is a good day to strive for balance and harmony in your daily and work routines. You may need someone's help or someone may ask you for help.

10 MARCH

You'll enjoy a meeting, and if your health has been on your mind this is a good day for an appointment. You will experience a trip down memory lane.

11 MARCH

Key discussions will merit an open mind; be prepared to be spontaneous. You will need facts to avoid making mistakes. It's a good day to boost your health.

12 MARCH

Health is a theme now and you may need to help someone or ask for help yourself. It's a good time to learn something new.

13 MARCH

Be adventurous and outgoing, as your optimism will be greatly appreciated.

14 MARCH

It is very important to have the correct information. Be open-minded but base your decisions on facts.

15 MARCH

You have a tendency to be super idealistic now and you may get a reality check. Be practical.

16 MARCH

You may discover that mistakes have been made, which will provide an opportunity to correct them. Avoid the resumption of a bad habit.

17 MARCH

Important news will arrive and a secret may be revealed. Be proactive but avoid stirring up conflict. You may enjoy a reunion.

18 MARCH

This is a good time to be practical with money and work. Be adventurous but avoid unpredictable people if possible.

19 MARCH

You will love the way some relationships blossom, yet others may be difficult. Luckily your communication skills will help you move through this phase.

20 MARCH

You may be surprised by the news you receive. You may hear from an old friend. It's a good day for a reunion or a trip down memory lane.

21 MARCH

The new moon will be in your sign so this is an excellent time to begin a new project. You may also be drawn to begin a new health or work routine.

22 MARCH

When the moon is in your own sign you tend to feel more positive, but you may also feel a little restless. It's a good day to avoid appearing bossy.

23 MARCH

This is a good time to find ways to adjust to circumstances. You may be drawn to joining new groups and socialising with a new circle.

24 MARCH

This is an ideal day to invest in good communication skills, especially in situations you find frustrating.

25 MARCH

Trust your intuition over the coming days and weeks; it is likely to be stronger than usual. This is another day to be careful with communications.

26 MARCH

This is a good weekend for health and beauty appointments. You may hear unexpected news or bump into an old friend.

27 MARCH

You will enjoy a reunion or a trip down memory lane. There is a therapeutic atmosphere around that is ideal for healthy activities.

28 MARCH

A key talk, trip or important news will arise. Some Aries will undertake key financial transactions.

29 MARCH

Trust your instincts. You may feel a little more sensitive than usual, so take things one step at a time.

30 MARCH

You're likely to receive unexpected news or bump into an old friend. Meetings and talks should go well; just avoid taking things personally.

31 MARCH

When the moon is in Leo you like to be more outgoing and upbeat and appear more assertive and positive. This is a good time to enjoy company.

April

1 APRIL

This romantic time is ideal for reunions and enjoying the arts and music. Just avoid romanticising life; be realistic also.

2 APRIL

This is another lovely day for get-togethers and meetings. If you are shopping you will find beautiful things. Just avoid overspending.

3 APRIL

Work and your chores will demand your attention and you can be productive. Just avoid a battle of words and be patient.

4 APRIL

This can be another productive day, so take the initiative with work and chores. However, you must again be patient with communications.

5 APRIL

An important meeting or news will command your full attention. This is a good day for health and beauty appointments. Someone may need your help.

6 APRIL

The full moon in Libra means you are turning a corner in a personal or business relationship. Avoid taking matters personally and look for balance.

7 APRIL

You will enjoy a fun surprise or meeting. This is a lovely time for romance. You may receive a compliment or financial boost.

8 APRIL

This is a lovely day to focus on your family and home. You may equally be drawn to travelling and to visiting a lovely place or person.

9 APRIL

You will enjoy being creative and spending time with like-minded people. It's also a good day for domestic improvements such as do-it-yourself projects.

10 APRIL

As a proactive person your approach can sometimes be seen as bossy. Take a moment to be diplomatic to avoid appearing heavy handed.

11 APRIL

This is likely to be a fun day. You may receive a compliment or financial boost. If the opposite occurs don't take it personally.

12 APRIL

This will be a busy, productive day. You can achieve a great deal. Be positive.

13 APRIL

Be practical and you will achieve your goals even if you seem to be working against the odds. Be optimistic.

14 APRIL

You often achieve your greatest success when you work the hardest. A current challenge will be overcome. It's a good time to sort out your finances.

15 APRIL

This is a good time to develop your communication skills as you are likely to meet people from many different walks of life.

16 APRIL

This is a lovely day for relaxation, romance and the arts, so be sure to organise a treat.

17 APRIL

You will feel more intuitive and in tune with others, so be sure to trust your instincts.

18 APRIL

The moon in Aries for the next two days will be motivational and you can achieve a great deal if you focus on your goals.

19 APRIL

Your sensitivities and vulnerabilities may surface, so be sure to be practical. You may be asked for help and may need advice yourself, which will be available.

20 APRIL

The total solar eclipse in Aries signals the end of a long chapter in your life. Be kind to yourself. Avoid arguments, as they will escalate.

21 APRIL

You may receive key news. Try to get important paperwork finalised if you don't wish to review it over the coming weeks.

22 APRIL

Communications and finances are likely to take your focus. You may be drawn to going shopping. Some household matters may need repair.

23 APRIL

This is a good day to check your financial situation. You'll enjoy a reunion or domestic get-together.

24 APRIL

This is an excellent day for meetings and communications, especially if you must review paperwork or agreements.

25 APRIL

This is a good day to make work agreements. You will enjoy a reunion.

26 APRIL

Be bold; you are communicating well even if you feel you are in a difficult situation.

27 APRIL

You may receive unexpected news or will bump into a friend. You may also receive an unexpected compliment or financial boost.

28 APRIL

You can achieve a great deal but your abilities may threaten others. Do not dim your light; be diplomatic instead.

29 APRIL

This is an excellent day for get-togethers at home or at someone else's house. It's also a good time for talks with family and for do-it-yourself projects. Just avoid minor accidents.

30 APRIL

You will enjoy getting things done at home and if you are working. Gardening and being in nature will appeal, as well as a healthy treat.

May

1 MAY

You may begin to see a friend or organisation in a new light. A meeting or news will clarify matters over the next two days.

2 MAY

Key news or a get-together will encourage you to reassess circumstances. This is a romantic time, so make a date!

3 MAY

You will not always agree with everyone, but as the day progresses you may find communications are a little easier.

4 MAY

Plan ahead to avoid delays and be clear to avoid misunderstandings. You like life to be straightforward and transparent, so when a mystery or complex situation arises it can be frustrating.

5 MAY

The full moon and lunar eclipse in Scorpio will be an intense one. Some talks may become exaggerated or even overblown. This is a romantic time but also very intense.

6 MAY

You will appreciate the opportunity to blow off some steam this weekend. Sports and your favourite activities will appeal.

7 MAY

You will appreciate the chance to focus on yourself or your home and family; however, some communications may be intense so take things one step at a time.

8 MAY

You will feel uplifted by engaging in pastimes you enjoy, so be sure to organise something you love.

9 MAY

You may receive a surprise, so be ready to think on your feet.

10 MAY

You will appreciate a more down-to-earth feeling around you that will help you to make informed decisions and get things done.

11 MAY

Be prepared to think outside the square. A friend or someone in a group or organisation may behave unpredictably.

12 MAY

This is a good day for work and health and also for making financial commitments.

13 MAY

This is another good day for reviewing finances and making commitments, especially those that concern your long-term outlook.

14 MAY

You will be feeling inspired and so will be drawn to the arts, music and spiritual development. You will enjoy relaxing.

15 MAY

News from your past will have a bearing on your present, especially your domestic life. It's a good day for home improvements.

16 MAY

As Jupiter enters Taurus your focus is likely to be drawn to financial planning and the need to be careful with investments.

17 MAY

You will be drawn to enjoying good food and good company.

18 MAY

This may be an intense day. Be prepared to reason with a group, organisation or family member for the best outcome.

19 MAY

The Taurus new moon signals that you are beginning a fresh chapter. You may be ready to make a key commitment. For some this will be financial in nature.

20 MAY

You will enjoy feeling a little freer in your movements. A lovely connection with someone special will be uplifting.

21 MAY

You'll enjoy socialising. However, some interactions may be intense so you must avoid arguments. You may be inclined to overspend at the shops.

22 MAY

There is an uplifting quality to the day. If you have the day off you'll enjoy investing in yourself and your home. Avoid arguments.

23 MAY

This is another good day to invest in yourself and your home and family, but you must avoid arguments as they will escalate.

24 MAY

You are generally known for being proactive and outgoing. Your sensitive character is lesser known, so look after yourself for this reason. Ask for help if it's needed.

25 MAY

You may feel more self-assured but must avoid appearing heavy handed, especially if arguments have been rife.

26 MAY

You may receive an unexpected visitor or will be spontaneous about your activities. You could receive good news.

27 MAY

This is a good weekend to mend bridges if necessary, even if you feel some areas are still not fair or equal.

28 MAY

This is a good day to review your finances, especially if you've been going into debt. Just avoid making arrangements that are too limiting.

29 MAY

This will be a good start to the week as you will be productive. Avoid being idealistic about what can be achieved in one day.

30 MAY

You'll appreciate the sense that some level of balance can be restored in your daily life, so take the initiative.

31 MAY

You may be asked for help and may need to ask for help yourself. It will be available.

June

1 JUNE

You like to see quick results for your hard work so you must avoid feeling frustrated if things go too slowly for you.

2 JUNE

You will enjoy a lovely get-together, but if things have been rocky avoid rocking the boat.

3 JUNE

The lead-up to the full moon is a passionate and intense time you'll enjoy if things have been going well. If not, you must avoid making incendiary remarks.

4 JUNE

The full moon signals a new chapter in a key agreement or relationship. You may be surprised by news.

5 JUNE

This is another intense or passionate day. Be prepared to be adventurous but also tactful.

6 JUNE

You will appreciate a more grounded and earthy feel to the day, especially if things have been dramatic. Be practical for the best results.

7 JUNE

This is a proactive day and you can achieve a great deal with your projects. Just avoid arguments as they will escalate.

8 JUNE

You'll enjoy doing something new and meeting different sets of people. Someone may be unpredictable but don't take this personally.

9 JUNE

This is a good day for a reunion and for romance and the arts. You may hear from an old friend and will enjoy the opportunity for some self-development or spiritual endeavour.

10 JUNE

You will gain insight into someone close and may understand them a little better. This is a good weekend for relaxing.

11 JUNE

A reunion or news from the past will be enlightening. You may enjoy a social event or trip.

12 JUNE

This is a proactive start to the week. You will gain the opportunity to enjoy your activities.

13 JUNE

You can achieve a great deal but may discover that not everyone is on the same page as you, so be patient and find some common ground.

14 JUNE

This is a good day to be more practical about your plans, especially those that concern others.

15 JUNE

You have high hopes, and a beneficial outcome for your projects relies on good communication skills. Be prepared to negotiate and avoid traffic delays and mix-ups.

16 JUNE

A financial matter is best approached carefully. Avoid gambling.

17 JUNE

Developments at work or regarding health are best approached carefully. This is a good time to invest in your personal relationships and home.

18 JUNE

Make a wish at the new moon in Gemini, which is excellent for turning a corner in a personal relationship and for making travel plans.

19 JUNE

You may receive good news at work or financially. If you are making important decisions, ensure you have the full facts and figures. Avoid making mistakes.

20 JUNE

Take a moment to look after your health and well-being. You will feel nurtured by your domestic surroundings.

21 JUNE

It's the solstice! If you take a moment to see matters from someone else's point of view you will gain perspective.

22 JUNE

You will enjoy being proactive and upbeat. Creative and personal developments will be optimistic or motivational.

23 JUNE

You will enjoy a trip or a visit. A development in your personal life will feel therapeutic.

24 JUNE

This is an excellent weekend for completing chores around the house and garden and boosting your health and well-being.

25 JUNE

You may be inclined to resume a bad habit that you are best avoiding. You can tend to be impulsive and must avoid this tendency. Aim for health and happiness.

26 JUNE

This is another day to avoid impulsiveness, especially with regard to your personal life and creative projects. You must also avoid gambling.

27 JUNE

You will enjoy meetings and talks, so organise a get-together.

28 JUNE

This is a good time for talks and meeting as you could make constructive progress.

29 JUNE

Work and discussions will go well, so take the initiative. This is a good time to boost your health and personal life.

30 JUNE

This is another lovely day for talks and meetings; you will enjoy a reunion. You may receive positive work news.

July

1 JULY

Expect key news to do with your home or family and, for some, there will be key work news or a trip.

2 JULY

You may be surprised by unusual developments, so be prepared and be practical.

3 JULY

The full moon in Capricorn will shine a light on your career and status. You may be preparing for a new direction.

4 JULY

Changes in your direction or that of someone close will merit a patient approach and preparedness to think outside the box.

5 JULY

Important decision-making merits careful research. You may find a friend or organisation particularly helpful.

6 JULY

Significant talks deserve careful preparation, so be prepared to back your ideas with facts. A domestic or personal development may bring out your vulnerabilities.

7 JULY

The next two days are good for talks and get-togethers. You may be surprised by pleasant news or a visit.

8 JULY

This is a good day for home repairs and improving family and domestic dynamics. You may receive good news.

9 JULY

You may experience some tension in relationships or regarding an organisation, so be prepared to use tact and aim to relax. Avoid pressure points.

10 JULY

You will enjoy seeing domestic matters improve. You'll gain more energy for work and chores over the coming days and weeks.

11 JULY

You are likely to feel more confident about expressing your views over the coming weeks, but you must avoid appearing bossy or domineering.

12 JULY

Your or someone else's vulnerabilities may surface, so be sensitive to your own needs and those of others. It's a good day for a health treat.

13 JULY

This is a good day to treat yourself to something that supports your health and well-being.

14 JULY

You may be pleasantly surprised by developments at home or with family. If work needs to be done ensure you have carried out adequate research.

15 JULY

You will enjoy socialising but must avoid inadvertently revealing someone's secret. If you're shopping, avoid overspending.

16 JULY

Trust your instincts, especially if you are unsure of someone. This may be a lazy day and you must avoid overindulgence, as you'll regret it!

17 JULY

You will gain an increasing sense of purpose over the coming weeks in your daily life. The Cancer new moon signals a fresh phase at home or with family. Avoid misunderstandings.

18 JULY

Some developments may be intense, so view them as the chance to turn a corner for a new beginning. Be proactive.

19 JULY

You will enjoy being busy and feeling more positive about life. You'll be drawn to music, the arts and creativity.

20 JULY

This is a lovely day to follow your inspiration. Romance will blossom, so why not organise a date?

21 JULY

You will be productive but must avoid pressuring yourself and others. Life is moving quickly so you must avoid minor accidents.

22 JULY

You are at a turning point, so take things in your stride. You may enjoy a therapeutic development and good news. It's a good day to consult an expert.

23 JULY

Be prepared to think on your feet. You may hear key work or health news. Avoid mix-ups by being super clear.

24 JULY

Someone may need your help, and if you need some advice it will be available so be sure to reach out.

25 JULY

You will appreciate the opportunity to provide a balancing and calming voice in potentially intense circumstances.

26 JULY

The moon in Scorpio for the next two days means someone close may express intense ideas and feelings. Be sure to back up your views with facts.

27 JULY

Be prepared to review a work, health or personal plan, especially if news comes to light that suggests more research must be done.

28 JULY

The key to success at the moment involves good communication skills, which will avoid arguments and tension.

29 JULY

You may need to choose between work and your personal life, so weigh your options carefully. Be prepared to go the extra mile.

30 JULY

You may be tempted to resume a bad habit. Take time out to boost your environment and health and well-being; you'll be glad you did.

31 JULY

The more practical you are, especially at work, the better the outcome. Negotiate a rational change of plan for the best results.

August

1 AUGUST

The full moon supermoon in Aquarius spells a new phase; the more innovative you are the better. You may receive good work or personal news.

2 AUGUST

This is a good time to discuss work and financial matters. You may need to review an agreement.

3 AUGUST

Be inspired but avoid seeing life through rose-coloured glasses. A work or health matter must be addressed carefully.

4 AUGUST

You will enjoy giving flight to your imagination but must avoid allowing it to run away with you, especially in your personal life. Avoid overindulging, as you'll regret it.

5 AUGUST

You will feel more motivated and upbeat about life and will appreciate the chance to meet up with friends and family. Music, the arts and dance will appeal.

6 AUGUST

This is a lovely day for rest and relaxation and, being the active person you are, you will enjoy being in nature and sports.

7 AUGUST

You will not always agree with everyone so this is a good day to be patient. Avoid emotional and financial gambling.

8 AUGUST

The key to success is thinking outside the box. Nevertheless, be prepared to take practical steps.

9 AUGUST

You may be surprised by news and developments, which is all the more reason to take things one step at a time.

10 AUGUST

You may receive good news as this is a better day for discussions and meetings than yesterday. You may enjoy a health or beauty treat.

11 AUGUST

Trust your intuition as it will not let you down. Be prepared to think on your feet.

12 AUGUST

This is a healing and therapeutic time for you both in your personal life and health-wise. Someone may need your help or advice.

13 AUGUST

You will enjoy a lovely get-together with family or friends. If you're creative you are likely to be busy. The arts and music will appeal.

14 AUGUST

This is a good time to focus on developing your skill sets at work. Just avoid arguments as they could escalate.

15 AUGUST

This is a lovely day for meetings and for getting ahead at work. It's also good for health and beauty appointments.

16 AUGUST

You may be surprised by developments but will appreciate the chance to do something different at work. This is a good day to focus on your health.

17 AUGUST

You will achieve a great deal as you have the ability to focus on details and be practical and methodical.

18 AUGUST

You may appear super organised to others yet you may feel distracted, so be sure to find balance.

19 AUGUST

You have new opportunities opening up so avoid feeling lost or that you have failed. Find balance. Someone will support your endeavours.

20 AUGUST

You have a tendency to be nostalgic or to focus on lost opportunities, so be sure to celebrate life as well. Just avoid overindulging as this is a real pitfall now.

21 AUGUST

You can make great progress in life as you change major routines and relationships but you must avoid power struggles.

22 AUGUST

You may discover you have over- or underestimated a situation. Avoid arguments and find a solution instead.

23 AUGUST

Try to get key paperwork finalised unless you wish to review matters over the next few weeks, especially at work. Key news is on the way.

24 AUGUST

An optimistic outlook regarding changes in the way you share duties and even finances will be successful.

25 AUGUST

This is an excellent time to invest in your work and your personal life and friendships. Be productive.

26 AUGUST

A practical approach to chores will be successful but avoid obsessing over details. Be prepared for change at work or in your daily life.

27 AUGUST

It is a good day to make a commitment but you must avoid limiting your options. You can complete a great deal of chores.

28 AUGUST

You will appreciate the opportunity to investigate new ideas and projects, so be open-minded and adventurous.

29 AUGUST

You may question your loyalty to certain people and to their plans. Just avoid making rash decisions.

30 AUGUST

This is a good day for self-development and spiritual activities. Trust your intuition.

31 AUGUST

The full moon supermoon in Pisces spotlights a new chapter in your daily life. Be inspired but also practical. It's a good day for a health appointment.

September

1 SEPTEMBER

You may need to review a work or health situation. Keep communications on an even keel to avoid arguments. Be patient.

2 SEPTEMBER

The moon in Aries may bring out your feisty side so avoid being baited by someone who is antagonistic.

3 SEPTEMBER

You will enjoy a reunion and will be productive at work.

4 SEPTEMBER

You may hear intense news from a friend or family member. It's a good time to invest in your health and well-being.

5 SEPTEMBER

You'll enjoy being active and outgoing. A friend or family member may have good news.

6 SEPTEMBER

You are likely to hear important news at work or regarding health. You may enjoy a get-together. This is a good time to be practical and realistic.

7 SEPTEMBER

You will enjoy a fun get-together. Creative Aries will be busy at work and with family.

8 SEPTEMBER

You may receive good news at work and will enjoy talks and discussions. A trip may be exciting and fun.

9 SEPTEMBER

This is a good day to focus on your home and family and to enjoy some me time.

10 SEPTEMBER

You will enjoy a reunion or a return to an old haunt. Avoid raking over old coals.

11 SEPTEMBER

You will enjoy taking the initiative with your projects and chores and may enjoy a reunion. Just avoid making rash decisions.

12 SEPTEMBER

This is an upbeat and proactive day but you must avoid spreading yourself too thin and creating tension.

13 SEPTEMBER

Are you putting yourself under too much pressure? If so, it's important to plan more relaxation in your life.

14 SEPTEMBER

The lead-up to the new moon is a good time to decide how best to run your daily life and work. Focus on creating a healthy environment.

15 SEPTEMBER

The Virgo new moon will help you turn a corner in your daily life, work or health so be practical and proactive.

16 SEPTEMBER

You may experience an unexpected change of routine. You will enjoy doing something different.

17 SEPTEMBER

Be mindful of other people's feelings and avoid both financial and emotional gambling.

18 SEPTEMBER

The Scorpio moon will bring out people's deepest feelings, so avoid arguments and look for constructive ways ahead.

19 SEPTEMBER

You will find out whether you have overestimated a situation as you will get a reality check. Avoid misunderstandings and delays by planning ahead.

20 SEPTEMBER

While you may feel adventurous not everyone else will, so be prepared to see developments in perspective. Avoid forcing issues.

21 SEPTEMBER

This is a good day for making progress at work and for socialising and networking, so make a date!

22 SEPTEMBER

Your endeavours are likely to succeed, especially if you are tactful and diplomatic. Be positive, as your enthusiasm will be catching.

23 SEPTEMBER

The sun in Libra over the next four weeks will encourage you to look for peace and balance, especially at work and in your relationships; it's a recipe for success.

24 SEPTEMBER

This may be a feisty day as someone may be feeling a little fiery. Avoid taking things personally and also avoid minor bumps and scrapes.

25 SEPTEMBER

Your expertise will be in demand and you may need to seek expert advice yourself. You must avoid making rash decisions. This is a good day for a health appointment.

26 SEPTEMBER

You will be drawn to an unusual character or group of people. Be prepared to consider fresh ideas.

27 SEPTEMBER

New ideas and interesting people will be inspiring, so be sure to be outgoing.

28 SEPTEMBER

You will be feeling inspired by music and the arts. You may also be forgetful, so be mindful of your keys and valuables.

29 SEPTEMBER

The Aries full moon signals the start of a new schedule in your daily life. It's a good time to turn a corner and to plan ahead so you have more peace in your life.

30 SEPTEMBER

You will enjoy doing something different this weekend. Just avoid locking horns with someone in a position of power.

October

1 OCTOBER

It's an excellent day for tidying up the house and garden and for beautifying your environment. Be spontaneous but avoid making rash decisions, as someone may surprise you.

2 OCTOBER

You may discover hidden information. This is a good day for research and for spiritual development. Avoid forgetfulness.

3 OCTOBER

You will enjoy socialising and networking. Focus on the details at work as you may be forgetful.

4 OCTOBER

The Gemini moon is excellent for communications and paperwork; just focus on the details to avoid mistakes.

5 OCTOBER

You may feel under pressure, so ensure you pace yourself to avoid feeling rushed. If you work hard you will be successful.

6 OCTOBER

Double-check that your aims are the same as someone you must collaborate with, otherwise you will be working at cross purposes.

7 OCTOBER

Be prepared to collaborate and co-operate. To be successful and avoid arguments, focus on common ground.

8 OCTOBER

The moon in Leo will encourage you to meet like-minded people. This is also a good day to rest and recuperate.

9 OCTOBER

This is a good day to look for ways to get on with people, as otherwise arguments could quickly escalate to conflict.

10 OCTOBER

Look for ways to agree and make a commitment with someone even if this represents a difficult choice.

11 OCTOBER

You or someone close may need help; rest assured, it will be available. It's a good day for a health appointment.

12 OCTOBER

Someone close may appear more passionate or intense than usual. Maintain clear communications to avoid misunderstandings.

13 OCTOBER

This is a good day for get-togethers and for socialising and networking. Just avoid making rash decisions.

14 OCTOBER

The solar eclipse represents a new chapter in a personal or business relationship. For some Aries it suggests you devise a fresh health schedule. It's a good day for a health appointment.

15 OCTOBER

You may be surprised by an impromptu visit or event. Be adaptable but avoid making rash decisions.

16 OCTOBER

The Scorpio moon may magnify feelings, so tread carefully to avoid intense interactions.

17 OCTOBER

You may be surprised by unexpected developments and may be required to maintain a peaceful environment as a result.

18 OCTOBER

You will appreciate the opportunity to enjoy your favourite activities such as sports. A reunion will be enjoyable, so make a date!

19 OCTOBER

A return to an old haunt or a reunion may bring mixed feelings. Avoid arguments, as these will escalate quickly.

20 OCTOBER

A personal or business partner has news for you that may represent considerable change moving forward.

21 OCTOBER

Communications and discussions may be intense. Avoid arguments, as these will be stressful. Romance could blossom. Avoid sensitive topics.

22 OCTOBER

This is a good day to discuss important matters as you are likely to come to an agreement if you avoid stubbornness in yourself and others.

23 OCTOBER

The next four weeks could be a passionate and dramatic time. If you dislike drama, find ways now to ground your plans and projects.

24 OCTOBER

This is a good day to make agreements and commitments both at work and in your personal life.

25 OCTOBER

You're not generally known as a dreamer but your imagination may run away with you unless you are careful. Be practical.

26 OCTOBER

Be prepared to take action, but you must have the full facts or you will make errors.

27 OCTOBER

This is a good time for a beauty or health treat but you must be clear about what you want. You may need to clear up a past error.

28 OCTOBER

The lunar eclipse signals a fresh chapter in your personal life. Things are going to move quickly, so avoid making rash decisions if you can.

29 OCTOBER

You will hear important news from someone close that may involve finances or a personal decision. Choose carefully.

30 OCTOBER

You will appreciate the opportunity to discuss matters with an organisation or friend who will be helpful.

31 OCTOBER

A pleasant change of routine will encourage you to be more spontaneous. This is a good time to look for financial and career advancement.

November

1 NOVEMBER

You may experience a work, personal or financial boost if you haven't already recently.

2 NOVEMBER

You will be feeling more in tune with someone close, making this a good time to discuss important domestic or personal matters. Just avoid arguments.

3 NOVEMBER

You will enjoy a get-together and this is a fun time for romance. However, it is also potentially an argumentative time. Ensure you have the facts to back up your views.

4 NOVEMBER

Someone close may surprise you or be unpredictable, so be prepared for a change of circumstance or plans.

5 NOVEMBER

Avoid taking someone's unpredictable or unusual behaviour personally. Someone may need your help or you may need to ask for help yourself.

6 NOVEMBER

This is a good day for boosting your work circumstances and health, so take the initiative.

7 NOVEMBER

This is a lovely day for a reunion and to get ahead with work projects.

8 NOVEMBER

You will be drawn to being more creative at work and to improving your health and appearance. Avoid arguments with an authority figure.

9 NOVEMBER

Certain meetings and talks may be intense or complex, so make an effort to engage in good communication skills. You may receive a financial boost.

10 NOVEMBER

You will be drawn to being talkative and outgoing but not everyone will feel the same. You may need to discuss shared or joint finances.

11 NOVEMBER

You may be surprised by a change of plan or by someone's news. Be spontaneous but avoid making rash decisions.

12 NOVEMBER

You may be super sensitive or notice people's feelings seem to be stronger. Nevertheless, this is a good day for talks and get-togethers.

13 NOVEMBER

The Scorpio new moon signals a fresh agreement either at work or in your personal life. You are likely to be surprised by news.

14 NOVEMBER

This is a good time to discuss your options and choices at work and financially.

15 NOVEMBER

This is a good day for meetings and discussions. Shared finances may need focus. It's also a good day for a beauty or health treat.

16 NOVEMBER

News will involve a little adjustment. Look for the positives and aim to collaborate for the best results.

17 NOVEMBER

Dream a little; your dreams could come true, especially in relation to work, romance and shared concerns. Just avoid excessive daydreaming.

18 NOVEMBER

You will enjoy an active weekend. If you have nothing planned yet take the initiative; you'll be glad you did. Romance could blossom.

19 NOVEMBER

You will enjoy being outgoing and upbeat. Just avoid arguments, as they could escalate quickly.

20 NOVEMBER

This is a good day for discussing important matters with a friend, group or organisation as you are likely to come to an agreement.

21 NOVEMBER

Be prepared to plan ahead as your preparations can take shape. It's a good time to make changes in key areas of your life.

22 NOVEMBER

Someone may be feeling a little vulnerable or sensitive. If it's you, take short breaks. Your advice may be needed. It's a good day for a health or beauty appointment.

23 NOVEMBER

If you focus on hard work you could attain a great deal. Avoid being cowed by restrictions but aim to work productively.

24 NOVEMBER

You will enjoy being adventurous but must be realistic in your planning. Be practical and you will scale mountains.

25 NOVEMBER

Your success depends on your plans being realistic, so double-check their viability; if all is well, put plans in motion.

26 NOVEMBER

Be prepared to be spontaneous even if you must take a calculated risk.

27 NOVEMBER

The Gemini full moon will spotlight the need to focus on finances and travel. For some this full moon signals the need to improve communication skills.

28 NOVEMBER

You may discover you have been talking at cross purposes with someone, which will give you the opportunity to put things right.

29 NOVEMBER

This is a good day to sort out shared duties and finances even if this seems a difficult task. You will succeed.

30 NOVEMBER

Be prepared to rectify past mistakes. You have the opportunity now to put practical measures in place.

December

1 DECEMBER

The more grounded and practical you are this month the more you will enjoy it.

2 DECEMBER

This is a good day for talks and discussions concerning finances, work and health. You will enjoy a get-together.

3 DECEMBER

Someone you find difficult to get on with may behave true to form, so maintain perspective. Avoid making snap decisions you may regret.

4 DECEMBER

Over the next few weeks you or someone close may be feeling more passionate and determined. It's a good time to get things done but you must avoid arguments.

5 DECEMBER

This is a good day to deepen your understanding of a work colleague or someone close, so make the effort to get closer and you will be rewarded.

6 DECEMBER

Be prepared to think both compassionately and analytically. Your intuition is spot on, so do trust it.

7 DECEMBER

Be positive, as you can make great headway both at work and in your personal life.

8 DECEMBER

Take the initiative as these are healing and therapeutic stars. You may even receive good news at work or financially.

9 DECEMBER

You will enjoy devoting some of your spare time to activities you love, so be sure to plan something fun.

10 DECEMBER

Important talks and get-togethers could result in solid plans being made. This is a good time for romance and for making a commitment.

11 DECEMBER

You are both charming and able to be realistic and practical now, so make the most of this engaging and proactive time.

12 DECEMBER

The Sagittarian new moon signals the start of a fresh chapter in a shared area of your life. Be prepared to reconnect with the past. Travel will appeal.

13 DECEMBER

You may receive key news to do with work, travel or someone special.

14 DECEMBER

Be adventurous and enjoy wonderful opportunities to broaden your horizons. Ensure you base your plans on facts, not opposition.

15 DECEMBER

There are therapeutic aspects to the day. You may reconnect with someone from the past. Work or health news will be constructive.

16 DECEMBER

Be open to the new and embrace fresh ideas, but if you are unsure of yourself then research circumstances.

17 DECEMBER

There are some hidden matters that may come to light, and if you uncover a mistake this is an excellent time to put things right.

18 DECEMBER

You may experience a financial improvement. This is a good day to review work and activities. A trip will be enjoyable.

19 DECEMBER

You may be inclined to be nostalgic, forgetful and absent-minded so be sure to take breaks when you can.

20 DECEMBER

You will enjoy meeting an upbeat crowd, and this is also a good day for romance.

21 DECEMBER

You may be surprised by developments and will enjoy being spontaneous. A personal or business partner may have unexpected news.

22 DECEMBER

You will enjoy a reunion and resuming favourite activities. You will also enjoy socialising.

23 DECEMBER

A change of pace is best negotiated by being practical and realistic with regard to travel and social engagements. This will avoid delays and frustration.

24 DECEMBER

You will enjoy the slower pace the day brings if you are not working. Workers are likely to be busy but you will enjoy the outcome.

25 DECEMBER

Merry Christmas! There is a beautiful romantic and nostalgic atmosphere to the day. Just avoid delays by planning ahead.

26 DECEMBER

You will enjoy get-togethers and reunions and romance can blossom. If you are travelling you will enjoy returning to an old haunt.

27 DECEMBER

The Cancer full moon represents the end of a long domestic cycle, so be prepared for something new. Exciting travel will appeal.

28 DECEMBER

A reunion will be poignant. You will enjoy romance and nostalgia will be strong. Avoid misunderstandings and delays.

29 DECEMBER

This is a lovely time for meetings and romance. If you are shopping avoid overspending, especially if you are in debt.

30 DECEMBER

The moon in Leo will bring your active and dynamic side out and you'll enjoy being in the outdoors and indulging in sports. The arts and romance will also appeal.

31 DECEMBER

Happy New Year! You may be drawn to being outgoing and socialising, but at the end of the day you may prefer to take things easy.

TAURUS

20 April - 21 May

FINANCES

Prepare for considerable changes in your finances as your daily and work routines will alter in 2023. You're likely to consider and begin a fresh approach to your career and activities, and as part of this you'll reconsider the importance of money management. This will be particularly important while Mars, Venus and the sun transit your second house of money during the first six months of the year, and also during October.

HEALTH

Jupiter in your sign from May onwards can add to a sense of joie de vivre but it can also lead to overindulging, especially for you as you love the good things in life such as good food and a little luxury. If you tend to lean towards too much chocolate or too much of a sedentary life, just be careful in the second half of the year that you don't put on weight!

LOVE LIFE

Once Jupiter enters your sign in May you'll appreciate a sense of joy and abundance and, with it, increased self-confidence and the chance to broaden your horizons. If you're single, this is an excellent year to look for fresh ways to meet new people as you'll be full of zest and lust for life. The eclipses in April and October will signal key turning points in your love life, times when you could make great change with long-term effect, so take the initiative then.

CAREER

As your daily life is due considerable changes so, too, is your career and general direction in 2023. You are ready to broaden your horizons and embrace activities and projects that bring an increased sense of fulfilment, and also of security and stability. Once Jupiter enters your sign in mid-May you will search increasingly for a sense of abundance in your daily life, which will reflect in your work choices. May will be a particularly important time for rearranging your priorities and for aiming for new goals in your career as you're likely to attain them in the long term.

HOME LIFE

Venus will be in your fourth house of domesticity from early June until early October, suggesting you will focus considerably on your domestic situation during these times, especially when Mars joins Venus in May to June and Mercury in July. While you will be keen at these times to make considerable change in your work and career, developments at home and in your personal or family life will merit careful appraisal and you must avoid making rash decisions or making change for the sake of it.

January

1 JANUARY

Strong feelings are likely to bubble up, so take things one step at a time. If you're working, expect a busy time.

2 JANUARY

It's a good day to put in place a careful new health routine. Avoid minor accidents, bumps and scrapes. You may return to an old haunt.

3 JANUARY

You will appreciate a breath of fresh air and the sense you are turning a new page. Be prepared to try something different.

4 JANUARY

This is a good day to reconnect with old friends and for work. It is also a good time for a health or beauty treat.

5 JANUARY

You will enjoy your favourite activities and the sense that you can be spontaneous and enjoy life. You may receive a surprise.

6 JANUARY

The Cancer full moon suggests you are ready to embark on a new understanding or agreement with someone. This is a good time to focus on nurturance.

7 JANUARY

You will enjoy travelling and your favourite pastimes, and if you're returning to work you will enjoy the change of routine.

8 JANUARY

You will enjoy resuming a project and a reunion. You may need to be super tactful and sensitive with someone.

9 JANUARY

This is a good day to invest time and energy in your work, career and favourite activities.

10 JANUARY

If you're working you will need to be super focused on your projects to avoid making mistakes. Focus on your health and avoid minor bumps and scrapes.

11 JANUARY

You may need to review a health situation. This is a good time to exercise your ability to be tactful to avoid arguments.

12 JANUARY

You may receive key news to do with work or from someone close and may need to review your plans.

13 JANUARY

This is a lovely day for socialising and networking and you'll enjoy indulging in favourite activities. Personal development may be a focus.

14 JANUARY

Your projects and chores are likely to go well. This is a good day to make a commitment to a friend or project.

15 JANUARY

Some plans may alter at short notice, so be prepared to be flexible and avoid taking developments personally. You may be called in to work unexpectedly.

16 JANUARY

Someone close may feel sensitive, so tread lightly. You may be feeling more passionate and motivated about your plans.

17 JANUARY

You may be feeling restless and prone to impulsiveness, so be careful with communications to avoid hurting someone's feelings. Avoid overspending.

18 JANUARY

You may receive news at work that could mean a change moving forward. A change in your general direction is likely.

19 JANUARY

Be sure to discuss your ideas with those concerned so that you are all on the same page. Above all, be practical.

20 JANUARY

Be prepared to embrace changes in your career and work or general direction and status. Be adaptable.

21 JANUARY

The new moon in Aquarius signals a fresh chapter in your general direction and status. This is a good time to make a wish. Be innovative.

22 JANUARY

A friend or organisation may be very helpful to you. This is a good day to make a commitment to a new path.

23 JANUARY

Be inspired by those you look up to as you will find direction as a result.

24 JANUARY

Trust your intuition, as it will not let you down. Avoid being easily influenced; maintain your own integrity.

25 JANUARY

This is a lovely day for get-togethers and meetings, both in your personal life and at work.

26 JANUARY

The moon in Aries will encourage you to reach out to people from your past, even if some conversations are difficult. You will enjoy a reunion.

27 JANUARY

Be prepared to reach out to those who need your help. If you need help it will be available. Avoid misunderstandings and minor accidents.

28 JANUARY

You'll be feeling more down to earth and may enjoy simply taking things easy, especially if you are adapting to new circumstances. Just be careful with communications.

29 JANUARY

You will appreciate creature comforts. You may hear unexpectedly from someone from the past and will enjoy a get-together.

30 JANUARY

Take the initiative as you will be productive. You may enjoy a change of routine and could receive unexpected news.

31 JANUARY

This is a good day for a reunion. You will enjoy socialising, so make a date! It's also a good day for a beauty treat.

February

1 FEBRUARY

You will enjoy getting together with someone who is helpful and perhaps an authority in their field. It's a good day for a health treat.

2 FEBRUARY

The moon in Cancer will help you to express yourself a little better and to also understand the motives of others.

3 FEBRUARY

You will gain deeper insight into people close to you both at home and at work, so be prepared to listen.

4 FEBRUARY

You will be drawn to doing something different this weekend or perhaps to meeting a new circle of people. You may even surprise yourself.

5 FEBRUARY

The full moon in Leo will magnify your feelings, especially concerning certain friends or organisations you are involved with and who you do not always agree with.

6 FEBRUARY

You are communicating well, making this a good time for meetings at work and in your personal life. Just avoid absent-mindedness.

7 FEBRUARY

You will not always agree with everyone. Just avoid being overly analytical and hypercritical of yourself and others.

8 FEBRUARY

You'll enjoy a change of pace or of place, and the more spontaneous you can be the more you will enjoy the day.

9 FEBRUARY

This is a good day for talks and meetings at work and with authority figures. You could make a valid commitment.

10 FEBRUARY

Key developments now could alter your career or even a future direction, so be careful with communications and discussions.

11 FEBRUARY

You like to be passionate about what you do and will enjoy being motivated by your activities. Just avoid being at loggerheads with someone you find difficult.

12 FEBRUARY

This is a sociable time, so if you have nothing planned yet then make a date!

13 FEBRUARY

You have a good connection with people at the moment so invest in your relationships.

14 FEBRUARY

Happy St Valentine's Day! Today and tomorrow are ideal for romance, and you'll enjoy the arts and music and meeting favourite friends.

15 FEBRUARY

This is an ideal day for meetings, especially if you have creative matters to discuss. You may be a little forgetful or have your head in the clouds, so avoid mishaps.

16 FEBRUARY

This is a good day to make a commitment to a friend or organisation. Just ensure you have the full facts.

17 FEBRUARY

Today's moon in Capricorn will bring out your practical side and you will be productive, but you will not suffer fools gladly so be tactful.

18 FEBRUARY

You will enjoy a reunion or a return to an old haunt. If you're shopping, avoid overspending.

19 FEBRUARY

This is another lovely day for a reunion. The arts, romance and beauty will appeal.

20 FEBRUARY

The new moon in Pisces signals a fresh chapter in your relationship with a friend or organisation. This is a good day for a health appointment.

21 FEBRUARY

You may be seen as being a little unpredictable or erratic, so ensure you avoid mix-ups and delays by planning ahead.

22 FEBRUARY

This is a better day for communications. Be prepared to take the initiative with a financial or social situation. If you're shopping, avoid overspending.

23 FEBRUARY

The moon in Aries will help you to get things done at work and with your health. However, you may feel feistier than usual so be patient.

24 FEBRUARY

You will enjoy a reunion. You may meet someone you are instantly drawn to and may return to an old haunt.

25 FEBRUARY

When the moon is in Taurus you feel more grounded and earthed. Today, though, you may feel restless, so be sure to do something you love.

26 FEBRUARY

Your main pitfall is being obstinate, so if you feel that way double-check you're not disadvantaging yourself.

27 FEBRUARY

You will enjoy meetings and discussions. It is a good day to immerse yourself in music and the arts.

28 FEBRUARY

You are communicating well and will be more inclined to embrace change, so why not try something new?

March

1 MARCH

Trust your intuition as it is likely to be spot on, but you must avoid impulsiveness and making snap decisions.

2 MARCH

You will enjoy a reunion or news from the past. It's a good day to improve your health and appearance.

3 MARCH

This is another good day for a reunion and also for a beauty or health treat. You may hear important news from the past. Someone may need your help.

4 MARCH

Be prepared to take the initiative, especially with personal and domestic matters.

5 MARCH

You will enjoy an unexpected meeting or event – that is, unless you dislike surprises.

6 MARCH

You may receive unexpected news from the past or regarding work. Expect a surprise.

7 MARCH

The full moon in Virgo signifies a fresh chapter in your personal life such as with family or a friend. Be prepared to turn a corner with a group or organisation.

8 MARCH

Be prepared to work hard to achieve your goals; you'll succeed with your chores as a result.

9 MARCH

You may be inclined to feel emotional or restless, so take a moment to channel your energy into work to achieve your goals.

10 MARCH

If you're feeling nostalgic, take a moment to discuss some of your memories with someone close. This is a good day for a health appointment.

11 MARCH

You may be pleasantly surprised by news. For some this will apply to work and for others to finances. You may enjoy an ego boost.

12 MARCH

There is a therapeutic atmosphere around you. You will enjoy a break. Health and well-being are themes in the air, and you may need to help someone or ask for help yourself.

13 MARCH

You will wish to be adventurous but you may also wish to avoid taking risks. You will find a happy medium.

14 MARCH

An outgoing approach will encourage you to socialise yet it is important to be tactful to avoid difficult communications. Base your decisions on facts.

15 MARCH

This is a lovely day for romance, the arts and music. However, you may be easily misled, especially financially, so be careful when making decisions.

16 MARCH

Aim to be super clear with communications to avoid misunderstandings. You may be under pressure and mistakes can be made. Avoid the resumption of a bad habit.

17 MARCH

You are likely to be busy socialising and networking. Avoid tiring yourself so you don't make mistakes. A reunion or meeting with an authority figure will be important.

18 MARCH

Be prepared to consider new ideas and activities as you will enjoy broadening your horizons.

19 MARCH

Socialising will appeal and this is a good day to deepen friendships, so be sure to make a date.

20 MARCH

A reunion or return to an old haunt will be significant. You can make progress at work so take the initiative.

21 MARCH

The Aries new moon signals a new health or work routine. Be prepared to turn the corner and leave the past behind.

22 MARCH

When the moon is in Aries you tend to feel a little restless, so ensure you channel energy into productive activities.

23 MARCH

You are entering new territory. For some this will apply to work and for others in your personal life. Welcome the new.

24 MARCH

Be prepared to adapt to a fresh circumstance, and as a result you will feel more positive.

25 MARCH

Someone from your past can be particularly helpful so ensure you reach out. You'll enjoy a reunion, but you must avoid thorny topics.

26 MARCH

This is a good time to follow your instincts, especially regarding friends and acquaintances.

27 MARCH

This is a good time for a health or beauty treat. Someone may need your help unexpectedly. If you need advice it will be available.

28 MARCH

A reunion or a trip down memory lane will be significant. Health or work news is on the way.

29 MARCH

You are better known for being dependable, so sometimes when you feel spontaneous you take people by surprise. Be prepared to express yourself compassionately for this reason.

30 MARCH

This is a good day to improve finances but avoid making rash choices. You may be surprised by developments or receive unexpected news.

31 MARCH

You will appreciate the opportunity to invest more time and effort in your personal life and home.

April

1 APRIL

There is a nostalgic aspect to your weekend. This is a good time to focus on self-development, the arts and romance.

2 APRIL

This is another lovely day for investing in yourself and in your health and well-being. You'll enjoy catching up with someone special.

3 APRIL

Be patient, as you are likely to be under pressure and must choose your words carefully. Avoid coercion.

4 APRIL

This can be a productive day and you can get a lot done. Be resourceful.

5 APRIL

There is a therapeutic aspect to the day. You may receive key health news and someone may need your help. A meeting will be significant. Singles may meet someone special.

6 APRIL

The full moon in Libra means you are turning a corner at work or regarding health. This is a good time to look for balance.

7 APRIL

You may hear unexpectedly from an old friend or will receive unusual news. The arts and romance will appeal.

8 APRIL

This is a good day for a short trip and for get-togethers, which you will enjoy.

9 APRIL

This could be a passionate and romantic time for you so why not organise a date?

10 APRIL

You will feel more dynamic and goal oriented, enabling you to reach your targets at work and in your daily life.

11 APRIL

Be prepared to see yourself in a new light. Key news from the past concerning work or your health will be relevant.

12 APRIL

You can get a great deal done and will enjoy some favourite activities, leading to a sense of achievement.

13 APRIL

Success lies in being prepared to innovate and to see your role from a fresh perspective.

14 APRIL

You will enjoy meeting with someone you look up to. However, you will not get on equally as well with everyone so be selective about the company you keep.

15 APRIL

You prefer to play your cards close to your chest. It's your choice who you let into your inner circle.

16 APRIL

This is a lovely day for relaxation and self-care. Be careful to avoid resuming old habits. Romance could blossom.

17 APRIL

You are a creative person and may tend to allow your imagination to run away with you now, so you must be practical.

18 APRIL

The moon in Aries for the next two days will be motivational and you'll feel the need to prove yourself, which you can do.

19 APRIL

Be prepared to discuss your secret fears. An expert or adviser will prove helpful, so avoid bottling up anxieties.

20 APRIL

The total solar eclipse in Aries will kick-start an important chapter in your life, for most Taureans in your daily life or work or health schedule. Avoid arguments, as they will escalate.

21 APRIL

Important communications are best tied up if possible to avoid having to review them in the weeks to come.

22 APRIL

You must be prepared to discuss your ideas with those they concern so you keep everyone in the loop.

23 APRIL

This is a good day to check your financial health. Seek help from an expert if necessary.

24 APRIL

Key financial decisions are likely now and an accountant could be helpful. You can improve your circumstances.

25 APRIL

You may receive news at work or regarding health. It's a good day to make a commitment as long as you have the full facts.

26 APRIL

This is a good time for meetings and a short trip. Just ensure you plan ahead well to avoid delays.

27 APRIL

You may receive unexpected news and may also receive an unexpected compliment or a financial boost.

28 APRIL

You'll enjoy the opportunity to spend some therapeutic time on yourself and with your family.

29 APRIL

You will enjoy doing something spontaneous such as taking a short trip or welcoming an unexpected visitor.

30 APRIL

A lovely connection with a family member or friend will boost your mood and you'll also enjoy improving your health.

May

1 MAY

You'll gain the opportunity to review some of your plans in the coming weeks, which will help to take the pressure off for now.

2 MAY

News or a meeting will catch your eye, helping you to review or understand the past. This is a good day to catch up on work and for a reunion.

3 MAY

This is a good day to find more balance in your daily life and schedule, as your efforts will succeed.

4 MAY

You may be inclined to overspend or overindulge, which you'll regret. It's a good day for research.

5 MAY

The full moon and lunar eclipse in Scorpio signal a fresh chapter in a relationship and, for some, a fresh daily or work schedule. You may receive a financial or personal boost.

6 MAY

Someone close may appear more emotional than usual and may surprise you as a result. This is a passionate and romantic weekend, so organise a date.

7 MAY

This is a good weekend to invest in your happiness and well-being, and to improve your self-esteem.

8 MAY

You will enjoy being with like-minded people and working towards similar goals.

9 MAY

You may reveal an aspect of your personality you don't often show and may even surprise yourself.

10 MAY

You'll appreciate a more down-to-earth feeling around you that will help you to make informed decisions and get things done.

11 MAY

You will be required to exit your comfort zone and will manage to succeed. Be prepared to spontaneous.

12 MAY

This is a good day to focus on good communication skills as you may be required to take the lead.

13 MAY

This is a good day for reviewing finances and making commitments, especially those that concern friends and organisations.

14 MAY

Your creative side and imagination will be useful and you'll enjoy socialising.

15 MAY

A domestic development and a connection with your past will deepen your understanding of yourself and someone special. You may enjoy a short trip somewhere pretty.

16 MAY

As Jupiter enters Taurus, prepare for an abundant 12-month phase. Decide now how you wish to expand your experiences and gain happiness.

17 MAY

Trust your instincts if you feel there may be a power struggle in the making. Find ways to negotiate around this.

18 MAY

This may be an intense day. Be prepared to reason with someone at work or in a domestic situation for the best outcome.

19 MAY

The Taurus new moon signals you are beginning a fresh chapter in your personal life. You may be ready to make a key commitment at work or regarding health.

20 MAY

Use your imagination and think outside the box to achieve solutions to problems. You will enjoy a lighter atmosphere.

21 MAY

Your attention will be going towards your personal relationships and home. There may be a battle of egos forming at home or at work so you must find a way to get around this.

22 MAY

This is a good day for talks and to find ways to overcome differences. You may enjoy a productive working day.

23 MAY

You must avoid office politics. If you don't work you must avoid domestic strife as conflict could flare up.

24 MAY

You may be known as a peacemaker yet you can be stubborn. If you're in conflict you must avoid allowing it to spiral as it will become long term.

25 MAY

You will appreciate the opportunity to spend time at home and with those you love. This is a good time for talks to overcome problems.

26 MAY

You may receive unexpected news or be spontaneous about your activities. You will enjoy an impromptu trip or visit.

27 MAY

This is a good weekend to reconnect with the family members and friends you are close to. You may enjoy a short trip.

28 MAY

Some restrictions in your life are difficult to negotiate, yet if you try you may make a breakthrough.

29 MAY

Play to your strengths by being practical as you will achieve a great deal as a result.

30 MAY

You'll appreciate being able to restore some balance in your daily life so take the initiative.

31 MAY

You may be asked for help and you may need help, advice or expert support yourself. It will be available.

June

1 JUNE

Delays and frustrations may be annoying, but if you're diligent you will succeed with your plans.

2 JUNE

You will enjoy a lovely get-together or will receive news from the past. You may meet someone you feel a strong connection with.

3 JUNE

This is a good time to review your finances and your relationships to ensure you are still on the right track.

4 JUNE

The full moon signals a new chapter in a key financial agreement or relationship. You may be surprised by news or will inadvertently surprise someone with your news.

5 JUNE

This is an intense or passionate day. Developments at home or at work will merit careful focus to ensure you're happy on the path you're pursuing.

6 JUNE

You will enjoy being able to see a more practical way forward once you ground yourself and are methodical with your plans.

7 JUNE

This is a good day to seek a fresh perspective regarding your career and general plans. Be prepared to think creatively.

8 JUNE

You will achieve your goals by being proactive and positive. Avoid feeling you are stuck.

9 JUNE

This is a good day for a reunion and for romance and the arts. You will enjoy the opportunity for some self-development or a spiritual endeavour.

10 JUNE

Look for inspiration from people you admire. You'll enjoy doing something different in your spare time.

11 JUNE

A trip somewhere different will be refreshing. You may even see yourself in a new light as a result.

12 JUNE

A proactive approach to both work and your home life will be rewarding. Be positive.

13 JUNE

Certain restrictions, rules or regulations may seem obstructive, but if you work within the confines of what is reasonable you will succeed.

14 JUNE

The moon in your sign for the next two days will help you get things done but you may tend to feel stuck. If so, be prepared to co-operate with others for the best results.

15 JUNE

You are communicating well and may receive good news financially. However, obstacles may annoy you so it's important to be adaptable and approachable.

16 JUNE

The influence of someone whose presence seems restrictive may be frustrating. You will appreciate the chance to spend time with less annoying people.

17 JUNE

You will enjoy spending time with family or someone special. This is a good weekend to leave work alone and devote time to those you love.

18 JUNE

Make a wish at the new moon in Gemini, which is excellent for turning a corner financially and in your personal life.

19 JUNE

You may receive good news at work or financially. If you are making important decisions, ensure you have the full facts and figures. Avoid making mistakes.

20 JUNE

The Cancer moon is an excellent time to look after yourself and your family. Take short breaks if you're tired.

21 JUNE

It's the solstice! Be prepared to go the extra mile to avoid an ego battle with someone in a position of power; you will be glad you did.

22 JUNE

You will feel rewarded by spending time investing in your own happiness. You will also enjoy fun activities such as music and dance.

23 JUNE

There is a healing and therapeutic atmosphere around and you'll enjoy reconnecting with someone special.

24 JUNE

This is an excellent weekend for finding out how to enjoy your time in constructive and manageable ways.

25 JUNE

You may be inclined to resume a bad habit that you're best to avoid. Some circumstances may remind you it's best to leave the past behind.

26 JUNE

Developments in your personal life may bring your impulsiveness or stubbornness to the surface. Avoid making snap decisions.

27 JUNE

You will enjoy a get-together, trip or visit. A debt may be repaid.

28 JUNE

This is a productive time, so focus on work and your chores as you can attain a lot.

29 JUNE

You may receive positive news from a group or organisation and can excel at work even if you feel you are under pressure. Take the initiative.

30 JUNE

This is a good day for a trip and also for a get-together and meetings. You may decide to make a commitment to a financial or work option.

July

1 JULY

You will enjoy a trip or a visit. For some this will be a trip down memory lane.

2 JULY

You may be surprised by unusual news from a family member or someone close to you. You will enjoy being outgoing but you must avoid minor bumps and scrapes.

3 JULY

The full moon in Capricorn will shine a light on your activities, plans for the future and relationships. You may be preparing for a new direction.

4 JULY

Be practical and patient about changes you wish to make as you could make great progress.

5 JULY

Be prepared to think outside the box about logistics and any conundrums that arise.

6 JULY

Someone may need your help and if you need advice it will be available, especially regarding certain matters to do with work or your personal life.

7 JULY

The next two days are good for get-togethers and domestic matters. You may be surprised by pleasant news or a visitor.

8 JULY

This is a good weekend for improving family and domestic dynamics. You may receive beneficial news. You may be feeling creative and active, so be prepared to plan fun events.

9 JULY

Trust your instincts, especially if you feel you're being misunderstood. Find ways to relate better with those you must be on good terms with.

10 JULY

You'll enjoy seeing personal and domestic matters improve. You'll feel more optimistic about your personal and family life in the coming days.

11 JULY

You will gain a deep understanding of someone over the coming weeks. In the meantime, avoid overanalysing and being super critical of others and yourself.

12 JULY

Misunderstandings and delays are possible, so be patient and super clear with communications. It's a good day for a health treat.

13 JULY

As the moon transits Gemini you may feel more talkative and likely to share your views. This moon will facilitate better communications.

14 JULY

You may be pleasantly surprised by developments at home or with family. It's in your interest to tread carefully with an authority figure or organisation.

15 JULY

You may be tempted by a little retail therapy, so leave the credit card at home if you're already in debt. You will enjoy catching up with an old friend.

16 JULY

This is a good time to research circumstances you are unsure of. Avoid overindulgence, as you'll regret it!

17 JULY

The Cancer new moon signals a fresh phase at home or with family. For some there will be important decisions to make regarding your personal life. Avoid misunderstandings.

18 JULY

Trust your instincts as they are on point. You may be inclined to avoid change, so remember to be adaptable.

19 JULY

You will enjoy an upbeat feeling to the day but you must avoid arguments with someone in a position of power as they will escalate.

20 JULY

This is a lovely day for improving domestic dynamics and also for interior decoration, both at home and at the office. Express your creativity!

21 JULY

This is a productive day but you must avoid feeling pressured and pressuring others. You may be prepared to make a long-term commitment.

22 JULY

This may be an intense day as changes at home or in your status take effect. You may enjoy a therapeutic development and good news. It's a good day to consult an expert.

23 JULY

You may receive unexpected news or a surprise visit. Be prepared to adapt to change and be spontaneous. Avoid misunderstandings by being clear.

24 JULY

There are certain people you know you can always rely on, so be sure to get in touch if you need a sounding board or support.

25 JULY

You often provide the voice of reason, and your skill set in this regard will be in demand today.

26 JULY

The moon in Scorpio for the next two days means life is likely to get busy, especially at work. People may be more intense, so maintain perspective.

27 JULY

You may need to review some of your decisions in your personal life or regarding a creative project due to news you receive.

28 JULY

Be prepared to think critically and clearly to ensure you stay on top of changes, both in your personal life and at work.

29 JULY

This is a good day to get your home and garden shipshape. You may need to exercise tact with someone regarding rules and regulations.

30 JULY

Taureans love a little indulgence and you may be tempted to resume a bad habit. Take time out to boost your health and well-being.

31 JULY

The more practical you are, especially at work, the better the outcome. Negotiate a rational change of plan for the best results.

August

1 AUGUST

The full moon supermoon in Aquarius spells a new phase in your career and status. Be innovative. You may receive good work or personal news.

2 AUGUST

This is a good time to discuss work and financial matters. You must avoid both financial and emotional gambling.

3 AUGUST

You may discover an inspired way to break a stalemate with someone, so think laterally.

4 AUGUST

This is a creative day, so allow your imagination to soar as you will be able to combine it with practicalities for the best results.

5 AUGUST

You'll be drawn to friends and activities that allow you to relax. Music, the arts and dance will appeal.

6 AUGUST

A strong connection with your past may be soothing but may also bring up strong emotions, so take things easy.

7 AUGUST

You have strong viewpoints and sometimes some compromises need to be made. Weigh your options carefully.

8 AUGUST

The moon in your own sign will enable you to be more practical, so take the initiative and avoid distractions.

9 AUGUST

Someone who can be unpredictable may behave true to form. Consider your reactions carefully.

10 AUGUST

This is a better day for discussions and meetings than yesterday. You may enjoy a reunion or a trip.

11 AUGUST

Trust your intuition as it will not let you down, especially if you're unsure of someone.

12 AUGUST

This is a good time to focus on your health and to promote a relaxing atmosphere at home.

13 AUGUST

This is a good day to mend bridges if you have argued with someone. You will enjoy a lovely get-together. Romance could blossom.

14 AUGUST

Be proactive and positive, as you can make headway in your chosen field.

15 AUGUST

This is a lovely day for romance and making home improvements. It's also a good day for talks and meetings.

16 AUGUST

Someone close may surprise you. The new moon in Leo signals you are turning a corner in a personal relationship or at home. This is a good day to focus on your health.

17 AUGUST

You will be practical and methodical and will accomplish a great deal. Focus on the details.

18 AUGUST

You may appear super organised to others and will be productive at work.

19 AUGUST

You will be drawn to establishing more balance in your daily life, which you'll enjoy.

20 AUGUST

You have a tendency to be nostalgic or to focus on lost opportunities, so be sure to celebrate life as well while avoiding overindulgence.

21 AUGUST

Be prepared to stand up to challenges and powerful people as you will succeed with your goals. Avoid power struggles.

22 AUGUST

You may find yourself drawn into an intriguing situation or even arguments. Be practical for the best results.

23 AUGUST

Try to get key decisions on the table unless you wish to review matters over the next few weeks, especially concerning your personal life.

24 AUGUST

An outgoing, optimistic attitude will lead to a productive day. Avoid distractions.

25 AUGUST

You can steam ahead with your projects as they are likely to succeed. This may, however, be an intense and passionate time. Romance could blossom.

26 AUGUST

You can build a sense of security and stability that you'll enjoy.

27 AUGUST

You may be prepared to make a serious commitment. You must avoid limiting your options, so ensure you have all the facts.

28 AUGUST

Be prepared to step into new territory at work or within your status.

29 AUGUST

Your bright ideas and clever plans can succeed, but success depends on careful planning.

30 AUGUST

You may be drawn to researching ways to find more stability and security in your personal life and may ask for a commitment.

31 AUGUST

The full moon supermoon in Pisces spotlights a new chapter in your personal life. Be inspired but also practical. It's a good day for a health appointment.

September

1 SEPTEMBER

Look for balance and harmony to avoid making a pressured situation worse. Work hard and you will attain your goals.

2 SEPTEMBER

The moon in Aries may spotlight new activities for you. You may be drawn to focusing more on your health and well-being.

3 SEPTEMBER

This is a lovely day to focus on yourself and on creating a stable and happy environment.

4 SEPTEMBER

You are likely to get ahead at work and a trip is likely to go well. A financial decision is best reviewed carefully.

5 SEPTEMBER

This is a good day for romance and for get-togethers with friends and family, so plan a date!

6 SEPTEMBER

You are likely to hear important news at work or regarding your family. A meeting will be significant and you may enjoy a reunion.

7 SEPTEMBER

You will enjoy a fun get-together. Creative Taureans will be busy with family and at home.

8 SEPTEMBER

This is an excellent day to organise meetings and to make progress with your plans. Romance could also blossom.

9 SEPTEMBER

You may be feeling super sensitive so take things easy. Someone may need your help, but if you need advice it will be available.

10 SEPTEMBER

A fun, upbeat development at home will raise morale, so plan a treat.

11 SEPTEMBER

This is a good day to initiate talks both with family and at work depending on where you feel discussions are most needed.

12 SEPTEMBER

The moon in Leo will contribute to you or someone close to you feeling a little more dynamic, so it's a good time to get things done.

13 SEPTEMBER

You can be super efficient and sometimes can be so meticulous that you appear critical. Avoid also seeing only criticism in others.

14 SEPTEMBER

The lead-up to the new moon is a good time to make a wish, especially regarding your personal life and creative projects.

15 SEPTEMBER

The Virgo new moon will help you to turn a corner in your personal life. Be practical and you could make a dream come true.

16 SEPTEMBER

You may be surprised by developments. Be open to new ideas, as you'll enjoy doing something different.

17 SEPTEMBER

You will not get on with everyone so you must avoid arguments. Be mindful of other people's feelings.

18 SEPTEMBER

The Scorpio moon will encourage you to be motivated at work. Just avoid taking on too much at once.

19 SEPTEMBER

This is a lovely day for the arts and for creative endeavours. Just avoid being forgetful and expecting everything to go your way.

20 SEPTEMBER

You may find people super dynamic and energetic. Your being grounded will help earth projects and plans, so be practical.

21 SEPTEMBER

This is a good day for making changes, especially at work and within your general direction and personal life.

22 SEPTEMBER

Be adventurous and you'll find ways to enjoy the end of your week.

23 SEPTEMBER

The sun in Libra will encourage you to look for peace and balance, especially in your daily schedule and relationships.

24 SEPTEMBER

This is a good day to look for balance, especially health-wise and in your diet.

25 SEPTEMBER

This is a good day to work constructively with people in a position of authority. You will enjoy a trip or a meeting, and it's a good day to talk.

26 SEPTEMBER

You'll discover unusual solutions to ongoing problems so be resourceful.

27 SEPTEMBER

You will enjoy getting together with inspiring people, and your creativity will be appreciated by others.

28 SEPTEMBER

This is a good day for spiritual development as you are in tune with your intuition and with the world around you. Trust your instincts.

29 SEPTEMBER

The Aries full moon signals the start of something new. You may be drawn to different groups, circles and people, so be outgoing.

30 SEPTEMBER

You'll enjoy taking time out for yourself and for your health and well-being. You may be drawn to spending more time on your appearance.

October

1 OCTOBER

It's an excellent day for cocooning at home and for home improvements. Just avoid making too many changes at once.

2 OCTOBER

This is a lovely day to enjoy music, dance and the company of those you love. Romance could flourish.

3 OCTOBER

This is a good day for building bridges with those you have argued with and for boosting work circumstances. Avoid being super idealistic.

4 OCTOBER

The Gemini moon is excellent for communications and researching financial matters.

5 OCTOBER

If some relationships have been strained, take things one step at a time to avoid misunderstandings.

6 OCTOBER

Double-check that your aims are the same as someone close or at work, otherwise you will be working at cross purposes.

7 OCTOBER

This is a good day to complete chores around the house and garden. Just avoid taking on more than necessary.

8 OCTOBER

This is a good day to make a commitment to a plan or to someone in particular, especially if you have all the facts.

9 OCTOBER

You are feeling outgoing but not everyone else is. You must avoid arguments, especially with someone in a position of power.

 70

10 OCTOBER

Look for balance and fair play in your interactions. If this is present it's a good time to make an agreement.

11 OCTOBER

Look after yourself and your interests. This is a good day for a health appointment. Be careful with communications, as you could make progress if you are.

12 OCTOBER

Work is likely to be busy and you'll feel passionate about certain plans and ideas, but you must be flexible and open to other people's ideas.

13 OCTOBER

This is a good day for socialising and networking. Your work plans could steam ahead but you should avoid making rash decisions.

14 OCTOBER

The solar eclipse represents a new chapter in your daily routine. For some this will mean changes at work and for others in your health schedule.

15 OCTOBER

You may be surprised by events or a change of plan and you may surprise others with your ingenuity. Be adaptable but avoid making rash decisions.

16 OCTOBER

The Scorpio moon will contribute to a feeling of passion and dedication to someone close or a project. Ensure you maintain perspective.

17 OCTOBER

You may receive unexpected news or will need to alter your usual routine. You may be required to maintain a peaceful environment as a result.

18 OCTOBER

This is a good day to take the initiative and to be bold. Just avoid causing arguments as a result.

19 OCTOBER

You can make headway but you must be sure you have the correct information. You will enjoy a reunion.

20 OCTOBER

You may need to review certain matters at work or regarding health as key news arrives. If you sense there is tension in the air, find ways to dissipate it.

21 OCTOBER

This is likely to be an intense day, so the more subtle you are with your communications the better for you. Avoid sensitive topics.

22 OCTOBER

You will enjoy a change of scenery and socialising. This is a good day to discuss important matters as you are likely to come to an agreement.

23 OCTOBER

The next four weeks could be a passionate and dramatic time, especially at work and, for some, in your personal life. Find ways to maintain balance in your life.

24 OCTOBER

This is a good day to make agreements and commitments at work and to a friend or organisation.

25 OCTOBER

You will appreciate the opportunity to dream a little but you must avoid being distracted at work.

26 OCTOBER

This is a busy time for you so it's important to pace yourself, otherwise tempers will flare.

27 OCTOBER

If you are tired, ensure you take breaks to avoid making mistakes. You may be feeling sensitive so you must avoid taking things personally.

28 OCTOBER

The lunar eclipse in Taurus signals a fresh chapter in your personal life if you were born in April and at work or health-wise if you are a May Taurean. Avoid making rash decisions.

29 OCTOBER

You will hear important news at work regarding health or from a partner. This may involve a change of routine or travel. Avoid arguments, as they will escalate.

30 OCTOBER

This is a good day to strategise and check you're on the right path, which will help you to avoid making rash decisions.

31 OCTOBER

Happy Halloween! You may enjoy a change of routine and may be surprised by news at work or in your personal life.

November

1 NOVEMBER

Be open to the new, and you may be surprised by what transpires!

2 NOVEMBER

You will be feeling more in tune with someone close, making this a good time to discuss important personal or work matters. Just avoid arguments.

3 NOVEMBER

You have bright ideas at the moment and it's a good time to put them in action. If someone disagrees with you be open-minded and ensure you have the facts.

4 NOVEMBER

Someone close may surprise you or behave erratically, so be prepared for a change of circumstance or plans. Romance can blossom.

5 NOVEMBER

You may be inclined to take other people's behaviour personally. This is a good time to seek rest and relaxation.

6 NOVEMBER

You can make a great deal of progress at work. This is a good day to improve your appearance, so take the initiative.

7 NOVEMBER

This is a good day for socialising and networking and for making long-term changes.

8 NOVEMBER

To ensure your projects progress smoothly, double-check you have all the correct information and that everyone is on the same page.

9 NOVEMBER

This is a good day for improving your career status and general direction. You may need to overcome your own insecurity, but when you do you will succeed.

10 NOVEMBER

You are likely to feel chatty and outgoing but not everyone will feel the same. You may need to answer to an authority figure.

11 NOVEMBER

Developments may come about quickly or unexpectedly. Be prepared to take the initiative but avoid making rash decisions.

12 NOVEMBER

You are likely to feel passionate about your projects and plans, so ensure you are practical and maintain perspective.

13 NOVEMBER

The Scorpio new moon signals a fresh chapter in your personal life and, for some, at work. Romance will appeal. You may be surprised by news.

14 NOVEMBER

This is a lovely day for romance and for getting head in collaborations at work.

15 NOVEMBER

This is another good day for meetings and discussions. You may need to discuss finances. It's also a good day for a beauty or health treat.

16 NOVEMBER

You have high hopes and these are likely to be realised, but you may need to work a little harder than you'd hoped.

17 NOVEMBER

This is a lovely day for romance and for meetings and socialising. You could make great progress at work as well.

18 NOVEMBER

You will feel passionate about your activities. Romance will flourish, however, you must avoid making rash decisions.

19 NOVEMBER

You will appreciate the opportunity to do something different and enjoy the company of like-minded people.

20 NOVEMBER

You are likely to experience a positive development that increases your status or deepens a beautiful relationship.

21 NOVEMBER

Romance, the arts and music will all inspire you to enjoy time with someone special.

22 NOVEMBER

It's a good day for a health or beauty appointment and for being optimistic and knowing you can overcome obstacles.

23 NOVEMBER

You can climb mountains, so be prepared to work hard as you could attain a great deal.

24 NOVEMBER

An adventurous and outgoing phase will bring your social side out. However, you must avoid misunderstandings.

25 NOVEMBER

Be prepared to rethink some of your plans, especially those where you must collaborate and cooperate with others. Be practical above all else.

26 NOVEMBER

You may need to be flexible and alter some of your usual schedule due to a change of plan.

27 NOVEMBER

The Gemini full moon will spotlight a fresh phase in your personal life. Be prepared to factually discuss options.

28 NOVEMBER

A friend, group or partner may require persuading about a plan of yours. Be prepared to back up your plans with facts.

29 NOVEMBER

You have high hopes and will need to optimistically promote your ideas and projects in order to gain support. Be positive.

30 NOVEMBER

This is a good day for discussions, especially with an employer or person in a position of authority. Be clear for the best results.

December

1 DECEMBER

You will appreciate the opportunity to enjoy some of your favourite activities. A trip somewhere beautiful will appeal.

2 DECEMBER

This is a good day for get-togethers and activities with like-minded people. You may be closer to making a financial or personal agreement.

3 DECEMBER

You may need to be careful with decisions to avoid a battle of egos. Sometimes it's wise to collaborate.

4 DECEMBER

This is the beginning of a more active and motivational time for you so be prepared to initiate plans and activities.

5 DECEMBER

Work is likely to present opportunities to show just what you can do. Avoid arguments with someone in charge as they will escalate.

6 DECEMBER

Your analytical mind is an asset to you and you'll find making decisions based on facts and figures profitable.

7 DECEMBER

You may need to be a mediator or play a conciliatory role, especially at work.

8 DECEMBER

These are healing and therapeutic stars, so be prepared to mend bridges. You may enjoy a reunion or a trip to an old haunt.

9 DECEMBER

Take time out to enjoy a favourite activity and meet with favourite people as you'll be glad you did.

10 DECEMBER

This is a good day for a health or beauty treat. You may enjoy a trip somewhere beautiful and enchanting.

11 DECEMBER

You will appreciate the opportunity to enhance your profile at work and also to improve your appearance. Meetings are likely to go well.

12 DECEMBER

The Sagittarian new moon signals the start of a fresh chapter in a relationship. You may be surprised by someone's news.

13 DECEMBER

A connection with your past or an old haunt may be on your mind. You may hear key legal, work or personal news.

14 DECEMBER

The moon in Capricorn will encourage you to be practical about your endeavours. You may be ready to organise a trip.

15 DECEMBER

There are therapeutic aspects to the day. Someone close may pay you extra attention and someone may ask you for help.

16 DECEMBER

You'll enjoy doing something different this weekend. Just ensure you keep everyone in the loop.

17 DECEMBER

Keep your plans clear as otherwise there may be misunderstandings. Avoid minor bumps and scrapes.

18 DECEMBER

You'll enjoy a lovely reunion or return to an old haunt. You may hear news from the past. A debt may be repaid.

19 DECEMBER

You will enjoy some of the mystical and magical aspects of this time of year and may be ready for a break or a fresh environment.

20 DECEMBER

There is a sociable yet busy aspect to the day that you'll enjoy. Romance could blossom, so take the initiative.

21 DECEMBER

A change of pace or of place may involve someone close or a surprise.

22 DECEMBER

You will receive news from someone close and may enjoy a reunion.

23 DECEMBER

You may need a day or so to acclimatise to a new pace or place, and someone will help you to do so.

24 DECEMBER

You will enjoy relaxing and slowing the pace but also a fun and sociable time.

25 DECEMBER

Merry Christmas! You will enjoy a relaxing day that adds a little touch of magic to the week.

26 DECEMBER

A reunion or nostalgic feeling will encourage you to deepen your relationship with someone special.

27 DECEMBER

The Cancer full moon represents the start of a new cycle in a relationship. For some a trip will be a catalyst. Avoid misunderstandings.

28 DECEMBER

You and someone close will wish to be outgoing and upbeat, however, someone close may not be on the same page so try to find common ground.

29 DECEMBER

This is a lovely time to make changes in your daily routine or circumstances. Romance and adventure will appeal; just ensure you have the full facts.

30 DECEMBER

The moon in Leo will bring out your adventurous side and you will love being active and outgoing.

31 DECEMBER

Happy New Year! This will be a sociable New Year's Eve for you, although as the day progresses you may be inclined to take it easy.

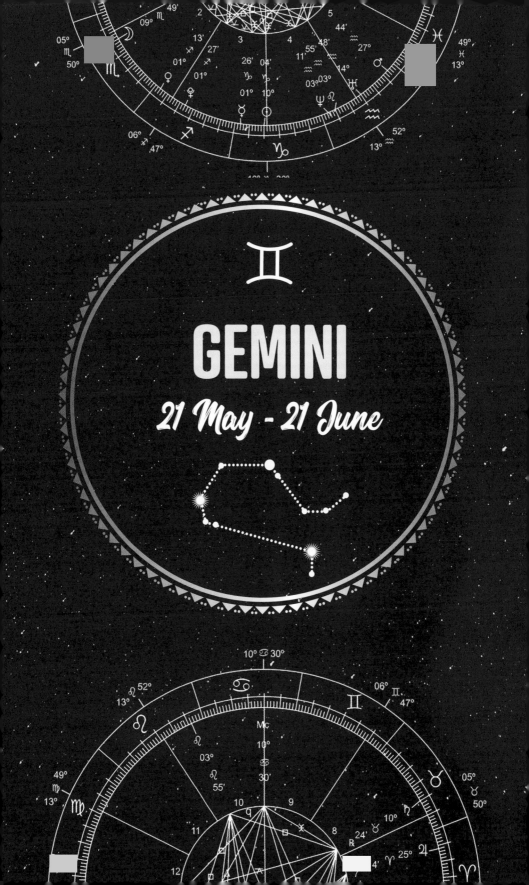

GEMINI

21 May - 21 June

FINANCES

Mars and subsequently Venus and Mercury in your second house of finances from the end of March until mid-July will place a great deal of focus on the importance of sound money management. There will be a tense period in May when you would be well advised to avoid impulsive investments, yet the new moon on the 19th will make a work or financial development very attractive. The most important news in 2023 financially is to embrace the new but also take things one step at a time, then you could build true and lasting wealth.

HEALTH

Prepare for a roller-coaster ride in 2023 as you make changes within your daily routine on a fundamental level. As you tend to live on your nerves, this could mean you burn the candle at both ends and then suffer from exhaustion, so be prepared to take breaks when you can. You are likely to be meeting all kinds of new people and finding fresh ways to collaborate, which puts you in your element socially and will contribute to a happier demeanour.

LOVE LIFE

This is a sociable year, one you'll love from the perspective of meeting new people. Being a social butterfly, you appreciate the chance to flap your wings. If you're single you're likely to meet someone upbeat and perhaps even passionate in April, May or October, and with Mars in your sign until the end of March you will be feeling more outgoing and optimistic and so are likely to attract similarly outgoing people. Venus in your sign from mid-April until early May makes this phase ideal for meeting someone new, then Mercury in your sign from mid-June for two weeks is another opportunity to meet people. Couples will enjoy feeling more adventurous, but if your relationship has been on the skids for a while then 2023 could be the year you go your separate ways.

CAREER

Neptune at the mid-heaven of your chart could lead to an idealistic approach to your career this year. You may even entertain something completely new or find something that has more meaning to you in your career development. However, you must be careful to research any changes you make as you could be seeing your career through rose-coloured glasses, especially at the end of April and in October. Keep your feet on the ground, though, and you could attain a true goal in 2023 and gain kudos as a result.

HOME LIFE

You will be undergoing an adjustment in how you share duties, responsibilities and personal and domestic space in 2023, so this is a year of great change in your home life. As Pluto changes signs from stable and sometimes stuck Capricorn at the end of March, expect to experience the desire to alter important shared concerns. For some this will be due to developments at work or financially, but they will have the knock-on effect of creating fresh developments at home.

January

1 JANUARY

Happy New Year! Prepare for considerable changes this year within your status, direction or career. You may experience signs of this today already.

2 JANUARY

You will enjoy socialising and meeting inspired and interesting people. Someone may need your help, and if you need support it will be available.

3 JANUARY

Be prepared to try something new. You are likely to be drawn to exciting activities and you'll appreciate expressing your creativity.

4 JANUARY

There is an upbeat and outgoing atmosphere to the day, so it's a good time to enjoy sports and your favourite activities.

5 JANUARY

You may hear unexpectedly from an old friend or will enjoy a lovely change of routine. Be spontaneous.

6 JANUARY

The Cancer full moon signals a new financial chapter in your life; you may also be preparing to alter how you share space and duties. This is a good time to focus on self-nurturance.

7 JANUARY

News from an old friend or a get-together will be enjoyable, so organise a date!

8 JANUARY

You may hear unexpectedly from someone from your past or will be surprised by a spontaneous meeting.

9 JANUARY

You are likely to resume a past schedule such as a work routine. You will enjoy a reunion with someone special.

10 JANUARY

This is a good time to organise how best to spend your time at home and to maximise time with those you love.

11 JANUARY

You may receive news to do with someone's health or well-being. The more tactful you are the better. Avoid misunderstandings.

12 JANUARY

You will gain the chance to feel more dynamic and proactive over the coming days and may already have experienced improved energy levels.

13 JANUARY

This is a good day for meetings and romance could blossom this evening, so why not organise a date?

14 JANUARY

This is a good time for collaborations and to share chores equally. You may be drawn to making a commitment to a project.

15 JANUARY

You may need to alter some of your plans at short notice. Be prepared to be flexible and avoid taking developments personally. You may be called in to work unexpectedly.

16 JANUARY

A change of routine will require you to be flexible and adaptable and to achieve results, so be prepared to do your best.

17 JANUARY

The more tactful and diplomatic you are the better for you as you will avoid difficult conversations.

18 JANUARY

You may receive news from someone close that will give you a heads-up about the best way to move forward.

19 JANUARY

This is a good time to be practical and to base your plans and decisions on facts, not supposition.

20 JANUARY

You'll enjoy the sense that your activities are changing and your horizons broadening, so plan ahead optimistically.

21 JANUARY

The new moon in Aquarius suggests that travel, study and entering new territory will appeal. You'll enjoy planning ahead.

22 JANUARY

You may be surprised by news you receive. A meeting will be encouraging.

23 JANUARY

You'll enjoy being adventurous and outgoing and will be prepared to investigate and research attractive avenues.

24 JANUARY

You will be inspired by those you spend time with so choose your company wisely. Avoid misunderstandings.

25 JANUARY

This is a lovely day for get-togethers and meetings both in your personal life and at work. Romance could flourish.

26 JANUARY

The moon in Aries will encourage you to socialise and network. You will enjoy meeting a diverse crowd.

27 JANUARY

Your opinion and expertise will be needed, and if you need advice it will be available. Avoid misunderstandings and minor accidents.

28 JANUARY

The more practical you are the best it will be for you. Just be careful with communications.

29 JANUARY

You will appreciate the time to relax and focus on your favourite activities. You may hear unexpectedly from the past and will enjoy a get-together.

30 JANUARY

You may hear unexpectedly from someone from the past and could enjoy a change of routine. You may receive unexpected news at work or regarding your health.

31 JANUARY

You can make great progress at work and will enjoy socialising and networking. A friend or organisation will be helpful.

February

1 FEBRUARY

You can make a great deal of progress at work so take the initiative. It's a good day for a health treat.

2 FEBRUARY

The moon in Cancer will bring out your intuition, so trust your instincts. Avoid overspending if you're shopping.

3 FEBRUARY

This is a good day to discuss your ideas with a group or a friend, but you must be prepared to be flexible.

4 FEBRUARY

You may be surprised by a change of schedule. You may be called in to work unexpectedly or will need to make a change to your usual routine.

5 FEBRUARY

The full moon in Leo will spotlight changes at home for some and at work for others. Be prepared to listen to another person's opinions to avoid arguments.

6 FEBRUARY

You will enjoy socialising and networking, and the arts, music and romance. Avoid being forgetful and absent-minded.

7 FEBRUARY

This is a good time to focus on details at work and with practical matters at home. Avoid being overly analytical and critical of yourself and others.

8 FEBRUARY

You will enjoy a change of pace at work or socially, and the more spontaneous you can be the more you will enjoy the day.

9 FEBRUARY

This is a good day for talks and meetings at work and with authority figures. You will enjoy a favourite activity and could make a valid commitment.

10 FEBRUARY

A trip, meeting or news from afar may be intense or complex, so give yourself time to investigate.

11 FEBRUARY

You will enjoy a change of pace but may need to take some time to unwind before you begin to enjoy your weekend.

12 FEBRUARY

There is a healing aspect to the day that will enable you to mend bridges if necessary and to focus on your health.

13 FEBRUARY

You will feel motivated to get ahead with your projects and chores and could be very productive, so take the initiative.

14 FEBRUARY

Happy St Valentine's Day! Today and tomorrow are ideal for socialising and networking. However, you must focus at work to avoid making mistakes.

15 FEBRUARY

You have a romantic view of someone and you may find out whether or not this is warranted. You will enjoy the arts and romance.

16 FEBRUARY

This is a good day to make a commitment to a work project or organisation; just ensure you have the full facts.

17 FEBRUARY

This is a good day to be practical about collaborations and to ensure you are on the same page.

18 FEBRUARY

You will enjoy socialising and engaging in your favourite activities. You are likely to feel increasingly creative and spiritually inclined.

19 FEBRUARY

This is a good day for get-togethers and for making practical plans with friends and for work projects.

20 FEBRUARY

The new moon in Pisces is a good time to begin a fresh venture, especially regarding favourite activities, travel and health.

21 FEBRUARY

You may be surprised by a change in your usual routine. Be prepared to be flexible.

22 FEBRUARY

This is a good day for talks and meetings, especially at work and regarding health and travel. A trip is likely to go well.

23 FEBRUARY

The moon in Aries will motivate you to get things done and to plan lovely activities.

24 FEBRUARY

You will enjoy a get-together. You may meet someone who appears familiar even if you have never met before. You may return to an old haunt.

25 FEBRUARY

When the moon is in Taurus you will feel more intuitive and able to read the room. Trust your impressions.

26 FEBRUARY

You will feel increasingly comfortable and relaxed, so be patient and aim to complete chores earlier in the day.

27 FEBRUARY

You will enjoy get-togethers or a short trip. You will also be drawn to music, romance and the arts.

28 FEBRUARY

The moon in your own sign will encourage you to be more outgoing and chatty. Just ensure you have all the information when you are making big decisions.

March

1 MARCH

You may be required to take the lead. Trust your intuition, as it is likely to be spot on.

2 MARCH

You will enjoy a reunion or news from a friend or organisation. It's a good day to research your circumstances and get help from experts.

3 MARCH

This is another good day for discussions, research and meetings. You may receive positive news at work. Someone may need your help.

4 MARCH

Be positive even if you feel the goal posts are moving. Your optimism will be infectious.

5 MARCH

You will appreciate news from your past or an unexpected meeting. Be spontaneous.

6 MARCH

You may need to alter your schedule at a moment's notice. Unexpected news is on the way.

7 MARCH

The full moon in Virgo spotlights a fresh chapter in your personal life such as with family or a friend. You may turn a corner with a creative project.

8 MARCH

You will be successful by collaborating and co-operating. Avoid being critical of yourself and others.

9 MARCH

You will not get on with everyone all the time, and your good communication skills will be in demand to avoid arguments.

10 MARCH

This is a lovely day for meetings and discussions. You may enjoy a short trip and a health boost.

11 MARCH

You will enjoy a reunion and the chance to do something different. A fun get-together will raise spirits.

12 MARCH

This is a good day for self-development and improving your health. You may need to help someone or ask for help yourself.

13 MARCH

An outgoing and upbeat approach will be effective and you can certainly achieve a great deal both at work and in your personal endeavours.

14 MARCH

Mars in your sign helps you to be motivated and productive, but it is important to be tactful to avoid difficult communications. Base your decisions on facts.

15 MARCH

You will enjoy a meeting and investing time in romance, the arts and music. However, you may be easily misled so be careful when making decisions.

16 MARCH

Mars in your sign is predisposing you to brush aside decision-making. You may be under pressure and mistakes can be made.

17 MARCH

Key news from a great friend or organisation will be significant. Avoid being easily led and making mistakes. You will enjoy a favourite pastime.

18 MARCH

You'll enjoy doing something different this weekend, so why not plan something special?

19 MARCH

A favourite activity will broaden your horizons and you'll enjoy meeting like-minded people.

20 MARCH

This is a good day for work and health improvements. You may be prepared to commit to a project. News may surprise you.

21 MARCH

The Aries new moon signals a fresh connection with a friend or organisation. Be prepared to turn the corner and leave the past behind.

22 MARCH

When the moon is in Aries you'll be outgoing and sociable, but you may appear a little feisty so be sure to channel your energy into productive activities.

23 MARCH

You are entering different territory. For some this will mean travel and exploration or a new project and for others a fresh development in your personal life.

24 MARCH

You may need to reconsider some of your loyalties as you forge fresh alliances.

25 MARCH

You have some lovely support and friendships. As you venture into fresh territory you will meet many new people. Avoid making rash decisions.

26 MARCH

The moon in your sign will bring out your sociable self and you'll enjoy being a social butterfly.

27 MARCH

This is a good time to focus on your health and appearance. Someone may need your help unexpectedly, and if you need advice it will be available.

28 MARCH

A get-together or trip down memory lane will be significant. Health, financial or work news is on the way.

29 MARCH

This is a good day to aim to co-operate and collaborate as you may actually feel like doing the opposite. Be prepared to compassionately express yourself.

30 MARCH

Be prepared for a surprise. You will enjoy doing something different and may receive a compliment. Just avoid making rash choices.

31 MARCH

This can be a sociable end to the week, but if you prefer to take things easy you'll enjoy the comforts of home.

April

1 APRIL

There is a lovely sociable aspect to your weekend. You will enjoy a reunion and indulging in a little luxury.

2 APRIL

The past will feel very present. You'll enjoy a get-together and a return to an old haunt.

3 APRIL

Be patient, as you may be under pressure and must choose your actions carefully. Avoid arguments and feeling that Rome can be built in one day.

4 APRIL

You will appreciate the opportunity to relax and enjoy the company of someone special.

5 APRIL

This is a good time to focus on your health and well-being. You may hear from the past. Someone may need your help.

6 APRIL

The full moon in Libra will remind you that you're turning a key corner in your life. Be prepared to improve your health or that of someone close.

7 APRIL

You will enjoy an uplifting meeting or receive good news. Just avoid forgetfulness.

8 APRIL

This is a good day for financial matters and for improving your daily life and health.

9 APRIL

You like to be passionate about your work and daily activities and will find the motivation and inspiration to enjoy life.

10 APRIL

You are relating well with people both at work and at home, so it's a good day to discuss important matters.

11 APRIL

You are likely to enjoy a trip somewhere beautiful and perhaps even down memory lane. A meeting or news will boost morale.

12 APRIL

Be practical at work and with your plans as you can get a great deal done. Just avoid overspending.

13 APRIL

You will enjoy leaving your comfort zone even if some discussions will merit tact and diplomacy.

14 APRIL

You will enjoy meeting someone you look up to. You could make great progress at work but you must be careful with money. Avoid compromising your principles.

15 APRIL

A change of pace or of scenery will encourage you to see the best in life.

16 APRIL

This is a lovely day for relaxation and self-care. Romance could blossom, so organise a date!

17 APRIL

You will enjoy being creative and dreaming a little, so you'll need to focus more at work on the details.

18 APRIL

The moon in Aries for the next two days will bring out your ability to socialise and network and to be positive and proactive.

19 APRIL

You will be happy to progress at a swift rate, however, not everyone will move at the same pace so be patient.

20 APRIL

The total solar eclipse in Aries will kick-start an important chapter in your life, for most Geminis in your daily life, work or health schedule and for some in the organisations you join.

21 APRIL

Important communications may be unexpected. You may be in a new circumstance, so be adaptable.

22 APRIL

The more practical you are the more you will enjoy your day. You will appreciate a health or beauty treat.

23 APRIL

The moon in Gemini will bring out your chatty self and you'll enjoy being more outgoing.

24 APRIL

You can make great headway with communications and meetings, especially financially. Just avoid overspending if you're shopping.

25 APRIL

It's a good day to make a personal or financial commitment as long as you have the full facts.

26 APRIL

Trust your instincts, especially financially. Avoid taking someone's news personally.

27 APRIL

You may receive surprise news and may also receive an unexpected compliment or financial boost.

28 APRIL

This is a good time to focus on your home and well-being. You may appreciate a visitor.

29 APRIL

You will enjoy doing something different, and the more spontaneous you are the more you'll enjoy a fresh opportunity.

30 APRIL

You will enjoy a return to an old haunt or a reunion and the feeling that you belong. Avoid overspending if you're shopping.

May

1 MAY

You may discover you have new interests and must make fresh plans as a result. You will get the chance to review circumstances.

2 MAY

News or a meeting will catch your eye, helping you to review or understand the past. This is a good day for a get-together.

3 MAY

This is a good day to find more balance in your personal life and family as your efforts will succeed.

4 MAY

You won't always agree with everyone's opinions nor will they agree with yours, so maintain perspective. Avoid mixed messages.

5 MAY

The lunar eclipse in Scorpio signals a fresh chapter in a daily, health or work schedule. You may receive a financial or personal boost.

6 MAY

This is a good weekend for getting things done around the house and garden. You may also enjoy sports and being outdoors.

7 MAY

You may be inclined to follow the crowd but may find more happiness in choosing your own path.

8 MAY

You are communicating well and will manage to review work and health plans if necessary.

9 MAY

You may hear unexpectedly from someone from the past, or regarding work or health.

10 MAY

Be practical, as you will achieve a great deal as a result. Avoid feeling pressured, especially at work.

11 MAY

Think outside the box, as this will help you overcome any conundrums. Trust your intuition.

12 MAY

This is a good day for meetings, both at work and in your personal life. You may need to review a plan.

13 MAY

This is a good day for reviewing your finances and it's a good day for making a financial or personal commitment. You may enjoy a reunion.

14 MAY

Trust your instincts, as you are intuitive at the moment. You will enjoy socialising, music and relaxing.

15 MAY

News at work will encourage you to be more outgoing, talkative and creative. You'll enjoy a get-together.

16 MAY

As Jupiter enters Taurus you'll focus increasingly on health, well-being and a balanced daily schedule. Spirituality will also be a drawcard.

17 MAY

Avoid taking on too much work and putting yourself under pressure over the next 12 months. Find time for the activities you love.

18 MAY

This may be an intense day. Be prepared to reason with someone at work or regarding a long-term project for the best outcome.

19 MAY

The Taurus new moon signals a fresh daily or health routine. You may be ready to make a key commitment at work or financially.

20 MAY

You'll enjoy the sense that your mojo is coming back as you will find expressing yourself easier this weekend. Enjoy!

21 MAY

While you are likely to feel more energetic others may be slightly intense or even argumentative, so you must avoid conflict as it will escalate.

22 MAY

You are likely to receive good news and will enjoy get-togethers and, for some, a short trip.

23 MAY

Someone close to you may appear more stubborn than they need to be. Luckily you are on top form with your communications and will manage to overcome adversity.

24 MAY

It's a good time to choose your loyalties wisely as you may be inclined to take someone's side due to misplaced loyalty. Avoid conflict, as it will escalate.

25 MAY

The Leo moon will bring out your inner dragon. You will be productive but could seem antagonistic. Be tactful.

26 MAY

Be prepared to be spontaneous as you may enjoy a last-minute change of schedule. You may receive an unexpected financial or personal improvement.

27 MAY

The more practical you are with domestic matters the better the outcome, and you will enjoy relaxing once your chores are completed.

28 MAY

A father figure or person in authority may seem to be flexing their muscles. Be diplomatic to achieve a good outcome.

29 MAY

You will appreciate planning a treat for yourself or someone special, so plan clever ways to relax later in the day.

30 MAY

You will appreciate being able to restore some balance in your personal life, so take the initiative.

31 MAY

You are known to be charming and your charm will be invaluable, especially if you feel a little under the weather.

June

1 JUNE

Plan travel and meetings well in advance to avoid delays and misunderstandings for the best results.

2 JUNE

You will enjoy a reunion. A health or work matter may need a review, so be prepared to go over old ground.

3 JUNE

This will be a productive day, and if you work in a creative field your imagination will do you proud.

4 JUNE

The full moon signals a new chapter in a key financial agreement or relationship. You may begin a fresh daily schedule. News might be unexpected.

5 JUNE

You or someone close is likely to express deep feelings. A trip or project may bring out a deep spiritual connection.

6 JUNE

Be prepared to put in the extra legwork, as you'll be glad about the results.

7 JUNE

This is a good day to seek a fresh perspective regarding a project or learning curve. Be prepared to think outside the box.

8 JUNE

Be proactive and positive. Avoid feeling you're stuck or being slowed down by an obstinate person or concern.

9 JUNE

This is a good day for socialising, for improving health and appearance and for romance and the arts.

10 JUNE

You will enjoy some self-development or a spiritual endeavour. Look for inspiration from the people you admire.

11 JUNE

You may be drawn to the past and travelling to somewhere familiar. A reunion will be enjoyable.

12 JUNE

You will appear to others as energetic and dynamic, which will increase your self-confidence and enable you to be productive and enjoy your day.

13 JUNE

Check that everyone is on the same page with your various plans and projects. You may need to work hard but you will succeed as a result.

14 JUNE

The moon in Taurus may accentuate your stubbornness or someone else's need for stability. Be prepared to be adaptable and flexible.

15 JUNE

You may receive positive work or health news. A reunion will be enjoyable, but you must avoid misunderstandings by being super clear.

16 JUNE

The Gemini moon for the next two days will encourage you to be chatty and sociable. You may undergo a financial improvement.

17 JUNE

You will appreciate the opportunity to spend time on yourself, including improving health and your wardrobe. You may begin to see yourself in a new light.

18 JUNE

Make a wish at the new moon in Gemini, which signals you are beginning an important fresh phase in your personal life.

19 JUNE

This is a good day to make a commitment to a person or project. Just ensure you have done your research and avoid delays and mix-ups.

20 JUNE

This is a good day to focus on planning events and meetings that will involve creativity and imagination.

21 JUNE

It's the solstice, a good time to consider how to self-nurture more and be more supportive of others. Avoid a battle of egos.

22 JUNE

You will feel motivated to get things done, and your connections with others both at work and at home will deepen.

23 JUNE

Someone may need your help, and if you need advice it will be available. There is a healing atmosphere and you'll enjoy reconnecting with someone.

24 JUNE

You will enjoy a change of pace and the chance to get things shipshape at home and in your environment.

25 JUNE

You are generally a good communicator, but sometimes even you can get things muddled. Avoid misunderstandings and delays.

26 JUNE

You may be surprised by a sudden or unusual change of schedule. News may be unexpected. Plan ahead to avoid traffic delays.

27 JUNE

You will enjoy meeting like-minded people, and it's a good day for get-togethers. You may meet someone familiar.

28 JUNE

Trust your intuition, as it will help you to make important decisions and form accurate impressions of people.

29 JUNE

This is a good day for work and to advance your projects. A group or expert may be particularly helpful.

30 JUNE

You may receive beneficial news at work or regarding finances. It is a good day for meetings such as interviews.

July

1 JULY

You may receive a financial or ego boost. A lovely get-together will provide a sense of stability. This is a good day to make a commitment.

2 JULY

You may receive an unexpected visitor or will need to change your routine at short notice.

3 JULY

The full moon in Capricorn will shine a light on your relationships. You'll begin a fresh chapter in an important relationship.

4 JULY

Be practical and patient about changes you wish to make as you could make great progress.

5 JULY

Be prepared to be flexible about various arrangements and activities. Embrace something new.

6 JULY

This is a good time to be careful with finances and with where you place your loyalties. Do-it-yourself projects may involve complexities but you will succeed.

7 JULY

You may hear unexpected news from the past. This is a good time to clear a debt and you may experience a financial improvement.

8 JULY

This is a good weekend for improving family and domestic dynamics. You may be drawn to some do-it-yourself projects or home renovation.

9 JULY

It will be to your benefit to tread carefully with some people and avoid sensitive topics for the best results.

10 JULY

This is a good day for creativity and financial matters. However, you must avoid being easily distracted.

11 JULY

Communications are likely to get busier over the coming weeks. You may be seen as being a little feistier, so maintain perspective.

12 JULY

Be prepared to take other people's opinions into account. You will not always agree with them, but you mustn't take their adverse comments personally.

13 JULY

As the day goes by you may see a shift in mood, going from feeling a little stuck to feeling more outgoing and optimistic.

14 JULY

You will enjoy an impromptu event but must keep those who rely on you in the loop. You may receive an unexpected compliment.

15 JULY

You are an independent character and like to organise your own activities. You'll feel more in tune with others as the day goes by.

16 JULY

If you are diligent with your various projects you will enjoy the outcome, so be positive.

17 JULY

The Cancer new moon signals the chance to forge fresh agreements with a friend or organisation. Some Geminis may find this a good time to reorganise finances.

18 JULY

Your willingness to discuss your ideas will be effective. You may be inclined to avoid change, so aim to be flexible.

19 JULY

You are generally known for being adaptable yet you may be inclined to get stuck on an idea now. Research the facts for the best results.

20 JULY

You will enjoy socialising and networking and may also appreciate a trip somewhere beautiful.

21 JULY

This is a good day to make an agreement at home or regarding work, especially if you have researched the facts.

22 JULY

Someone may express intense emotions or will require your help and advice. Avoid clinging to the past for the sake of it.

23 JULY

You may need to alter your plans abruptly. A domestic matter will require attention. Avoid arguments and misunderstandings.

24 JULY

Focus on activities and people who make you happy. Avoid making a tense situation worse; look for balance.

25 JULY

Be optimistic about projects at work and at home by focusing on being creative and proactive.

26 JULY

You will feel more passionate about your projects and personal life, so aim to engage in activities you love.

27 JULY

You'll enjoy a reunion and the chance to review some domestic matters. You will progress by relying on facts, not assumptions.

28 JULY

Be careful to check you are loyal to certain values and principles and avoid standing up for someone who does not support you.

29 JULY

Be prepared to work hard at achieving your goals and you may be surprised at what you can achieve.

30 JULY

Changes you are making at home and in your personal life will be successful, but you must be patient and avoid giving mixed messages.

31 JULY

The Capricorn moon will encourage you to be practical both at home and at work. Avoid being distracted by other people's business.

August

1 AUGUST

The full moon supermoon in Aquarius spells a new phase in your activities. A trip or fresh agreement may be on the cards.

2 AUGUST

You may receive important news at work or at home. It's a good time to be practical with any commitments you are about to make.

3 AUGUST

Be prepared to think outside the square, especially if a difficulty arises.

4 AUGUST

You may be seeing someone or a project through rose-coloured glasses. Romance and the arts will thrive.

5 AUGUST

This is an active and outgoing weekend. It's also a good time for home improvements.

6 AUGUST

You'll enjoy socialising and networking and may enjoy something different or a new social circle.

7 AUGUST

Be prepared to listen to the opinions and ideas of others but also to stick with trusted methods to avoid making mistakes.

8 AUGUST

You will enjoy spending some quiet time to refuel your energy levels. Time spent at home will be enjoyable. Avoid arguments at work.

9 AUGUST

You may be surprised by someone's intense viewpoints or by a change of schedule or plan. Be prepared to state your case if you feel you're being hard done by.

10 AUGUST

This is a good day for a reunion and to improve domestic circumstances. You will be productive both at home and at work.

11 AUGUST

You are communicating well at the moment but may be seen as being critical of others and of yourself, so maintain perspective.

12 AUGUST

This is a good time to focus on promoting a relaxing atmosphere at home. You may enjoy an impromptu visit or surprise guest.

13 AUGUST

You will enjoy a lovely get-together and improving domestic dynamics or decor.

14 AUGUST

Be prepared to back up your ideas and projects with enthusiasm and be positive, as you can make headway in your chosen fields.

15 AUGUST

It's a good day for talks and meetings, especially regarding home improvements. Romance could flourish.

16 AUGUST

The new moon in Leo signals you are turning a corner at work or at home. Be prepared for a surprise and to support your plans.

17 AUGUST

The more precise you can be the better will be the outcome. Ensure you base your ideas on facts.

18 AUGUST

You can make a great deal of progress with a creative project and at work. You'll enjoy a reunion.

19 AUGUST

This is a productive and also sociable weekend that you'll enjoy. The arts and music will be drawcards.

20 AUGUST

A social or domestic circumstance will demand you be tactful. If you have made a mistake, this is the time to rectify it.

21 AUGUST

Gain the information you need, especially regarding domestic and shared matters, as this will put you in a strong position.

22 AUGUST

Avoid being drawn into an intriguing situation or even arguments by being practical and down to earth.

23 AUGUST

You may find your focus goes on details and as a result information may come to light that you must act upon. It is better earlier than later.

24 AUGUST

This is a good time to be practical and put your energy into projects you feel passionate about.

25 AUGUST

You can steam ahead with projects you are truly invested in as they are likely to succeed. Romance, work and family relationships could blossom.

26 AUGUST

As the weekend goes by you will appreciate an increased sense of security, especially in your personal life.

27 AUGUST

This is a good time to make a serious commitment, especially regarding your home or work life and status.

28 AUGUST

Be prepared to step into new territory at work or within your status. Be prepared to stand up to the naysayers.

29 AUGUST

Your clever plans can succeed; be innovative and think outside the square if problems arise. You will feel motivated to find peace over the coming weeks.

30 AUGUST

You may be drawn to being a little idealistic, so double-check your plans are practical and, if so, set them in motion.

31 AUGUST

The Pisces full moon supermoon spotlights your social life. Be open to meeting new people. Avoid taking random comments personally.

September

1 SEPTEMBER

It's a great day to show just what you're capable of both at work and in your personal life, but you must avoid arguments.

2 SEPTEMBER

You'll enjoy socialising and a reunion but should avoid making rash decisions.

3 SEPTEMBER

This is a lovely day to focus on taking a little downtime and enjoying your domestic environment.

4 SEPTEMBER

You are likely to get ahead at work. You will enjoy a trip or a reunion. This is also a good day for a health appointment.

5 SEPTEMBER

This is a good day for talks and discussions, especially around family and to do with property and travel.

6 SEPTEMBER

You will appreciate a visit or trip. This is a good time to discuss changes at home and at work.

7 SEPTEMBER

A trip will be enjoyable. Your connection with a sibling or neighbour can improve. It's a good time to discuss domestic finances.

8 SEPTEMBER

A link with your past could be lucky, and key news or a meeting will be decisive.

9 SEPTEMBER

Use your intuition, especially at work and with domestic or family matters, as it is working well now.

10 SEPTEMBER

You may be feeling super sensitive so plan to take things easy. Be practical and inspired with arrangements that are already in play.

11 SEPTEMBER

This is a lovely day for romance and creative projects. You'll be drawn to music and dance. Do-it-yourself projects are likely to go well.

12 SEPTEMBER

Your enthusiasm is infectious and will enable you to overcome any obstacles. Be positive.

13 SEPTEMBER

Your efficiency is outstanding; just avoid taking on too much at once.

14 SEPTEMBER

The lead-up to the new moon is a good time to make a wish, especially regarding your personal and social lives and creative projects.

15 SEPTEMBER

If you have been planning a family, romance or changes at home, be practical and a dream could come true.

16 SEPTEMBER

You may be pleasantly surprised by news. Be open to fresh ideas. You will enjoy a change of routine.

17 SEPTEMBER

You have some particular plans and mostly they coincide with your other plans, but you may need to compromise.

18 SEPTEMBER

You will be productive, especially regarding chores and work, so lean in! Just avoid forgetfulness.

19 SEPTEMBER

You'll enjoy dreaming and pursuing your goals but you must be super clear to avoid misunderstandings and delays. Creative projects and romance will flourish.

20 SEPTEMBER

A little synchronicity will help your efforts along so you remain focused on your goals.

21 SEPTEMBER

You will see your projects and certain relationships flourish, so be prepared to take the initiative.

22 SEPTEMBER

You may need to work that little bit extra hard but it will be worth it. You will find ways to enjoy your Friday.

23 SEPTEMBER

The sun in Libra will encourage you to look for peace and balance, especially in your personal life.

24 SEPTEMBER

This is a good day to focus on good communication skills to avoid hurt feelings. Avoid taking other people's rash comments personally.

25 SEPTEMBER

Choose your words carefully and you could make great progress both at home and at work.

26 SEPTEMBER

An unexpected project or development will keep you on your toes, so be spontaneous.

27 SEPTEMBER

You are thinking creatively and imaginatively and will enjoy upbeat activities.

28 SEPTEMBER

You are inspired, making this a good time for self-development and spiritual enquiry. Trust your instincts.

29 SEPTEMBER

The Aries full moon signals the start of a new phase in your personal life. You may be drawn to fresh groups, circles and people.

30 SEPTEMBER

You are dynamic and productive right now but may appear a little feisty to others, so be sure to maintain perspective.

October

1 OCTOBER

You may experience a surprise or undergo a challenge, but rest assured you will gain ground and attain your goals. It's a good day for a trip or talks.

2 OCTOBER

It's a good day to get on top of chores both at home and at work. Just avoid misunderstandings and delays.

3 OCTOBER

You will appreciate the chance to get involved in your favourite activities and interests. Make the most of your day by being practical and realistic.

4 OCTOBER

The Gemini moon will put you in a positive frame of mind, but you must be careful with financial matters.

5 OCTOBER

Work towards an outcome and you may experience a financial or work improvement.

6 OCTOBER

This is a good day to focus on collaborations. You may need to compromise with someone for the best results.

7 OCTOBER

Some chores may be more difficult than others, but rest assured you'll find ways to overcome a hurdle.

8 OCTOBER

Take the initiative and you could enjoy some lovely activities and get-togethers. It's also a good day to relax.

9 OCTOBER

You may need to focus on the details of paperwork and talks. Avoid arguments, as they will escalate.

10 OCTOBER

Be prepared to be tactful and pay attention to details for the best results. You could make an important commitment.

11 OCTOBER

You may feel sensitive, especially in large groups. Avoid taking people's random comments personally.

12 OCTOBER

You will gain a sense of being passionate about your projects but you must be careful to avoid mix-ups.

13 OCTOBER

This is a good day for getting ahead at work and making concrete plans for fun events.

14 OCTOBER

The solar eclipse represents a new chapter in your personal life. Be prepared to look after yourself.

15 OCTOBER

You may be surprised by events or a change of plan. Some communications may be out of the ordinary.

16 OCTOBER

You will feel motivated to get things done and may need to adjust part of your schedule to do so.

17 OCTOBER

Quirky news or an unexpected change of plan may cause problems, so keep an eye on your goals.

18 OCTOBER

This is a good day to improve your health and well-being and to focus on finding help for yourself or someone else if necessary.

19 OCTOBER

You will enjoy a reunion. Certain news will be encouraging but you must base your decisions on facts, not assumptions.

20 OCTOBER

A meeting or news will demand that you find common ground, as the alternative is to enter into conflict that could be long standing.

21 OCTOBER

This may be an intense day, so ensure you find ways to unwind.

22 OCTOBER

Be practical and look for security and stability in your path moving forward to gain direction.

23 OCTOBER

The next four weeks could be a passionate and dramatic time, especially in your personal life or with family. Find ways to maintain balance in your life.

24 OCTOBER

This is a good day to make agreements and commitments at work and with family.

25 OCTOBER

There will be great merit in concentrating on details to avoid mistakes being made, even if they are not of your doing.

26 OCTOBER

This is a busy time for you and you may feel under pressure, so ensure you take breaks.

27 OCTOBER

You will enjoy socialising. Someone may need your help, and if you need help or advice it will be available.

28 OCTOBER

The lunar eclipse in Taurus signals a fresh chapter in your daily routine or health schedule. You may be drawn to a new group or organisation. Avoid making rash decisions.

29 OCTOBER

You will enjoy doing something different. A fun meeting will bring fresh air into your weekend.

30 OCTOBER

The next two days are ideal for making long-term changes, either at home or in your work life.

31 OCTOBER

Happy Halloween! You may be surprised by changes at home or in your personal life. It's a good time to welcome in the new.

November

1 NOVEMBER

The Gemini moon will bring your chatty, upbeat self out and you can attain a great deal. Just avoid being easily distracted.

2 NOVEMBER

Trust your intuition, especially with regard to money and work.

3 NOVEMBER

Be prepared to work hard as you can attain your goals, especially with creative projects. Romance will blossom, so organise a treat!

4 NOVEMBER

A change of routine or of place may surprise you or be unexpected.

5 NOVEMBER

Be prepared to see other people's points of view. You will attain your goals even if you feel you are under pressure.

6 NOVEMBER

This is a good day for important talks in your personal life and with family. You will enjoy a favourite activity.

7 NOVEMBER

You are thinking creatively and may enjoy some beneficial news. It's a good day to improve your appearance.

8 NOVEMBER

You have admirable goals in your personal life but you may need to focus more on work. You'll find balance in the coming weeks.

9 NOVEMBER

Be prepared to negotiate and agree with others within reason. This is a good day to transform your health and appearance.

10 NOVEMBER

Some tough talks to do with work or a person in a position of authority are best approached carefully.

11 NOVEMBER

You may wish to perform your chores quickly and make changes swiftly, but you must avoid making rash decisions.

12 NOVEMBER

You are likely to feel passionate about your plans, so ensure they are practical as well.

13 NOVEMBER

The Scorpio new moon signals a fresh chapter in your work or daily schedule and, for some, with health. You may be surprised by news.

14 NOVEMBER

Be bold about the changes you wish to make. This is a good day for research.

15 NOVEMBER

This is a good day for meetings and discussions, especially at work. It's also a good day for a beauty or health treat.

16 NOVEMBER

You are communicating well but not everyone else is, so you'll need to be patient with a friend or organisation.

17 NOVEMBER

You can make great headway at work by thinking creatively. This is a good day for romance and for meetings and socialising.

18 NOVEMBER

You'll be drawn to going to the beach and/or engaging in active pursuits. Socialising and spending time with like-minded people will appeal.

19 NOVEMBER

This is a good time to focus on improving interpersonal dynamics. Be prepared to think outside the box and meet new people.

20 NOVEMBER

Meetings at work are likely to go well, so take the initiative if you have important topics to discuss.

21 NOVEMBER

You may be feeling a little idealistic, so ensure you're also being realistic.

22 NOVEMBER

You will be drawn to adventure and new activities. If you need advice it will be available. Someone may need your help.

23 NOVEMBER

If you work hard at your goals you will certainly attain them. Just avoid cutting corners and frustration over rules and regulations.

24 NOVEMBER

You are likely to feel more gregarious and may be prone to risk-taking. To avoid misunderstandings, ensure you are on the same page as someone at work.

25 NOVEMBER

You are super productive now but must avoid feeling frustrated by restrictions or an authority figure such as an employer. Be patient.

26 NOVEMBER

Keep someone close to you in the loop, especially as you may prefer to be spontaneous.

27 NOVEMBER

The Gemini full moon signals a fresh phase in your personal life. Avoid making snap decisions.

28 NOVEMBER

You must be prepared to collaborate and cooperate at work, so discuss your plans and back them up with facts.

29 NOVEMBER

You can achieve your goals by working hard to prove your worth.

30 NOVEMBER

This is a good day for discussions with someone close such as a partner or colleague.

December

1 DECEMBER

As the weeks go by this month you'll feel more grounded, especially within your relationships. Just avoid stubbornness.

2 DECEMBER

This is a good day for talks with those in a position of authority. You may be closer to making a financial or personal agreement.

3 DECEMBER

As there is an intense aspect to the day, avoid rushing and find time to relax. Arguments could escalate, so avoid conflict.

4 DECEMBER

This is the beginning of a more active and motivational phase, so be prepared to initiate plans and activities.

5 DECEMBER

This is a good time to make a personal or work commitment as it is likely to succeed. It's also a good day for planning, especially financially.

6 DECEMBER

This is a creative and productive time for you. Just avoid unwarranted criticism of yourself and others.

7 DECEMBER

You will be looking for peace and harmony so avoid taking other people's problems on as your own. Avoid mix-ups.

8 DECEMBER

You may achieve a breakthrough either at work or in your personal life, so be positive.

9 DECEMBER

Be prepared to invest time and energy in those you love. You'll enjoy romance, music and the arts.

10 DECEMBER

This is a lovely day for romance and enjoying doing what you love, so ensure you organise a treat.

11 DECEMBER

Communications are going well at the moment, so be sure to organise talks and other communication.

12 DECEMBER

The Sagittarian new moon signals the start of a fresh chapter in a relationship or work situation, especially if you were born in mid-June. News may surprise you.

13 DECEMBER

Someone you share duties or space at home with has news for you. You will get the chance to review matters in the weeks to come.

14 DECEMBER

Be practical with your endeavours, especially those you share with others.

15 DECEMBER

There are therapeutic aspects to the day. Someone close may need your help, and if you need support it will be available.

16 DECEMBER

Be prepared to be flexible and enjoy something new this weekend such as socialising with a fresh group of people.

17 DECEMBER

You are a tactful character but sometimes even your patience is tried. If you are socialising, avoid overindulging as you will regret it!

18 DECEMBER

This is a lovely day for celebrations, meetings and a reunion, so take the initiative and plan a get-together.

19 DECEMBER

You'll feel you are in your element by taking the reins. Travel may appeal, as will socialising. Just avoid thorny topics.

20 DECEMBER

If you are working this will be a productive day. It's also a good day for a beauty treat and romance.

21 DECEMBER

A change of pace or of place will be enjoyable but may involve a surprise. Avoid making rash decisions.

22 DECEMBER

You will enjoy a get-together and a trip somewhere different. It's a busy time, so pace yourself.

23 DECEMBER

You will enjoy a reunion even if there is a little tension in the day. Be open to the new.

24 DECEMBER

You'll appreciate a feeling of stability and security even if there is a little uncertainty in the air or you miss someone.

25 DECEMBER

Merry Christmas! This is a romantic day on which you'll enjoy all the comforts and trimmings.

26 DECEMBER

You will appreciate a financial improvement and shopping may be a drawcard. You'll enjoy a reunion.

27 DECEMBER

The Cancer full moon represents the start of a new cycle in a relationship and, for some, financially. You will enjoy a trip but you must avoid delays and mix-ups.

28 DECEMBER

You may be inclined to experience delays and misunderstandings so you must plan ahead and be super clear.

29 DECEMBER

This is a lovely time to make changes in your daily routine. Just ensure you have the full facts when you are making serious decisions. Romance will blossom.

30 DECEMBER

The moon in Leo will encourage you to be outgoing and positive, especially in your relationships.

31 DECEMBER

Happy New Year! You will enjoy spending time with those you love the most and may even be a homebody this year.

CANCER

21 June – 22 July

FINANCES

You'll feel inspired in 2023 to invest wisely and make your money work for you. Once Saturn enters Pisces in early March and with Jupiter being adventurous at the zenith of your chart, you will be drawn to spending and investing in activities that resonate more deeply with you. As Jupiter leaves Aries and steps into practical Taurus in mid-May you will be drawn to earthing your projects and ventures and to being realistic. However, in the second half of the year you will need to double-check that your investments and activities are practical or you may be inclined to see money through rose-coloured glasses and overspend.

HEALTH

Chiron at the zenith of your chart all year points to a keen interest in health and well-being throughout the year, and to the chance to broaden your understanding of your own input into your physical, mental and emotional health and also into that of others. A particularly busy time health-wise is likely to be in early March and early April, so find ways then to focus on well-being as this will be a healing time. The end of June, early July and early December are also particularly therapeutic times.

LOVE LIFE

The year generally begins with the spotlight on your love life, as the full moon in your sign will bring out emotions. This makes early January a good time to carry out a health check on your love life and to tweak any aspects you'd like to refresh. The period from April to the new moon in Cancer on 17 July will provide excellent opportunities to revitalise your love life, so whether you're single or married this is the time to look for ways to zhuzh up your love life. Early December could be particularly romantic, so if you're single be sure to connect then.

CAREER

Your professional collaborations are due a change in 2023, so be prepared to transform aspects of your career that no longer resonate with you. This could mean a change of job, a fresh venture or simply a new boss, but you will find that you can step up the career ladder this year and especially during May and June and the end of August and September. Just avoid making rash decisions, especially in May and July. You may even get the chance to review an aspect of your career so it suits you better, so be proactive about finding a position you love. Your home life is due some changes and these will impact on your career, or vice versa. You must avoid making sudden decisions.

HOME LIFE

Changes in your personal and/or home life are likely in April and May this year, and these will provide an ideal opportunity to find more balance and harmony in these important parts of your life. If you have been hoping to travel and are able to this year you'll love the opportunity to wander far from home, but on your return you will also appreciate the security and stability a property provides. A change at work could mean a change at home, and the best months for do-it-yourself projects and home improvement are during the last quarter of the year. You may enjoy visits and guests more than usual at these times.

January

1 JANUARY

Happy New Year! It's an intense or even passionate start to the year. Someone close is likely to express strong feelings. It's a good day to rest if you can.

2 JANUARY

It's a good day to boost your health. Someone may need your help, and if you need help it will be available.

3 JANUARY

A fresh situation in a relationship will encourage you to be a little more outgoing.

4 JANUARY

This is a good day for get-togethers and getting ahead at work.

5 JANUARY

You will enjoy a change of routine and being spontaneous, and meeting a fresh group of people.

6 JANUARY

The Cancer full moon suggests you are ready to turn a corner in your personal life. You may also be ready for a fresh start at work.

7 JANUARY

A trip to an old haunt will be enjoyable. You may receive key news and will enjoy improving your health and well-being.

8 JANUARY

You may bump into an old friend or receive unusual news. Be prepared for a change of schedule.

9 JANUARY

This is a good day for romance and enjoying quality time doing what you love with people you love.

10 JANUARY

This is a good time to be meticulous with communications and finances and focus on your health to avoid minor bumps and scrapes.

11 JANUARY

You may need to review a health or personal situation. Avoid taking other people's random comments personally.

12 JANUARY

You may receive key news to do with work or health and may need to review your plans.

13 JANUARY

You may be drawn to an attractive and charming character. You'll enjoy spending time on your favourite activities.

14 JANUARY

Your projects and chores are likely to go well. This is a good day to discuss serious topics such as finances.

15 JANUARY

Some plans may alter at short notice, so be prepared to be flexible and avoid taking developments personally.

16 JANUARY

You will not always agree with everyone. Luckily you have charm on your side.

17 JANUARY

You are communicating well at the moment but must avoid being pressured into making rash decisions and mistakes.

18 JANUARY

You may receive news from a personal or business partner. You may need to review a work or health plan.

19 JANUARY

This is a good day to be practical, especially at work and regarding health. Someone close will prove to be supportive.

20 JANUARY

Someone close has plans that may affect yours. It's a good time to be adventurous and outgoing.

21 JANUARY

The new moon in Aquarius signals a first chapter in a relationship. This is a good time to make a wish. Be innovative.

22 JANUARY

This is a good time to organise finances and shared responsibilities. It's also a good day to make agreements as long as you have researched the facts.

23 JANUARY

Be inspired by people close to you but also maintain your strong vision. Find the balance.

24 JANUARY

You are an insightful and sensitive person so you must trust your instincts, especially concerning important decisions.

25 JANUARY

This is a lovely day for romance and for organising shared concerns.

26 JANUARY

The moon in Aries will encourage you to be productive, but you must avoid taking on too much work. Take breaks.

27 JANUARY

You may receive news at work or regarding health. Your help may be required. A teacher or authority figure has news for you.

28 JANUARY

A friend or group will be supportive of you. Just be careful with communications, especially with someone close.

29 JANUARY

You will enjoy spending time with like-minded people. However, a friend or family member may need your attention.

30 JANUARY

You are able to communicate well at the moment and may be surprised by the positive results your efforts produce.

31 JANUARY

You can make great headway at work and with your projects, so take the initiative. You will enjoy a favourite activity.

February

1 FEBRUARY

This is a good day to discuss sensitive topics and for mending bridges. A teacher or employer may be helpful.

2 FEBRUARY

The moon in your sign will encourage you to express yourself well and to gain insight into others.

3 FEBRUARY

Your feelings or those of someone close may be intense, so if you're at work maintain a professional stance.

4 FEBRUARY

A friend or organisation may have unexpected news. Be prepared to be spontaneous but avoid making rash decisions.

5 FEBRUARY

The full moon in Leo signals a fresh chapter in your personal life or financially. Avoid gambling and arguments, as you may regret both.

6 FEBRUARY

This is a good day for meetings at work and in your personal life. Just avoid being forgetful and absent-minded.

7 FEBRUARY

You may wish to gain a commitment or certainty from someone, so the more you lay your cards on the table the better it will be.

8 FEBRUARY

You may be surprised by an impromptu get-together or by news from an organisation.

9 FEBRUARY

This is a good day for negotiations and financial discussions. A commitment may be possible.

10 FEBRUARY

Discussions to do with money, shared duties or a relationship may be intense, so take breaks to avoid arguments.

11 FEBRUARY

Strong emotions may detract from an otherwise upbeat day, so find ways to channel feelings into productive activities.

12 FEBRUARY

You'll enjoy a favourite activity such as a trip somewhere beautiful. Spiritual endeavours will flourish.

13 FEBRUARY

You have a good connection with certain people at work, so trust that you have support.

14 FEBRUARY

Happy St Valentine's Day! You will enjoy being adventurous in the love stakes. Avoid taking matters too seriously.

15 FEBRUARY

You can make great progress in your career and chosen activities. This is a good day to improve your appearance and profile.

16 FEBRUARY

A commitment can be made, but you must ensure the agreements are clear.

17 FEBRUARY

Today's moon in Capricorn will help you to feel more grounded and able to work with certain people's unpredictability.

18 FEBRUARY

You will enjoy a favourite activity. This is a good day for a trip somewhere different and for talks and meetings, especially to do with money or legal matters.

19 FEBRUARY

You may be seen in a new light or see someone close differently. It's a good day to deepen relationships.

20 FEBRUARY

The new moon in Pisces signals a fresh chapter in an inspired project. There are healing aspects to the day. An expert will be helpful.

21 FEBRUARY

You may discover information that does not add up. You'll progress by establishing common ground.

22 FEBRUARY

This is a better day for communications. A work or personal matter can progress.

23 FEBRUARY

The moon in Aries will help you to get things done. However, you may feel feistier than usual so be patient.

24 FEBRUARY

You will enjoy getting together with someone special whom you are instantly drawn to.

25 FEBRUARY

This is a lovely weekend to enjoy mixing with a new group of people even if it means leaving your comfort zone.

26 FEBRUARY

A lovely get-together or chat with a like-minded friend or colleague will raise morale.

27 FEBRUARY

Romance is alive and you'll enjoy speaking to someone special. A creative project or collaboration will progress.

28 FEBRUARY

The moon in Gemini may bring your restlessness to the surface, making this a good time to find fun ways to be productive.

March

1 MARCH

You may feel a little more emotional than usual, so take things carefully. Trust your intuition, as it is spot on.

2 MARCH

You will receive key news from a friend, group or organisation. Be prepared to think outside the box.

3 MARCH

Developments at work and socially could put you in a stronger position, so avoid seeing only the negatives. Advice is available.

4 MARCH

This is a good day to be active with communications, especially with friends and an organisation.

5 MARCH

You may receive unexpected news or bump into an old friend.

6 MARCH

This is a good day to be spontaneous and for meetings. You may receive a surprise.

7 MARCH

The full moon in Virgo spotlights a fresh chapter in your domestic life. Be prepared to think creatively.

8 MARCH

Domestic changes may be due to reforms at work. Someone will support your efforts.

9 MARCH

This is a good time to look for balance in your personal life and not to take random comments personally.

10 MARCH

You will enjoy a social get-together. A work development may boost your confidence.

11 MARCH

You will appreciate the opportunity to be spontaneous and reconnect with the past.

12 MARCH

There is a healing aspect to the day. You'll enjoy meeting people who have a therapeutic effect and it's a good day for self-development.

13 MARCH

You can certainly achieve a great deal both at work and in your personal endeavours. Avoid allowing problems to seem insurmountable.

14 MARCH

You'll gain information that can help you but you will need to research circumstances to avoid making mistakes.

15 MARCH

A work meeting could be ideal, but if mistakes have been made remedies must be found. You will enjoy romance, the arts and music. Avoid misunderstandings.

16 MARCH

It will be important to get down to basics and work hard. Avoid an ego battle.

17 MARCH

The more practical you can be the greater will be your success. Avoid making assumptions. You will receive important news to do with work, health or your status.

18 MARCH

You may hear unexpectedly from someone from the past. A new approach to an unpredictable person may be effective.

19 MARCH

Someone close has something to confide in you. You will enjoy making new friends.

20 MARCH

This is a good day for work talks as you can make a great impression and changes are likely, so be spontaneous for the best results. You will enjoy a reunion.

21 MARCH

The Aries new moon is a good time to start something fresh, especially at work and concerning a different direction. Avoid making snap decisions.

22 MARCH

You are productive and can achieve a great deal, so take the initiative.

23 MARCH

You may be entering new territory in a partnership or relationship. Be prepared to make progressive choices.

24 MARCH

You may need to update your loyalties, especially if you feel conflicted about a relationship.

25 MARCH

Trust your intuition and find new ways to express yourself, especially if you're unsure about your decisions.

26 MARCH

This is a good day to reconnect with someone special.

27 MARCH

You are likely to review certain work or health practices. Be prepared to try something new.

28 MARCH

A get-together will be enjoyable. You may need to make a financial agreement with a friend or organisation.

29 MARCH

The moon in your sign will bring out your sociable side but you may feel a little sensitive at work, so keep your professional hat on.

30 MARCH

Be prepared for a surprise. A meeting may be spontaneous. You'll appreciate the chance to put new ideas in motion.

31 MARCH

Your enthusiasm will be appreciated at work. You may need to be tactful with someone close to avoid arguments.

April

1 APRIL

There is a lovely sociable aspect to your weekend. You will enjoy the arts and music and indulging in a little luxury.

2 APRIL

This is likely to be another sociable day. You will enjoy a get-together or a return to an old haunt.

3 APRIL

You must choose your words carefully as you may be under pressure. You may uncover a secret.

4 APRIL

Domestic matters can move ahead, especially if you focus on the facts and details and avoid obsessing over needless doubts.

5 APRIL

This is a good time to focus on your health and well-being. Someone may need your help, and if you need advice it will be available.

6 APRIL

The full moon in Libra signals a key turning point in your personal life. You may be ready to begin a new creative project or invest more time in your family.

7 APRIL

This is a good day to be spontaneous and outgoing as the developments may be unexpected. You may receive beneficial news; just avoid forgetfulness.

8 APRIL

You may receive positive news from the past. It's a good day for a reunion and for catching up on chores.

9 APRIL

You may need to go with the flow to avoid an argument, within reason.

10 APRIL

An adventurous start to the week will produce good work and the chance to improve your work and health circumstances.

11 APRIL

You're able to get on well with people and make wise choices. Just avoid exaggerated or unrealistic expectations.

12 APRIL

Be practical at work and with your plans as you can get a great deal done. Just avoid underestimating your abilities.

13 APRIL

This is a good day to get down to the nitty-gritty with your various projects and commitments and to ensure you're all on the same page.

14 APRIL

Someone in a position of authority or an expert will help you. A commitment may be made. Avoid compromising your principles.

15 APRIL

A change of pace or of place will encourage you to meet new and diverse characters and enjoy something different.

16 APRIL

You'll enjoy socialising and being involved with the arts, music and dance. Romance could blossom, so organise a date!

17 APRIL

You are an intuitive character and this will be a very useful quality, especially at work.

18 APRIL

The moon in Aries for the next two days will bring out your productivity and highlight your skill sets. Just avoid favouring work over family if possible.

19 APRIL

This is a proactive time, but you must avoid taking on more than you can manage. Look for collaborations and cooperation.

20 APRIL

The total solar eclipse in Aries will kick-start an important chapter in your life, for most Cancerians in your social life and for some in the organisations you join.

21 APRIL

Check your loyalties. Important communications may come quickly, so be responsive and avoid being pressured.

22 APRIL

You will appreciate a slower pace this morning. Collaborations and partnerships could improve with careful talks.

23 APRIL

You may feel more proactive and chattier and will enjoy reviewing some of your decisions and improving your health.

24 APRIL

This is a good day for talks and communications and also for a health or beauty appointment.

25 APRIL

It's a good day for your favourite activities, and if you need someone's cooperation you're likely to get it.

26 APRIL

Trust your instincts but avoid making decisions without investigating the facts.

27 APRIL

An impromptu invitation or surprise news will be uplifting. Be open to fresh activities.

28 APRIL

Trust your intuition with regard to a health matter. This is a good day to get expert advice.

29 APRIL

You'll enjoy being spontaneous and meeting up with a fun crowd. Just avoid making snap decisions and rushing.

30 APRIL

You will appreciate the chance to slow down and find time for someone special. A trip may be delayed.

May

1 MAY

Someone close may reveal a change of plans. You'll get the chance to review circumstances over the coming weeks.

2 MAY

You will enjoy a reunion and one of your favourite activities. A trip may take you somewhere beautiful.

3 MAY

You'll enjoy investing time and energy in yourself and your home life, which will replenish your energy levels.

4 MAY

You may discover a secret or information that reveals a mistake was made, making this is an ideal time for research and correcting errors.

5 MAY

The lunar eclipse in Scorpio signals a fresh chapter in your personal life or a creative project. You may receive praise for past work that was done well.

6 MAY

You will enjoy being close to water and, if this is not possible, immersing yourself in the arts, music and romance.

7 MAY

This is a good time for self-development. Avoid taking someone else's moods personally.

8 MAY

You have what it takes to be successful with your projects and activities so be positive and proactive.

9 MAY

News from a group, friend or organisation may surprise you. You can remain constant despite unpredictable circumstances.

10 MAY

Your organisational skills will be in demand and appreciated.

11 MAY

Someone's unpredictability may again be an issue, but if you approach circumstances in a down-to-earth and practical way you will succeed nevertheless.

12 MAY

This is a good day to review some of your projects and loyalties to ensure you're still on track. An old friend may be in touch.

13 MAY

This is a good day to make great progress with your work and projects, so be proactive and positive. A debt may be repaid or you may receive a compliment.

14 MAY

Be inspired and follow your instincts and your activities will be enjoyable and will succeed.

15 MAY

This is an excellent day to be proactive and work towards your goals. You may receive key news that is encouraging.

16 MAY

As Jupiter enters Taurus you are about to begin a more abundant and settled phase at work and in your general direction, so be sure to plan ahead.

17 MAY

A diligent and comprehensive approach to your circumstances will be rewarded. Avoid entering conflict as it will escalate quickly.

18 MAY

This may be an intense day. Someone close may have different viewpoints to yours, so avoid arguments and find common ground instead.

19 MAY

The Taurus new moon signals a fresh chapter in your relationship with a friend or organisation. Be practical and forge a fresh agreement.

20 MAY

You will enjoy a more light-hearted and sociable few days, especially if you avoid sensitive topics with someone close.

21 MAY

You will feel more inclined to be outgoing, but if your views cause problems it's a good time to discover new ways to express yourself positively and constructively.

22 MAY

This is a good time to be active and positive, as your actions can have beneficial results.

23 MAY

Your optimism is infectious but some people may see it as feistiness, so avoid arguments if this is the case.

24 MAY

You may feel super sensitive yet you can achieve your goals, so put your feelings aside if they are distracting you.

25 MAY

This can be another productive day but it may also be a little dramatic, so avoid adding to drama if possible.

26 MAY

You will receive unexpectedly good news, and if you need help it will be available.

27 MAY

You'll enjoy focusing on the practicalities of daily life such as shopping and cleaning, and once your chores are done you will enjoy relaxing.

28 MAY

A shared situation or duty will need to be addressed, and once you have done that you'll enjoy spending time with someone special.

29 MAY

A measured and balanced approach to your daily chores and work will be productive. Just avoid daydreaming.

30 MAY

Your home is a beautiful place to relax and rest in, and if you have felt under the weather this is an excellent day to restore your energy levels.

31 MAY

A sensitive and compassionate approach to friends and family will be successful and could overcome disagreements.

June

1 JUNE

It's a good day to review finances, and if you're shopping avoid overspending.

2 JUNE

You'll appreciate the chance to talk to someone who plays a big role in your life. Just avoid sensitive topics for the best results.

3 JUNE

You will enjoy feeling motivated. It's a good day for personal development and sports.

4 JUNE

The full moon begins a new chapter that will alter your daily routine in the weeks to come. You'll enjoy a spontaneous get-together.

5 JUNE

You or someone close is likely to express deep feelings. This is a good day for romance, unless anger gets the better of you.

6 JUNE

Be practical and focus on your chores as you can attain many goals.

7 JUNE

Consider whether a fresh approach to a personal or business partner could work. If so, try something new.

8 JUNE

Be proactive and positive, as you have every chance to get on better with those close to you.

9 JUNE

This is a good day for meetings. You'll enjoy the arts, music and romance but may be a little forgetful.

10 JUNE

Be prepared to dream a little as you will feel inspired. A friend or group may have an uplifting effect.

11 JUNE

Someone close has news for you. If you're single you may reunite with an ex or will review better ways to get ahead.

12 JUNE

Be positive and proactive, as you will appear to others to be energetic and dynamic and will enjoy a productive day.

13 JUNE

This is a good day to evaluate your own values and check you're on the same page at those around you.

14 JUNE

The moon in Taurus will bring out your ability to be focused and practical but may also bring out people's stubbornness, so be flexible.

15 JUNE

This could be a busy day but it will also involve delays, so be patient as you can make great progress.

16 JUNE

The Gemini moon will bring a sociable couple of days, although it will be best to avoid misunderstandings.

17 JUNE

You may need to review important plans, and luckily you'll have a good sounding board in a friend or colleague.

18 JUNE

Make a wish at the new moon in Gemini, which signals a fresh phase at work or regarding your health.

19 JUNE

Be willing to research circumstances to ensure you make the most of any new opportunities at work and to improve your health.

20 JUNE

You'll feel more in your element but others may be under pressure, making this a good time to support them whenever possible.

21 JUNE

It's the solstice! As the sun enters your sign you'll gain energy over the coming weeks but must avoid a battle of egos.

22 JUNE

You will need to be on your toes. Luckily, you'll feel motivated to get things done and your relationships could deepen.

23 JUNE

There is a healing atmosphere and you will enjoy reconnecting with someone special. An expert or adviser will be helpful.

24 JUNE

This is a good weekend for domestic improvements in both decor and interpersonal dynamics. You may enjoy gardening as well.

25 JUNE

Be clear with communications as there may be misunderstandings. You may be prone to forgetfulness.

26 JUNE

This is another day to be careful with communications. News may be unexpected. Plan ahead to avoid traffic delays.

27 JUNE

A friend or adviser will be particularly helpful. You will enjoy a reunion or news from the past.

28 JUNE

This is a creative time that is excellent for pursuing the arts and music. It's also a good time to deepen relationships.

29 JUNE

Be proactive and optimistic as you can make great progress at work and with your projects. It's a good day to mend bridges.

30 JUNE

You may receive good news at work or regarding finances. It's a good day to indulge in your favourite pastimes.

July

1 JULY

This is a lovely weekend for socialising. If you're working it will be a productive day. A debt may be repaid.

2 JULY

Be prepared to discuss someone else's opinions to avoid conflict but do not compromise your values. A trip or meeting may be delayed.

3 JULY

The full moon in Capricorn shines a light on a business or personal relationship. Many will begin a fresh chapter in a daily schedule.

4 JULY

Be practical and patient about changes you wish to make as you could make great progress.

5 JULY

Be prepared to listen to someone close as they may have important but surprising news.

6 JULY

This is a good time for health and well-being appointments. Avoid taking delays and other people's random comments personally.

7 JULY

You may hear unexpected news from a friend or organisation. You'll enjoy an impromptu meeting.

8 JULY

This is a good time to review your finances and for catching up with friends and neighbours. You will enjoy a short trip.

9 JULY

Some conversations may require a little more tact and sensitivity to ensure the relationship remains unscathed.

10 JULY

This is a good day to put your best foot forward, especially at work, as you appear to others to be charming and influential.

11 JULY

A financial matter may require attention to avoid overspending.

12 JULY

Your help and advice may be required, and rest assured you are the best person for the job. If you need help it will be available.

13 JULY

You have every reason to focus on details, especially at work, and will enjoy relaxing in the evening. Avoid being super critical.

14 JULY

A lovely spontaneous event will raise morale. However, you will need to be careful with communications and finances.

15 JULY

Trust your instincts and go with the flow a little this weekend. You will enjoy a fun event.

16 JULY

Be prepared to adjust to other people's circumstances and plan ahead to avoid delays.

17 JULY

The Cancer new moon signals a fresh agreement within a business or personal relationship. Some Cancerians may find this a good time to reorganise finances.

18 JULY

Someone may express intense feelings so be prepared to listen, but you must also consider your own feelings and values.

19 JULY

Communications will benefit from special attention to avoid misunderstandings. Plan ahead to avoid travel delays.

20 JULY

This is an excellent day for getting ahead; however, ensure you're not seeing life through rose-coloured glasses. Avoid overspending.

21 JULY

This is a good day to make a commitment either at home or at work; just avoid feeling pressured.

22 JULY

Intense or deep feelings are likely to arise this weekend. There is potential for misunderstandings, so ensure you're on the same page.

23 JULY

You may be surprised by developments. Plan travel to avoid delays. Misunderstandings or a change of plan are likely.

24 JULY

You will be drawn to looking for more balance in your personal life and relationships, and there's no time like the present!

25 JULY

Your link with someone from the past need only continue if you feel this is a mutually supportive relationship. It's a good day for talks.

26 JULY

You'll enjoy channelling your energy into activities you love, so make a plan!

27 JULY

You will enjoy a reunion and the chance to return to an old haunt. You must base your decisions on facts, not hopes.

28 JULY

This is a good time to reassess where your loyalties lie but you must avoid obsessing over the details. Be proactive.

29 JULY

You will reap the rewards of hard work and diligence this weekend.

30 JULY

This is a good time to work towards good relationships as your efforts will be successful.

31 JULY

The Capricorn moon will encourage you to be practical with chores. Avoid being distracted by other people's business.

August

1 AUGUST

The full moon supermoon in Aquarius spells a new phase in the way you share duties and, for some, financially. A trip or fresh agreement may be on the cards.

2 AUGUST

This is a good time for discussions, especially those in which you wish to come to an agreement either in your personal life or financially.

3 AUGUST

You may need to leave your comfort zone a little but your efforts will be worthwhile.

4 AUGUST

You may tend to wear your heart on your sleeve, so if you're working be sure to keep your professional hat on.

5 AUGUST

This is another day when your emotions may get the better of you. You will enjoy music, the arts and romance.

6 AUGUST

You may be drawn towards improving your appearance and well-being. Someone may ask for your help, and if you need help it will be available.

7 AUGUST

Be prepared to listen to other peoples' opinions and ideas but also to stick to your principles. It's a good day to review your finances.

8 AUGUST

You'll enjoy a trip or meeting that enables you to appreciate a sense of calm and security. Avoid pandering to your fears.

9 AUGUST

You may be surprised by an unexpected change of plan, so be prepared to think on your feet.

10 AUGUST

This is another good day for a trip or meeting. Check the fine print if you are making large purchases.

11 AUGUST

This is a good time to look after your own interests and improve your health and well-being.

12 AUGUST

There is a therapeutic aspect to the day. You may experience a boost in status or a compliment or financial improvement. Avoid overspending.

13 AUGUST

You will enjoy a feel-good factor and may even have a debt repaid. You'll enjoy a trip or get-together.

14 AUGUST

You have a natural empathy with people but must avoid being easily influenced. You may enjoy a financial or work improvement.

15 AUGUST

It's a good day to talk and for meetings, especially regarding travel and finances. Romance could flourish.

16 AUGUST

The new moon in Leo signals you are turning a corner financially or in your personal life. Be prepared for a surprise and to support your viewpoints.

17 AUGUST

The more practical you can be the better will be the outcome. Ensure you base your ideas on facts, especially financially.

18 AUGUST

You can make a great deal of progress with meetings and your involvement with an organisation or a friend. Relationships can improve.

19 AUGUST

Base your plans on realistic expectations as you may be super idealistic. You will enjoy the arts, music and romance.

20 AUGUST

You'll enjoy a favourite pastime and the company of someone you love but you must avoid overspending and having unrealistic expectations.

21 AUGUST

You are a positive and friendly character but you may not agree with everyone, so tact will help with negotiations.

22 AUGUST

This is a good time to review your finances and agreements, especially if you feel there has been a misunderstanding.

23 AUGUST

You may receive important news at home or regarding work. It's an excellent time to discuss practical plans.

24 AUGUST

This is a good time to seek the support and advice of dependable people, especially if some aspects of your life are unpredictable.

25 AUGUST

You'll enjoy the company of people you love. It's an excellent time for romance and for improving domestic dynamics.

26 AUGUST

This is a productive weekend and you'll achieve your goals by being focused. However, distractions could slow the pace.

27 AUGUST

This is a good time to review your finances and make a commitment to a solid plan.

28 AUGUST

You'll appreciate the opportunity to work with people and spend time with those who are grounded and realistic.

29 AUGUST

This is a good time for collaborations and for making plans at home and with those you love.

30 AUGUST

Be prepared to look at some of your activities and shared arrangements in a new light, especially if difficulties have arisen.

31 AUGUST

The Pisces full moon supermoon spotlights your favourite activities such as travel. Be prepared to dream but be realistic with the planning.

September

1 SEPTEMBER

While your focus is increasingly on your home you may need to complete chores first to enjoy company or a relaxing time later.

2 SEPTEMBER

You will be drawn to enjoying upbeat and active pursuits and spending time improving your immediate environment.

3 SEPTEMBER

You will be drawn to a beautiful place and to spending time improving your environment, as well as adding a touch of sumptuousness to your home.

4 SEPTEMBER

This is a good day to reconsider some of your plans, especially to do with travel. You will enjoy a reunion or a catch-up.

5 SEPTEMBER

Talks and meetings are likely to go well, especially in connection with your home or family.

6 SEPTEMBER

You'll appreciate a visit or a trip. This is a good time to discuss changes at home and regarding travel and finances.

7 SEPTEMBER

You will enjoy a trip. Your connection with a sibling or neighbour can improve. It's a good time to discuss finances and your home.

8 SEPTEMBER

This is a lovely day for socialising and making improvements at home, and simply for relaxing at the end of the day.

9 SEPTEMBER

You'll feel more in tune with someone you share common interests with and will enjoy focusing on your health and well-being.

10 SEPTEMBER

You will enjoy being outgoing and sociable. Someone close may wish to have more time with you and may express strong feelings.

11 SEPTEMBER

This is a good day for making home improvements and for talks with family and housemates. Just avoid being impulsive.

12 SEPTEMBER

You will appreciate feeling optimistic, especially about finances, and you can certainly overcome debt but you must maintain a stable budget.

13 SEPTEMBER

Pay attention to detail as this will be rewarding and you'll avoid making mistakes. This is a good time to plan a trip.

14 SEPTEMBER

You'll appreciate the advice of someone more experienced than you, especially in connection with domestic and travel matters.

15 SEPTEMBER

The new moon in Virgo signals a fresh chapter at home or with a key relationship. Be practical and a dream could come true.

16 SEPTEMBER

You may be pleasantly surprised by news or a get-together. You'll enjoy making changes at home or visiting someone else's home.

17 SEPTEMBER

Take time to sort out your differences with someone important to you. Financial matters will deserve attention.

18 SEPTEMBER

You'll feel passionate about your projects but not everyone will feel the same way, so be prepared to compromise.

19 SEPTEMBER

This is a good time to be creative, so if you work in the arts you're likely to be productive. However, you may need to overcome an obstacle first.

20 SEPTEMBER

Circumstances are likely to develop quickly over the next two days, so be sure you're happy with their direction or apply the brakes.

21 SEPTEMBER

This is a lovely time to spend with someone you love. A domestic or personal situation can blossom.

22 SEPTEMBER

You're firing on all cylinders at the moment and will be productive, but you must avoid minor bumps and scrapes.

23 SEPTEMBER

The sun in Libra will encourage you to look for peace and balance, especially at home.

24 SEPTEMBER

You're enthusiastic and energetic but must avoid rushing, as otherwise minor accidents could occur. You may be asked for help.

25 SEPTEMBER

This is a good day for a trip and for meetings but you must take nothing for granted and work hard for your goals.

26 SEPTEMBER

Someone close to you may surprise you. You may be drawn to retail therapy but must avoid overspending.

27 SEPTEMBER

This is a good day to discuss important shared concerns such as space at home and finances.

28 SEPTEMBER

You'll enjoy music and the arts but must focus a little more than usual on the details to achieve your goals. Avoid daydreaming.

29 SEPTEMBER

The Aries full moon signals the start of a new phase in your career, status or general direction. Ensure you research your options carefully.

30 SEPTEMBER

You are dynamic and outgoing and will enjoy the company of good friends, but if you're tired this is a perfect day for rest.

October

1 OCTOBER

A change in your environment will raise morale, and if you have been arguing with someone it will break the tension.

2 OCTOBER

You may be seeing life through rose-coloured glasses and could attain an ideal outcome but you must be realistic, especially at work.

3 OCTOBER

Events are likely to move quickly so ensure you have the facts to avoid making mistakes, especially financially and at work. You may receive good news.

4 OCTOBER

The Gemini moon will put you in a chatty frame of mind, and you'll enjoy catching up with friends and family.

5 OCTOBER

Take the time to find out where you stand if you're unsure. It's difficult to second guess someone.

6 OCTOBER

You are getting on perfectly with some people but not so well with others. Try to find common ground.

7 OCTOBER

It's in your interest to get on with someone at home, within a group or with a friend. Be diligent and you will succeed.

8 OCTOBER

You may enjoy relaxing and improving your health. Meetings are likely to go well but you must avoid sensitive topics.

9 OCTOBER

A disagreement needn't turn into an argument; focus on the facts and you can find common ground.

10 OCTOBER

This is a good time to make an agreement or commitment as long as fair play prevails.

11 OCTOBER

Choose carefully between duties at home and at work, as one environment may need more of your attention. Avoid taking random comments personally.

12 OCTOBER

You may notice a change of atmosphere at home. It's a lovely time to cocoon and overcome tension.

13 OCTOBER

Be proactive, as your efforts will be successful. A domestic or personal matter can be resolved.

14 OCTOBER

The solar eclipse represents a new chapter in your home or family life. Be prepared to establish peace. Avoid minor bumps and scrapes.

15 OCTOBER

You may receive a surprise visitor or unexpected news from a friend or organisation. Be prepared to research further for the best results.

16 OCTOBER

You'll get on top of the changes in your environment and could even establish an ideal outcome, so be positive.

17 OCTOBER

Good communication skills will help you to navigate unexpected circumstances. Look for peace and balance in your environment.

18 OCTOBER

A hobby or favourite pastime will raise morale, so be sure to pursue activities you love.

19 OCTOBER

You will enjoy a reunion or a visit at home. Avoid allowing a degree of uncertainty to reign and be optimistic.

20 OCTOBER

News to do with your home or family is important. If it is unclear, ensure you do your research.

21 OCTOBER

It's important to double-check that the information you receive is correct. Changes at home are likely, but avoid feeling pressured to make key decisions before you're ready.

22 OCTOBER

You will feel drawn to moving forward with your plans, especially to do with family and long-term decisions. You'll enjoy a trip or get-together.

23 OCTOBER

The next four weeks will be a creative and active phase, so be prepared to innovate and enjoy life.

24 OCTOBER

This is a good day to make agreements and commitments, especially in connection with your projects, home and family.

25 OCTOBER

Be inspired but also practical, otherwise complexities may become even more of a conundrum.

26 OCTOBER

This is a busy time and you may feel under pressure from others and also from your own high expectations, so ensure you take breaks.

27 OCTOBER

It's the end of the week so you'll be happy to give your projects one last push, but you must avoid taking on too much.

28 OCTOBER

The lunar eclipse in Taurus signals a fresh chapter in your social life and friendships. You may be drawn to developing fresh loyalties but must avoid making rash decisions.

29 OCTOBER

Developments in your personal life and socially will take much of your focus. Be prepared to discuss your plans with those they affect.

30 OCTOBER

The next two days are ideal for making long-term changes, either at home or in your work life.

31 OCTOBER

Happy Halloween! You may be surprised by a change of routine and will enjoy developments at home or at work.

November

1 NOVEMBER

A backlog of work may distract you from current endeavours but it will be to your benefit to clear paperwork.

2 NOVEMBER

This is a good day to discuss personal and creative matters as you are in tune with people you must get on with.

3 NOVEMBER

Important meetings or news will illuminate your best path forward. You must avoid being easily influenced.

4 NOVEMBER

You may be surprised by news or a visit. You may need to make a compromise with someone close.

5 NOVEMBER

Be prepared to see other people's points of view but avoid taking their opinions personally. You may be asked for help.

6 NOVEMBER

This is a good day for important talks to do with property or family. Romance could flourish, so plan a date!

7 NOVEMBER

You are communicating well and are creative and appear charming to others, so be proactive and take steps forward, especially at work.

8 NOVEMBER

You may need to work within certain frustrating rules and regulations, but if you're diligent you will succeed with your goals without conflict.

9 NOVEMBER

Negotiations and talks will go well, so this is a good day for discussions and meetings. Be prepared to be tactful.

10 NOVEMBER

You may need to undergo some difficult communications. Focus on fair play and the facts for the best results.

11 NOVEMBER

You'll enjoy being spontaneous and will appreciate a sense of freedom, but you must avoid making rash decisions.

12 NOVEMBER

You'll enjoy your favourite activities and being creative and spending time with the people you love.

13 NOVEMBER

The Scorpio new moon signals a fresh chapter in your personal life or a creative project. You may be surprised by news.

14 NOVEMBER

Be proactive at work and make changes in your daily schedule. This is a good day for sports and to look after your well-being.

15 NOVEMBER

This is a good day for meetings and discussions and also to improve your domestic circumstances.

16 NOVEMBER

Discussions with a friend or organisation may test your communication skills, but if you remain diligent you will succeed despite delays or misunderstandings.

17 NOVEMBER

This is a good day for making progress with your ventures. You may enjoy being creative. Romance will appeal and could flourish.

18 NOVEMBER

This is a passionate and creative time, so be sure to organise enjoyable events. Romance will blossom.

19 NOVEMBER

Someone who is quirky and whose company you enjoy will add to a fun day.

20 NOVEMBER

Changes you wish to make are going to be easier to implement, so take the initiative. This is another romantic day.

21 NOVEMBER

Be prepared to dream a little and be inspired, but you must avoid forgetfulness and misunderstandings.

22 NOVEMBER

The sun in Sagittarius for the next four weeks will bring out your optimistic side. However, you may feel a little vulnerable.

23 NOVEMBER

Someone may need your help and your hard work will be appreciated. If you need advice it will be available.

24 NOVEMBER

Be prepared to be tactful even while you are being bold, as this will avoid social gaffes.

25 NOVEMBER

You are super productive now but must avoid feeling frustrated by restrictions or an authority figure such as an employer. Be patient instead and work hard towards your goals.

26 NOVEMBER

You may be surprised by developments concerning a friend, group or at home. Be prepared to work hard towards the outcome you desire.

27 NOVEMBER

The Gemini full moon signals a fresh phase in your daily routine. You'll enjoy a meeting and news but you must avoid making snap decisions.

28 NOVEMBER

Trust your instincts as they are spot on, but equally rely on hard work and observation to avoid making mistakes.

29 NOVEMBER

Your go-ahead attitude is getting you noticed, but some people prefer tradition and may appear stubborn so weigh your options carefully.

30 NOVEMBER

This is a good day for discussions with someone close such as a partner or colleague. Just ensure you have the facts.

December

1 DECEMBER

You'll find it easier over the coming weeks to communicate with people you've found to be stubborn in the past.

2 DECEMBER

You will find making agreements a little easier, so if you need someone's cooperation this is the day to ask for it! Just avoid a battle of egos.

3 DECEMBER

If you disagree with someone you must avoid conflict, as it will escalate quickly. Find ways to establish common ground instead.

4 DECEMBER

This is the beginning of a more passionate and romantic phase for you so take the initiative!

5 DECEMBER

This is a good time for planning and for making a commitment.

6 DECEMBER

You will be looking for peace and harmony over the next two days and will be prepared to compromise.

7 DECEMBER

It's a good day to discuss your feelings, but you must avoid gossip at work and taking other people's problems as your own. Avoid mix-ups.

8 DECEMBER

You may achieve a breakthrough either at work or in your personal life, so be positive.

9 DECEMBER

You'll enjoy indulging in activities you love, perhaps even enjoying some early seasonal cheer.

10 DECEMBER

This is a lovely day for romance and enjoying doing what you love, so be sure to organise a treat.

11 DECEMBER

It's a good day to organise talks and other communications, and also for creativity and get-togethers.

12 DECEMBER

The Sagittarian new moon signals the start of a fresh chapter in your personal life and may involve a surprise.

13 DECEMBER

Important news or a change in your usual routine will merit focus. Try to get important communications finalised to avoid having to review them later.

14 DECEMBER

Be prepared to go the extra mile to get work done, even if you feel unmotivated.

15 DECEMBER

You'll enjoy being sociable and upbeat. Perhaps a work development will be uplifting. Avoid overindulging in seasonal cheer.

16 DECEMBER

This is a good weekend to try something new and avoid simply repeating the same patterns of previous years.

17 DECEMBER

It's a good day to take things one step at a time as you may be absent-minded or forgetful. Focus on good health and happiness.

18 DECEMBER

This is a lovely day for travel and get-togethers. You'll enjoy a reunion. It's a good day for health appointments.

19 DECEMBER

You will enjoy being outgoing and upbeat but must avoid appearing bossy, especially at work.

20 DECEMBER

You'll enjoy focusing on someone special such as a friend, lover or family member.

21 DECEMBER

A change of pace or of place will be enjoyable, although some arrangements may change at the last minute. Avoid making rash decisions if possible.

22 DECEMBER

Get-togethers, reunions and, for some, news at work will be enjoyable. Plan ahead to avoid delays.

23 DECEMBER

A change of pace or of place will require you to adapt, and you'll enjoy settling into your festive weekend.

24 DECEMBER

Someone close will be a catalyst for you feeling safe and secure, so you can enjoy this Christmas Eve.

25 DECEMBER

Merry Christmas! This is a romantic day, and a trip or magical development will raise morale. Just avoid misunderstandings and hard feelings.

26 DECEMBER

It's a good day for talks and reminiscing and also for reunions, so take the initiative and plan a date!

27 DECEMBER

The Cancer full moon represents the start of a new cycle in your personal life and, for some, in your daily routine. You will enjoy get-togethers but must avoid delays and mix-ups.

28 DECEMBER

You'll feel motivated to change your circumstances and routine but you must avoid rushing.

29 DECEMBER

This is a lovely time for romance and for being optimistic about your personal life. Don't allow disappointments to hold you back.

30 DECEMBER

The moon in Leo signals an outgoing and positive weekend, so be sure to organise a fun event.

31 DECEMBER

Happy New Year! You'll enjoy an active and upbeat New Year's Eve but must keep everyone in the loop.

LEO

22 July - 23 August

FINANCES

The eclipses in May and October suggest you are ready to make considerable changes to the way you share your finances and investments. This may be because you will be rearranging your career and ventures or because you receive an inheritance or other financial adjustment. During the months of January, March, July and August you will be particularly focused on managing finances and prospectively also improving them, so be prepared to initiate change by researching your options carefully.

HEALTH

It's likely the health of someone close to you will be your main focus in 2023 as you'll gain the opportunity to look after them and their circumstances, and with Pluto in your sixth house of health all year it's important you also care for your own health. You'll be drawn to trying new treatments and potentially even altering your usual health routine by considering a fresh approach to care, especially in March and April.

LOVE LIFE

Be prepared to enter fresh territory in your love life: you have become comfortable with a certain routine and approach but that is all set to change in 2023! You'll find new self-expression and may even surprise yourself with some of the people and ideas you're drawn to. Singles may be tempted to experiment with new relationship structures and couples to step into fresh terrain within your existing relationship, spicing up your love life in the process. You'll find the period from the end of March to the end of April will bring the most change.

CAREER

Uranus at the zenith of your chart all year means you're ready to make changes to your career and to the bigger picture too – your status and general direction. In 2023 you'll gain the perfect chance to do just that, especially in the second half of the year, which will give you the first few months to plan ahead. The eclipses in April and October suggest your relationships will transform as adventure beckons, be this in the shape of travel, new legal agreements or study. You're set to broaden your horizons, and the more you embrace change the better for you!

HOME LIFE

The busiest months in 2023 will be during the last quarter of the year, and you'll appreciate the opportunity then to make changes in this important area of your life. These may come about principally due to developments at work and a change of direction for you, but will mean a considerable amount of effort and emotion is likely to be imbued in your domestic life. The new moon on 12 December will be particularly poignant, as changes will accentuate the fact you are starting a fresh phase at home.

January

1 JANUARY

Happy New Year! A change in your usual New Year's Day routine is likely. You may be drawn to making a considerable alteration to your environment.

2 JANUARY

You will enjoy reconnecting with someone or even a change of scenery. Just be careful of minor bumps and scrapes. Someone may need your help or you may need to ask someone for help.

3 JANUARY

This is a good time to consider venturing into a new work environment and also to consider a fresh health routine.

4 JANUARY

A trip somewhere beautiful will be a real drawcard. You will enjoy some fun and upbeat activities.

5 JANUARY

A change of pace or of place will be enjoyable. You may be preparing to return to work and may receive unexpected news.

6 JANUARY

The Cancer full moon suggests you're ready to turn a corner in your work or health routine. Consider a schedule that is healthier.

7 JANUARY

You will appreciate the chance for a reunion and may receive important health news or experience a change of environment.

8 JANUARY

You will enjoy being spontaneous and doing something different and may be pleasantly surprised by developments.

9 JANUARY

This is a lovely day for romance and work meetings. You may also be drawn to improving your appearance and health.

10 JANUARY

This is a good time to be meticulous with communications and finances and to slow down, especially if you've been overtiring yourself.

11 JANUARY

You can make great progress at work and with your activities but you must avoid travel delays and misunderstandings and misjudging a situation.

12 JANUARY

This is a good time to pick up where you left off with a work project or health routine, and to boost your energy levels.

13 JANUARY

You may be drawn to an attractive and charming character; romance is alive! You will enjoy the arts and the company of inspiring people.

14 JANUARY

This is a good time for making a commitment to an exciting venture and also for getting work done around the house and garden.

15 JANUARY

Some plans may alter at short notice. Be prepared to be flexible and avoid taking developments personally.

16 JANUARY

You are likely to feel more passionate about domestic and personal matters. Avoid allowing this to get in the way of good relationships and work.

17 JANUARY

You may be under pressure to achieve fast results but it's a case of the tortoise making better progress now.

18 JANUARY

You may receive news that could be intense, so take time out when you can. It's a good time to move forward with written and creative ideas.

19 JANUARY

You prefer to be dynamic and energetic, so sometimes slowing down may feel counterproductive. It has its merits, which you will begin to see.

20 JANUARY

It's a good time to be adventurous and outgoing, and to consider a fresh project at work and even a new appearance or health routine.

21 JANUARY

The new moon supermoon in Aquarius signals a refreshing chapter in your daily, work or health schedule. Make a wish and be innovative.

22 JANUARY

This is a good time to look at your career, direction and finances in a new light. It's also a good time to make fresh commitments, as long as you are sure of the facts.

23 JANUARY

Be inspired by people close to you and be guided by your intuition, as you see more than many others do at the moment.

24 JANUARY

You are an insightful and sensitive person so you must trust your instincts, especially concerning important decisions.

25 JANUARY

You'll be inspired to learn more and to delve more deeply into your own self-development to create a sense of accomplishment.

26 JANUARY

The moon in Aries will bring out your dynamism. A teacher or authority figure may be helpful. Avoid minor bumps and scrapes.

27 JANUARY

Trust your intuition, as it is spot on. News at work or regarding health will need focus. You may need to help someone or will need advice yourself.

28 JANUARY

Keep your feet on the ground and you'll enjoy doing something different, but you must avoid stubbornness.

29 JANUARY

A practical approach to your chores will be super effective and you'll enjoy a sense of achievement as a result. A social event will be fun.

30 JANUARY

Meetings and get-togethers will be productive and you may experience a pleasant surprise at work.

31 JANUARY

This is a good day for collaborations, travel and moving any legal matters forward. It's also a good day for romance.

February

1 FEBRUARY

This is a good day to gain advice from an expert or adviser. It's also a good time to overcome differences and for self-development.

2 FEBRUARY

You are thinking intuitively and can gain insight into someone close and deepen relationships, but you must avoid forgetfulness.

3 FEBRUARY

It's the end of the week, so if you're tired or feeling sensitive you know why. Be sure to pace yourself.

4 FEBRUARY

Someone close may surprise you with their news or due to a sudden change of circumstance.

5 FEBRUARY

The Leo full moon signals a fresh chapter in your personal life and, for some, at work. Be prepared to discuss options and avoid a Mexican stand-off.

6 FEBRUARY

This is a good day for research and to find out where you stand with someone. Meetings are likely to go well.

7 FEBRUARY

You are thinking critically, which will be good for financial plans, but you must avoid being critical of yourself or others.

8 FEBRUARY

You may be surprised by an impromptu get-together or by news at work. Collaborations are likely to go well.

9 FEBRUARY

Work meetings and talks with people in authority such as employers are likely to go well, so take the initiative.

10 FEBRUARY

News at work or regarding health will signal considerable change. A fresh daily routine or meeting will be significant.

11 FEBRUARY

You will be drawn to bringing more peace, harmony and balance into your life and this is a good day to do just that.

12 FEBRUARY

Romance can blossom, so be sure to organise a lovely treat. It's a good day for creative and spiritual ventures.

13 FEBRUARY

You have a good connection with certain people yet others may be annoying, so choose your company carefully.

14 FEBRUARY

Happy St Valentine's Day! It's a lovely day for romance, so take the initiative. If you're missing someone take time out to look after yourself.

15 FEBRUARY

This is one of the most romantic times of the year, so be sure to organise a treat. You may be prepared to make a commitment to someone.

16 FEBRUARY

A commitment can be made but you must ensure agreements are clear to avoid regret.

17 FEBRUARY

Today's moon in Capricorn will encourage you to be practical regarding changes and developments.

18 FEBRUARY

You will enjoy a favourite activity. This is a good day for meetings, and for travel and visiting a beautiful place.

19 FEBRUARY

You'll enjoy a change of pace or of place. Beauty, the arts and romance will all appeal.

20 FEBRUARY

The new moon in Pisces signals a fresh chapter in a shared situation or collaboration. It's a good day to consult an expert.

21 FEBRUARY

Be on your toes as a sudden change of pace or unexpected news may distract you. Avoid travel delays and mix-ups.

22 FEBRUARY

This is a better day for communications. A work, health or personal matter can progress.

23 FEBRUARY

The moon in Aries will motivate you to broaden your horizons and learn more about your circumstances.

24 FEBRUARY

This is a lovely day for a reunion, and for spiritual development and enjoying doing what you love.

25 FEBRUARY

You will appreciate the opportunity to make plans for the long term, especially regarding your direction and status. Be practical.

26 FEBRUARY

This is a good time to evaluate who and what means the most to you and to make arrangements accordingly.

27 FEBRUARY

This is a good day for research and romance and for important talks. You may also be drawn to making important financial decisions.

28 FEBRUARY

The moon in Gemini will bring out your chatty side, making this a fun time for collaboration. Avoid revealing too many secrets.

March

1 MARCH

You're thinking intuitively, which gives you an advantage, but you may feel a little more sensitive as well so maintain perspective.

2 MARCH

A trip, activity or favourite pastime will be a drawcard. Be prepared to think outside the box.

3 MARCH

A meeting will be productive and may involve the necessity to show sympathy for someone else's situation. Advice will be available.

4 MARCH

There are therapeutic aspects to the weekend that you'll enjoy. You may travel somewhere beautiful. A friend will show support.

5 MARCH

You will enjoy being spontaneous and outgoing and may be surprised by events.

6 MARCH

Be proactive and optimistic about collaborations, especially at work, as you could make great progress.

7 MARCH

The full moon in Virgo spotlights a fresh chapter in a relationship and, for some, financially. Be prepared to think creatively.

8 MARCH

Domestic changes may be due to developments at work. Someone you care about will support your efforts.

9 MARCH

You will appreciate finding the time to focus a little on yourself, your health and well-being. Be prepared to take breaks.

10 MARCH

You'll enjoy talks and get-togethers. A trip, negotiation and research are likely to go well.

11 MARCH

You will appreciate the opportunity to broaden your horizons. A trip, reunion and socialising will appeal, and a spontaneous event will also be enjoyable.

12 MARCH

There is a healing aspect to the day. Spiritual and self-developmental activities will be fulfilling. Be prepared to avoid travel delays by planning ahead.

13 MARCH

This is a sensitive time, so it is a good time to focus on looking after yourself and others. Study and research will be rewarding.

14 MARCH

This is a good time for research but mistakes are possible, so double-check information. Avoid minor bumps and scrapes by focusing.

15 MARCH

This is a super romantic day but you must avoid misunderstandings. You will enjoy the arts and music. Avoid being misled.

16 MARCH

You may be easily distracted by someone who gives mixed messages. Aim to get the facts right to avoid making mistakes.

17 MARCH

Key news to do with finances and shared concerns such as duties is on the way. Focus on the facts and avoid assumptions. A meeting will be significant.

18 MARCH

You'll appreciate the chance to alter your usual routine and deepen your connection with someone special.

19 MARCH

You'll be more expressive about your feelings in the coming weeks, starting today. You may confide in someone or someone may confide in you.

20 MARCH

This is a good day for collaborations and work talks, and you may experience a pleasant surprise. You will enjoy a reunion.

21 MARCH

The Aries new moon is a good time to start something fresh, especially regarding a favourite project, activity, travel and study. Avoid making snap decisions.

22 MARCH

You are productive and can achieve a great deal so take the initiative, but you must avoid alienating someone who supports you.

23 MARCH

This is a good time to enter fresh territory, especially at work and regarding your health and well-being even if this feels intense.

24 MARCH

You may need to review your loyalties, especially if you feel conflicted about a relationship such as with someone in your family.

25 MARCH

You may notice a softening in someone's attitude to you, but if the opposite occurs seek the support of a loyal person.

26 MARCH

You are dynamic and productive but sometimes your energy can be overwhelming to those close to you, so find the balance.

27 MARCH

You may feel vulnerable yet you may receive good news. It's a good time to review certain work or health practices.

28 MARCH

A development at work or in your status means you must communicate clearly. It's a good day for talks and travel. Avoid delays by planning ahead.

29 MARCH

You have many strong feelings bubbling under the surface, and unless you express these creatively you risk appearing angry or emotional.

30 MARCH

Be prepared for a surprise. A meeting will be enjoyable, and you can make great progress both at work and in your personal life.

31 MARCH

Your optimism and enthusiasm are infectious. Just avoid alienating those you work with or must rely on.

April

1 APRIL

You will enjoy being active and outgoing. Sports and getting together with like-minded people will appeal. If you're shopping, avoid overspending.

2 APRIL

This is another sociable and active day. You will enjoy get-togethers but must avoid misunderstandings.

3 APRIL

You may discover you're talking at cross purposes with someone important so ensure you are on the same page.

4 APRIL

The more precise you are the better the outcome, especially at work and with financial matters.

5 APRIL

A trip or a visit, meeting and talks will be productive but may also bring out your sensitivity, so take things carefully.

6 APRIL

The full moon in Libra signals a new chapter in a key relationship such as at home or at work. It's a good time to seek perspective and balance.

7 APRIL

This is a good day to express yourself and enjoy favourite activities. You may be surprised by a chance encounter or unexpected development.

8 APRIL

You will enjoy socialising and networking, and if you're working you're likely to be busy. Just avoid impulsiveness.

9 APRIL

You will enjoy the creature comforts. Romance can blossom but you must avoid sensitive topics if you are meeting with family members.

10 APRIL

There is an outgoing and upbeat atmosphere, so make the most of this proactive time and pursue your projects optimistically.

11 APRIL

Key developments regarding study, travel, spiritual or even legal matters point to changes to come in your status and general direction.

12 APRIL

Be practical, as you'll be super productive as a result. Be positive also.

13 APRIL

New ventures and ideas will appeal, and the secret of success lies in good preparation and research.

14 APRIL

You will not always agree with everyone and you may need to compromise, but you must avoid compromising your principles.

15 APRIL

An adventurous and outgoing approach to your activities will be rewarding. You'll enjoy spending time with someone special.

16 APRIL

This is a lovely day for romance and for relaxing, so go ahead and plan a treat!

17 APRIL

You may have your head in the clouds a little, so be prepared to focus a little harder on the work at hand.

18 APRIL

The moon in Aries for the next two days will bring out your dynamism. You'll be productive but must avoid appearing overbearing.

19 APRIL

This is a proactive time. Your activities and wish to expand your horizons will be motivating, which you will enjoy.

20 APRIL

The total solar eclipse in Aries will kick-start an important chapter in fresh activities and the direction you favour, including your career. Choose wisely.

21 APRIL

You are in a position to review where you stand. You'll enjoy meeting someone special and discussing your options.

22 APRIL

As you will see over the coming weeks you'll have many new opportunities that arise, so be prepared to look outside the box.

23 APRIL

Being with a diverse and chatty group of people will boost your mood, so take a moment to get in touch.

24 APRIL

This is a good day for talks and communications. It's also a good time for health and beauty appointments.

25 APRIL

This is a good time to collaborate and seek agreement with those you must get along with. An expert may be super helpful.

26 APRIL

Trust your instincts but avoid making decisions without having all the facts. If you feel a little emotional, be sure to take time out.

27 APRIL

You may receive unexpected news from work or from a friend that will be uplifting.

28 APRIL

The moon in your sign for the next two days will encourage you to be outgoing and upbeat, so take the initiative with your projects.

29 APRIL

Surprise developments at work or socially will be enjoyable. Be prepared to be spontaneous.

30 APRIL

Attention to detail will be productive but you must avoid being super critical of yourself and others, as this will be counterproductive.

May

1 MAY

You may begin to look at your commitments in your daily life in a new light. Rest assured you will gain time to review them over the coming weeks.

2 MAY

You may receive good news from work, a far distance away or in relation to a collaboration.

3 MAY

You'll appreciate a sense of fair play, but if it seems elusive avoid retaliation and research ways to succeed.

4 MAY

This is a good day for research, especially about hidden, legal or love matters. Avoid giving mixed messages even if you're receiving them.

5 MAY

The lunar eclipse in Scorpio signals a fresh chapter in your domestic life. This is a good time to meet an active and upbeat crowd. Avoid overindulgence.

6 MAY

You will enjoy doing something different and being more outgoing even if you also crave a little peace and quiet at home.

7 MAY

You'll enjoy daydreaming a little and improving your appearance, environment and health.

8 MAY

Be adventurous and believe you have what it takes. You may surprise yourself with your abilities.

9 MAY

You will receive surprise news from an organisation or employer. There are many changes about to occur, so be sure to look for opportunities.

10 MAY

It's always the tortoise that wins the race, so the steadier and more stable you are the more ground you will cover.

11 MAY

Be prepared to look outside the box at your options both health-wise and at work. Draw on your creative abilities.

12 MAY

This is a good day to review some of your projects. You may enjoy a reunion or return to an old haunt.

13 MAY

A trip or reunion will be enjoyable. This is a good time to look for support from those close to you and to offer it in return.

14 MAY

This is a good time for romance, but if you're at work you will need to focus a little harder. Avoid forgetfulness.

15 MAY

Key news that concerns your career, travel, study or general direction will be enlightening. You will enjoy romance or a get-together.

16 MAY

As Jupiter enters Taurus you are about to begin a learning curve that will prospectively bring abundance and wisdom your way.

17 MAY

While you are known for being dynamic you can also be stubborn, so if you encounter problems just double-check you're not being obstinate.

18 MAY

You'll be motivated to succeed but mustn't forget how important relationships are, so avoid putting someone offside.

19 MAY

The Taurus new moon signals a fresh chapter in your status, career or general direction. Be practical and forge a fresh agreement.

20 MAY

You will enjoy a lovely, therapeutic activity that will be relaxing. This is a good day for clearing chores.

21 MAY

This is a good day for making changes at work and within your status. Just avoid taking things too seriously and avoid conflict, as it will escalate.

22 MAY

You will enjoy pursuing your favourite activities such as sports and a short trip will be fun. This is a good day for promoting yourself at work.

23 MAY

You are a force to be reckoned with and will be super productive now but you must avoid putting colleagues or even employers offside.

24 MAY

Your drive is peaking, but if you have been experiencing conflict it's time to dial down your approach as others may find you threatening.

25 MAY

This is a good time to improve your appearance, well-being and status. A new look or health schedule may suit.

26 MAY

You'll receive unexpectedly good news and may also enjoy an impromptu get-together.

27 MAY

You will appreciate the opportunity to come to an agreement with someone you must share duties and even finances with.

28 MAY

Hard work will reap excellent results, but you must avoid arguments with someone you share duties or space with. Find a happy medium.

29 MAY

You are motivated and determined and can make great progress with your projects. You'll feel more relaxed later in the day.

30 MAY

You are communicating well, so reach out to those you know are like-minded and helpful.

31 MAY

A trip, chat or message that provides a sense of peace and balance will be rewarding, so take the initiative.

June

1 JUNE

Aim to work hard, especially on your interpersonal skills, and your efforts will be rewarded.

2 JUNE

A meeting, reunion or news at work or regarding your general direction and status will be important.

3 JUNE

You will enjoy feeling motivated, especially with domestic matters and improving a romantic or shared situation.

4 JUNE

The full moon in Sagittarius begins a new chapter in your personal life or a creative project. News may be unexpected. You'll enjoy a get-together.

5 JUNE

This is a good day to focus on your health, well-being and appearance. You may be motivated at work but must avoid arguments.

6 JUNE

The Capricorn moon will put you in a practical frame of mind and ensure you are capable of dealing with all eventualities.

7 JUNE

Be prepared to exit your comfort zone either at work or in your daily activities or health situation.

8 JUNE

You'll appreciate the company of a chatty and outgoing character. You will enjoy trying something new.

9 JUNE

This is a good day for meetings, both in your personal life and at work. However, you may be slightly idealistic so ensure you are being realistic.

10 JUNE

You will enjoy a romantic weekend and immersing yourself in music and good company. A trip somewhere beautiful will appeal.

11 JUNE

A change of pace or of place may take you to a familiar haunt. You will enjoy a reunion.

12 JUNE

Be positive and proactive and you'll enjoy a productive day. Avoid treading on someone's toes by mistake.

13 JUNE

You are dynamic and outgoing but your energy may threaten someone's fragile ego. Be prepared to be tactful and diplomatic.

14 JUNE

If you have felt that life is stuck it is important you take steps to move forward. It's a good day for research.

15 JUNE

A trip is likely to be enjoyable but you must double-check schedules to avoid delays and disappointments.

16 JUNE

You'll enjoy socialising with an upbeat, chatty crowd, but some Leos will need to attend to duties first.

17 JUNE

This is a good day to review some of your responsibilities and discuss agreements, but you must have an open mind for a positive outcome. A trip or visit will be enjoyable.

18 JUNE

Make a wish at the new moon in Gemini, which signals a fresh phase in your social life or in connection with a group or friend.

19 JUNE

This is a productive day but you must avoid second guessing someone and must double-check details if you are making key commitments.

20 JUNE

Powerful emotions are bubbling under the surface either in you or someone you work with, so aim to take breaks when possible.

21 JUNE

It's the solstice! Be prepared to see another person's viewpoint for the best results. Be diligent at work and you could scale mountains.

22 JUNE

A dynamic outlook will encourage you to embrace challenges but you must avoid making snap decisions.

23 JUNE

You'll enjoy therapeutic yet upbeat activities such as sport. You'll also enjoy a reunion or good news at work.

24 JUNE

This is a good weekend to review your finances and loyalties. Just avoid being super critical of yourself and others. You'll enjoy good company.

25 JUNE

Be clear with communications as there may be misunderstandings. You may also be forgetful.

26 JUNE

You'll appreciate the chance to excel even if circumstances change but you must avoid restlessness and impulsiveness.

27 JUNE

You'll enjoy a reunion or news at work and may meet someone who seems familiar even if you've never met before.

28 JUNE

This is an excellent time for getting things done at home and for improving domestic and sibling relationships.

29 JUNE

You will appreciate the outcome of a self-development class or study. It's a good day for meetings, health and beauty appointments and to mend bridges.

30 JUNE

A get-together either at work or socially will be productive and constructive. You may draw up a fresh agreement.

July

1 JULY

You'll enjoy a trip, visit or change of pace. A reunion will be memorable.

2 JULY

Be prepared to think on your feet as you may need to alter your plans at a moment's notice. Avoid making snap decisions.

3 JULY

The full moon in Capricorn shines a light on your daily life, work and health schedules. You may begin a fresh agreement with a friend or organisation.

4 JULY

Be prepared to cooperate and collaborate. You will appreciate being more flexible with arrangements as the day goes by.

5 JULY

Changes in your usual routine or news from someone close are best navigated carefully to avoid making mistakes.

6 JULY

This is a good time for health and well-being appointments. Avoid jumping to conclusions and be prepared to research circumstances.

7 JULY

You may hear unexpected news to do with work or a change in your status. You'll enjoy an impromptu meeting and socialising.

8 JULY

This is a good time for catching up with friends and chores. You may enjoy a short trip and improving your appearance and health.

9 JULY

A little give and take with your plans will ensure everyone gets to do what they want. If you must catch up on work you will.

10 JULY

You're thinking creatively, which will be reflected in your activities and at work. Take short breaks to overcome pressure.

11 JULY

As Mercury enters your sign communications will become the focus, and you may receive key health or work news.

12 JULY

Your help and advice may be required, and rest assured you can provide it. If you need help it will be available from an expert.

13 JULY

You may begin to see issues in a new light and will be able to move forward as a result. Avoid being super critical.

14 JULY

You'll enjoy being spontaneous and may receive good news to do with work, health or your status, but you must be prepared to work hard and be diligent.

15 JULY

You'll be drawn to spending time with people you love and to avoiding complex discussions, opting to look after yourself first.

16 JULY

This is a good time for spiritual development and for deepening your understanding of someone close and yourself. Avoid overindulgence, as you'll regret it!

17 JULY

The Cancer new moon signals a fresh daily, health or work schedule. Be prepared to be super clear to avoid misunderstandings.

18 JULY

You may wear your heart on your sleeve and will be drawn to expressing your feelings. You may re-evaluate your long-term plans.

19 JULY

Healing, self-development and generally helping others and yourself to feel more fulfilled will be a drawcard. Be inspired.

20 JULY

You'll enjoy a reunion and romance could truly blossom, so organise a date! The arts, music and creativity will all appeal.

21 JULY

This is a good day to focus on finances, and if you've overspent to establish a fresh budget.

22 JULY

There is healing potential this weekend but intense feelings may arise. Avoid arguments, as they will escalate quickly. Find common ground, as you could make solid agreements now.

23 JULY

A change of routine or in your personal circumstances is best navigated carefully to avoid mistakes and mix-ups.

24 JULY

You're looking for more balance in your relationships and there's no time like the present to find a way.

25 JULY

You'll gain insight into the best way to achieve a positive outcome in a relationship. Take short breaks during the day to gain perspective.

26 JULY

You'll feel more passionate about your projects and personal life so seek balance, especially at work, by channelling energy into your projects.

27 JULY

Financial and personal matters will deserve attention, and if you're uncertain of your position you must research further.

28 JULY

Focus on good communication and negotiation skills as these will help you to feel fulfilled, both at work and at home.

29 JULY

Be prepared to listen to someone else's opinion, as the more you work collaboratively together the better will be the outcome.

30 JULY

This is a good time to get on top of chores and to research your personal and financial plans. Avoid distractions.

31 JULY

The Capricorn moon will encourage you to be practical and maintain focus on long-term plans and goals.

August

1 AUGUST

The full moon supermoon in Aquarius spells a new chapter in a relationship for July Leos and a fresh daily routine for August Leos. You may receive a financial or ego boost.

2 AUGUST

This is a good time for discussions regarding finances, contracts and personal agreements.

3 AUGUST

You may tend to be seeing life through rose-coloured glasses at the moment so be prepared to be realistic as well.

4 AUGUST

This could be a lovely, romantic time; however, you may be easily distracted so be sure to focus hard at work.

5 AUGUST

You will enjoy being active and outgoing this weekend, so why not plan sports, travel and fun events?

6 AUGUST

This is a good day for personal development. You may be asked for help. If you're studying you will make progress.

7 AUGUST

Be prepared to listen to the opinions and ideas of others even if you disagree, as you could find common ground.

8 AUGUST

Someone in a position of authority has news and a friendly approach will be productive. You may receive a compliment or financial boost.

9 AUGUST

You may be surprised by unexpected developments and may need to review your position.

10 AUGUST

This is a better day for communications, especially with those in authority. Be sure to check the fine print if you are making purchases and avoid overspending.

11 AUGUST

There is a lighter, chattier atmosphere you'll appreciate, and you'll enjoy socialising and networking.

12 AUGUST

You will appreciate the opportunity to improve your appearance and self-development. An expert or adviser will be helpful.

13 AUGUST

This is another excellent day for self-improvement, both of your appearance and spiritually. Romance could blossom.

14 AUGUST

You will feel increasingly in your element as the day goes by, so avoid allowing Mondayitis to rule your day.

15 AUGUST

It's a good day to talk and for meetings, especially regarding finances. You may receive a compliment or financial boost.

16 AUGUST

The new moon in Leo signals a fresh phase in your personal life. Be prepared for a surprise that will affect your career or general direction.

17 AUGUST

The more precise you can be the better will be the outcome. Ensure you base your ideas on facts, especially financially.

18 AUGUST

You can make a great deal of progress with meetings and at work. Focus on the facts if you are making a large investment.

19 AUGUST

You're approaching your chores this weekend realistically, which will enable you to enjoy relaxing and romance later in the day.

20 AUGUST

This is a romantic time when you'll enjoy the arts and the company of special people. Base decisions on facts, not assumptions.

21 AUGUST

A little tension in relationships can be motivational and productive, but if the stress is overwhelming it must be addressed.

22 AUGUST

This is a good time to review finances and agreements, especially if you feel there has been a misunderstanding.

23 AUGUST

You'll find out whether you have over- or underestimated someone. Avoid overspending and double-check financial figures.

24 AUGUST

You will find merit in being more actively engaged in finding peace and harmony at home.

25 AUGUST

A change of routine or circumstances will lift morale. You may receive a financial or ego boost.

26 AUGUST

Being active, including outdoor ventures and sports, will be a drawcard. This is a good time to review finances.

27 AUGUST

This is a beneficial time to review commitments and to formulate a solid plan.

28 AUGUST

Focus on the practicalities with chores as this will enable you in the afternoon and evening to focus a little more on your favourite activities.

29 AUGUST

You will enjoy a change of pace and being innovative and trying something new.

30 AUGUST

You'll be more sympathetic towards people's ideas and opinions, which will help you to navigate through the day both at home and at work.

31 AUGUST

The Pisces full moon supermoon spotlights a key relationship. Be prepared to dream but be realistic with planning and finances.

September

1 SEPTEMBER

A trip or meeting may seem to be a challenge, but if you put the hard work in your efforts will be rewarded.

2 SEPTEMBER

You'll appreciate the opportunity to work off excess energy at the gym or beach or by enjoying fun activities.

3 SEPTEMBER

This is a good time to invest in yourself. You may be drawn to retail therapy, self-improvement or simply travelling somewhere beautiful.

4 SEPTEMBER

Your life will move forward, especially if things have been slow, so be ready to make key decisions. You may review a financial or work situation.

5 SEPTEMBER

Talks and meetings are likely to go well, especially in connection with finances, beauty and work.

6 SEPTEMBER

Key news or a meeting will arise. A financial or personal matter will be open for review.

7 SEPTEMBER

This is a good day for a beauty treat and improving your appearance. Romance will blossom. It's also a good day to discuss finances.

8 SEPTEMBER

This is a lovely day to make progress at work, in your career and status. You may receive good news or a financial boost.

9 SEPTEMBER

Trust your instincts, especially with regard to a group, friend or organisation.

10 SEPTEMBER

Your emotions may be strong, so find time to channel them into productive outcomes and avoid mood swings and needless arguments.

11 SEPTEMBER

This is a good day for a reunion and getting on top of financial and personal matters. If you're shopping, avoid overspending.

12 SEPTEMBER

You will appreciate feeling optimistic about your long-term goals but must avoid feeling too frustrated by some limitations.

13 SEPTEMBER

This is a good time to pay attention to details, especially financially if you're considering a commitment or investment.

14 SEPTEMBER

This is a good day to consider a commitment to a financial or personal venture.

15 SEPTEMBER

The new moon in Virgo signals a fresh chapter in a financial or personal arrangement. Be prepared to be practical.

16 SEPTEMBER

You may be pleasantly surprised by news at work or financially. You may hear from someone unexpectedly.

17 SEPTEMBER

Someone may have very high expectations of you. Avoid feeling you cannot achieve your goals: you can.

18 SEPTEMBER

This is a good time to focus on creating a calm and productive atmosphere in your environment. Take short breaks when you can.

19 SEPTEMBER

You will discover whether you've over- or underestimated someone, especially due to financial or personal circumstances. Romance will blossom, so organise a date!

20 SEPTEMBER

You may need to choose between loyalties, so ensure you choose wisely. This is a good time for do-it-yourself projects and home improvements.

21 SEPTEMBER

This is a good time to make changes in your daily life, health and work. You may receive beneficial financial news.

22 SEPTEMBER

Be adventurous and positive. Nobody is quite as optimistic as you, so take the initiative with your ventures and personal life.

23 SEPTEMBER

The sun in Libra will encourage you to create more peace and harmony in your personal relationships. You may be drawn to travelling over the coming weeks.

24 SEPTEMBER

You are energetic now and must avoid rushing to avoid minor accidents. A short trip or meeting will be healing. Look for expert advice if it's needed.

25 SEPTEMBER

Be careful with expenditure, as you may be tempted to overspend. Take the time to do your research if you are making new agreements.

26 SEPTEMBER

Someone close to you may surprise you. You may be drawn to retail therapy but must avoid overspending.

27 SEPTEMBER

Refreshing developments in your personal life will be uplifting and you'll enjoy being spontaneous.

28 SEPTEMBER

If you work in the arts you will be super inspired, but if you work with facts and figures be prepared to concentrate more than usual.

29 SEPTEMBER

The Aries full moon signals a fresh phase in key relationships, and this will include focus on travel, study and, for some, legal matters.

30 SEPTEMBER

You'll feel motivated to be outgoing and make changes at home, such as do-it-yourself projects. You may enjoy a visit to someone else's home.

October

1 OCTOBER

It's a lovely day to catch up with someone special, but you must avoid making rash decisions that affect those you live with.

2 OCTOBER

You may not have all the facts, so if you're making key decisions you may need to do more research. Romance and artistic ventures will appeal.

3 OCTOBER

You may receive good news at work or concerning health or financially – or all three! Developments may happen fast, so be sure you have all the facts.

4 OCTOBER

The Gemini moon is excellent for research and meetings but you may need to be discreet.

5 OCTOBER

Take someone's circumstances into account to avoid hurt feelings and being distracted from your goals.

6 OCTOBER

Be prepared for a busy and even intense day, but rest assured your efforts will be worthwhile.

7 OCTOBER

It's in your interest to get on with someone who is influential, such as someone in authority. Be diligent with your projects and you will succeed.

8 OCTOBER

Take time out for yourself. Avoid arguments at home or if you're working, as these will escalate quickly.

9 OCTOBER

This will be a busy and productive day. However, arguments could flare up from nowhere so be prepared.

10 OCTOBER

This is a good time to make an agreement or commitment as long as fair play prevails. Key financial decisions may be made.

11 OCTOBER

Events may bring out your vulnerabilities, so be sure to take short breaks when possible. Avoid taking random comments personally.

12 OCTOBER

You may notice a change of atmosphere at home. You're likely to feel more passionate about your activities and beliefs. Avoid misunderstandings.

13 OCTOBER

This is a good time to actively make changes at home that can provide more stability and security.

14 OCTOBER

The solar eclipse represents a new chapter in your home or family life. For some this may involve a chance to travel or to study. Avoid minor bumps and scrapes.

15 OCTOBER

You may be surprised by developments. Maintain a steady approach to your goals and your efforts will be worthwhile.

16 OCTOBER

Be prepared to go the extra mile for those you care about as your interest will be appreciated.

17 OCTOBER

Your key to success lies in good communication skills, especially at work. Avoid impulsiveness, as this may backfire.

18 OCTOBER

An optimistic approach to creating the home life you want will be productive, but you must avoid power struggles over the coming days.

19 OCTOBER

You will enjoy a reunion, trip or visit. This is a good time for research and to avoid misunderstandings.

20 OCTOBER

A trip or reunion will be enjoyable but you must avoid sensitive topics, especially at work.

21 OCTOBER

You'll enjoy a change in your usual routine, but if you're travelling you must double-check details to avoid delays and mix-ups. It may be an intense day.

22 OCTOBER

You'll enjoy a trip or get-together and may also enjoy a financial or ego boost.

23 OCTOBER

The next four weeks will be a busy time when you will enjoy leaving your comfort zone and improving relationships.

24 OCTOBER

This is a good day to make agreements and commitments with personal or business partners. You may commit to a trip.

25 OCTOBER

Be inspired but also practical, as otherwise complexities may become a conundrum.

26 OCTOBER

Someone you share duties or space with may take more of your attention than usual, so tact and diplomacy will be invaluable.

27 OCTOBER

Relationships may require more of your focus and effort than usual, but if you remain positive you will overcome any prospective difficulties.

28 OCTOBER

The lunar eclipse in Taurus signals a fresh chapter in your activities, pastimes and, for many, your general direction such as your career. Avoid making snap decisions.

29 OCTOBER

Events will unfold swiftly. You may experience a key change at home and may be under pressure, so be careful with long-term decisions.

30 OCTOBER

The next two days are ideal for making long-term changes, especially at work, financially and in your personal life, so take the initiative.

31 OCTOBER

Happy Halloween! You may receive unexpectedly good news at work or a financial boost.

November

1 NOVEMBER

You may feel super sensitive to undercurrents, so be sure to maintain perspective.

2 NOVEMBER

This is a good day to discuss personal and domestic matters as you are in tune with people you must get on with.

3 NOVEMBER

You may need to make key decisions concerning your home, career, general direction and finances. If you are unsure, seek expert advice.

4 NOVEMBER

Unexpected news will shed light on complex issues. You may receive an unexpected visitor or make changes at home.

5 NOVEMBER

Developments at home and in your interests and hobbies will merit a careful approach. If you feel times are challenging, rest assured you can succeed with hard work.

6 NOVEMBER

This is a good day to make changes to your usual daily schedule and for improving your appearance. You may experience an ego or financial boost.

7 NOVEMBER

This is a good time for get-togethers at home and for sharing duties and responsibilities carefully. It's also a good time for home improvements.

8 NOVEMBER

You'll become more aware of the necessity for fair play, both financially and in your personal life, and will be drawn to the arts and romance.

9 NOVEMBER

Be prepared to consider another person's opinions, as good listening skills will enable you to improve relationships.

10 NOVEMBER

You're likely to feel more outspoken, especially at home. However, some people may find this confronting, so be sure to use tact as well.

11 NOVEMBER

Expect a surprise or change of circumstance at home or at work. Developments will arise quickly, so be adaptable but avoid making rash decisions.

12 NOVEMBER

You'll have strong feelings about a domestic or family matter, and the more you research your ideas the better it will be otherwise mistakes can be made.

13 NOVEMBER

The Scorpio new moon signals a fresh chapter in your domestic life. This may come about in surprising ways or through changes outside your control.

14 NOVEMBER

You are proactive at the moment and can make positive changes, especially regarding family and your personal life, but you must avoid gambling.

15 NOVEMBER

You'll enjoy a trip or meeting or the chance to improve your domestic life.

16 NOVEMBER

Some of your meetings and talks will revolve around how to improve your home life. It's a good time to think big but to also be realistic. A trip may be delayed.

17 NOVEMBER

Be positive about your plans moving forward as you may be surprised by how easily they can fall into place, especially at home and regarding travel.

18 NOVEMBER

Sudden or unexpected developments at home will encourage you to be more spontaneous. It's a good day for relaxation but also for home improvement.

19 NOVEMBER

You'll enjoy the company of an upbeat character. Family or your home life will take much of your focus.

20 NOVEMBER

This is a good day to make changes in your usual routine at work and at home. Be prepared to go with a changing scenario.

21 NOVEMBER

You may be inclined to dream a little, which is positive with creative projects, but you'll need to be down to earth with facts and figures.

22 NOVEMBER

A meeting or trip may bring your vulnerabilities to the surface. Avoid taking events and random comments personally. Plan ahead to avoid travel delays.

23 NOVEMBER

Someone stubborn may behave true to character. Avoid arguments, as there are more constructive ways to gain agreement.

24 NOVEMBER

You are proactive and productive, but over the next two days you may discover some minor obstacles and therefore must be patient.

25 NOVEMBER

This is a good time to be productive and active, especially at home, but you must avoid getting too frustrated by delays, rules and restrictions.

26 NOVEMBER

You're communicating well at the moment but, nevertheless, misunderstandings can occur. A trip may be delayed or you will need to work harder at gaining someone's support.

27 NOVEMBER

The Gemini full moon signals a fresh phase in your social or personal life and, for some, in your career. Misunderstandings and delays are likely, so plan ahead.

28 NOVEMBER

This is a sociable, chatty time ideal for networking and improving your relationships.

29 NOVEMBER

You have high expectations of yourself, and you'll gain insight into whether these are realistic or whether you need to adjust your expectations.

30 NOVEMBER

You'll enjoy a change of routine and the chance to gain a deeper understanding of someone close.

December

1 DECEMBER

You'll find communications more down to earth over the coming weeks, which will enable you to express yourself better.

2 DECEMBER

This is a lovely day for get-togethers, especially with friends and family and someone special. You could make a long-term commitment.

3 DECEMBER

This may be a tense day, especially if you're travelling or altering your usual routine. Avoid allowing arguments to escalate.

4 DECEMBER

You'll feel more passionate about your plans and projects over the coming weeks but so will others, so avoid arguments.

5 DECEMBER

This is a good time for get-togethers and, for some, a trip. If you have recently argued with someone it's a good day to mend bridges.

6 DECEMBER

Be prepared to look for a balanced outcome and let bygones be bygones.

7 DECEMBER

Be sensitive to the feelings of others as it can be a gift. You may find a supportive role is welcome.

8 DECEMBER

This is a therapeutic, healing time and you can make great inroads into your relationships, especially at home.

9 DECEMBER

Conversations or a trip or get-together will be memorable. You'll enjoy transforming your home or environment.

10 DECEMBER

Domestic developments are likely to be upbeat, and you'll enjoy preparing your home or environment for the upcoming seasonal activities.

11 DECEMBER

It's a good day for paperwork and improving both your health and appearance. You may enjoy improving home decor as well.

12 DECEMBER

The Sagittarian new moon signals the start of a new chapter in your personal, family or love life. You may be surprised by developments at work.

13 DECEMBER

Important work or health news or a change in your usual routine will merit focus. Try to get important communications finalised to avoid having to review them later.

14 DECEMBER

This is a good time to get super organised at work and at home so that the seasonal period is enjoyable.

15 DECEMBER

There is a therapeutic aspect to the day. An expert or adviser will be helpful. Avoid rushing to avoid minor accidents.

16 DECEMBER

You'll enjoy diverse company, and activities such as sports and self-development will appeal.

17 DECEMBER

Developments such as delays may bring your sensitive side to the surface. Avoid taking people's random comments personally and be super clear to avoid mix-ups.

18 DECEMBER

Communications and meetings are likely to go well. You may enjoy a reunion or good news at work.

19 DECEMBER

Take the initiative, as you will be productive and able to reach your goals.

20 DECEMBER

Get-togethers with friends and family will be enjoyable and you'll appreciate creature comforts, the arts, music and dance.

21 DECEMBER

A change of pace or of place will be enjoyable, although some arrangements may change at the last minute. You may receive an unexpected visitor.

22 DECEMBER

You'll enjoy a change of pace and a reunion. Avoid overindulging and gambling, as you'll regret both.

23 DECEMBER

You may be conscious of your own or someone else's new status. Remain grounded and you will enjoy your weekend.

24 DECEMBER

This is a lovely day for romance and for spending time with friends and family. Enjoy!

25 DECEMBER

Merry Christmas! There is a sentimental and romantic atmosphere to your Christmas Day that you'll enjoy. Music, dance and the arts will appeal.

26 DECEMBER

Domestic and family developments will be uplifting but you must avoid overindulging and overspending.

27 DECEMBER

The Cancer full moon signals the start of a fresh chapter in your social or family life and, for some, in relation to the groups and organisations you're a part of.

28 DECEMBER

You'll be drawn to the arts, music and romance. Some meetings, get-togethers and talks may be delayed and, for some, overwhelming, so take breaks when possible.

29 DECEMBER

This is a lovely time for a change of pace or of place and you'll feel more outgoing and optimistic.

30 DECEMBER

The Leo moon will bring out your active and upbeat side, making today ideal for sports, socialising and favourite hobbies.

31 DECEMBER

Happy New Year! A fun, active New Year's Eve will be a drawcard. Just avoid being perfectionist and enjoy the festivities.

VIRGO

23 August - 23 September

FINANCES

You'll experience considerable change financially in 2023, especially in the months of April and October, as you'll gain the opportunity to reconfigure your investments and the way you earn money. This will be due to opportunities arising that allow you to embrace fresh collaborations work-wise. You will also need to rejig shared finances such as payments for utilities and joint bank accounts as there are likely to be considerable changes in your personal life.

HEALTH

You'll find the time to focus more wholly on your health and well-being and to initiate a fresh schedule that may involve some unusual treatments. In 2023 you'll discover a deeper understanding of the link between mind and body. From 7 March onwards you'll feel more comfortable about your health routine, and this circumstance will enable you to focus on other aspects of your life. You may need to tweak some elements of your health regime in early November and then again in December.

LOVE LIFE

Be prepared to embrace a fresh understanding and relationship with those you hold dear in 2023. This circumstance may well come about due to a change in how you share responsibilities and also communal space at home. Your values are changing, and you may value peace, harmony and stability in relationships more than ever. Your relationship status will change, especially in April and October/November, so singles looking for a new partner will be active then and couples will appreciate the chance to embrace a fresh chapter.

CAREER

You'll enjoy being creative and inventive and choosing something different in 2023, and the more you embrace the new in all aspects of your life, especially in January and December, the more you'll enjoy this year. Otherwise the option will be to go with the flow, and while this may take some of the risk-taking out of your career situation it could lead you somewhere you're unhappy with as you will feel unfulfilled. Be proactive, and actively seek fresh projects; you'll be glad you did!

HOME LIFE

Your home life is likely to see considerable changes in 2023 due to developments in your family and personal lives and the way you share your personal space. The start of the year is ideal for deciding how you wish to proceed, as the sun in Capricorn in your domestic sector will help you to make practical and realistic decisions. The new moon in Capricorn on 23 December 2022 may already have seen fresh ideas take root. You'll see the need to make decisions that affect your home life mid-year and at the end of December, prospectively due to a change in status.

January

1 JANUARY

Happy New Year! Strong emotions are likely. Romance and family time will be focuses.

2 JANUARY

This is a good day for discussing shared concerns; however, you or someone close may be feeling sensitive so take things one step at a time.

3 JANUARY

Consider looking at your personal life and commitments in a new light, as you may have a light-bulb moment.

4 JANUARY

This is a lovely day for romance and for getting together with your favourite people.

5 JANUARY

You'll enjoy going somewhere different and may also receive unexpected news.

6 JANUARY

The Cancer full moon suggests you are ready to turn a corner in relation to a friend, organisation or family member. Be prepared to discuss your options.

7 JANUARY

You'll enjoy a reunion and the opportunity to review your circumstances, and focusing on paperwork will be productive.

8 JANUARY

You'll enjoy being spontaneous and doing fun activities and may be pleasantly surprised by developments.

9 JANUARY

This is a creative day. You may be drawn to improving your appearance and health. It's a good day for making improvements at work.

10 JANUARY

You'll enjoy the variety in your day and being in new or different circumstances.

11 JANUARY

This is a busy and diverse time, so it's in your interest to take extra care with communications to avoid misunderstandings and hurt feelings.

12 JANUARY

Your activities and general direction are about to alter course, and you'll appreciate being busier over the coming weeks.

13 JANUARY

The arts, romance and music will appeal. This could be a good time to enjoy creative and family activities.

14 JANUARY

You'll appreciate the results of spending time working on family dynamics and your environment.

15 JANUARY

A change of pace or of place may come about unexpectedly. Be on your toes. You may receive an unexpected visitor or take an unplanned trip.

16 JANUARY

An outgoing and upbeat approach to a trip or change in your environment will be productive.

17 JANUARY

A return home or to a familiar setting will create a sense of stability, but you must avoid rushing so you don't make mistakes.

18 JANUARY

You may receive news regarding family or someone close. This is a good time to focus more on your family and home life.

19 JANUARY

A practical approach to chores and domestic responsibilities will be productive, and someone close will be happy of your support.

20 JANUARY

This is a good time to view your personal life such as a family commitment in a new light.

21 JANUARY

The new moon supermoon in Aquarius signals a fresh chapter in your personal life or creative project. Make a wish. Be innovative.

22 JANUARY

This is a good time to consider a commitment at work or to bettering your health and appearance. You will be drawn to a new environment or learning curve.

23 JANUARY

You'll appreciate the opportunity to dream a little but you must avoid forgetfulness, especially at work.

24 JANUARY

Someone close will require your help with understanding complex matters. Romance will be a drawcard, although there is a sentimental atmosphere.

25 JANUARY

You can make the changes you wish to see in your personal and work lives, so take the initiative.

26 JANUARY

The moon in Aries spotlights your empathy for others but you must avoid being misled.

27 JANUARY

Your help will be required, and if you need help or support it will be available.

28 JANUARY

It's a good day to make domestic improvements, and you may receive help and support from unexpected sources.

29 JANUARY

A trip or change in your usual activities may involve some delays but will be refreshing.

30 JANUARY

You'll gain a sense of progress as your activities may advance surprisingly swiftly.

31 JANUARY

Activities such as sport and self-development will go well now and you may be drawn to improving your wardrobe and appearance. Romance will blossom, so plan a date!

February

1 FEBRUARY

Your expertise will be in demand, and if you need help from an expert or support it will be available.

2 FEBRUARY

As an earth sign you like to be practical above all else, yet your intuition is spot on so be sure to trust it.

3 FEBRUARY

You will appreciate the opportunity to touch base with someone special but may need to be adaptable with arrangements.

4 FEBRUARY

You may receive unexpected news or experience an unusual change of schedule. Be prepared to collaborate but avoid arguments.

5 FEBRUARY

The Leo full moon signals a fresh chapter in your daily, health or work schedule. Be prepared to discuss options and avoid a Mexican stand-off.

6 FEBRUARY

This is a good day for romance and creative and artistic projects. You'll enjoy being with like-minded people.

7 FEBRUARY

The moon in your sign will encourage you to be practical above all else. Be prepared to see a situation from someone else's point of view.

8 FEBRUARY

You may be surprised by news from a partner and will enjoy leaving your comfort zone at work.

9 FEBRUARY

Meetings both at work and with experts and those in authority are likely to go well. Just avoid gambling.

10 FEBRUARY

Key meetings and news will signal changes to come. You may experience an intense discussion or development, so maintain perspective.

11 FEBRUARY

You will be drawn to expressing your true feelings to someone close, and the more you can find common ground or simply agree to disagree the better.

12 FEBRUARY

It's a lovely day for sharing your interests with those close to you. This is a good time for self-development, spiritual pursuits, romance and the arts.

13 FEBRUARY

You may experience a mild case of Mondayitis, yet with some application you will be super productive whether at home or at work.

14 FEBRUARY

Happy St Valentine's Day! It's a lovely day for romance, so make a statement. Be brave.

15 FEBRUARY

This is one of the most romantic times of the year for you, so be sure to organise a treat. Avoid unrealistic expectations. You may be prepared to make a commitment to someone.

16 FEBRUARY

A commitment at work or regarding a health schedule may be productive, but you must obtain all the details and avoid assumptions.

17 FEBRUARY

You'll enjoy investing your time, energy and emotion in domestic or family matters. Just avoid taking someone's random comments personally. Romance could blossom.

18 FEBRUARY

Sports, gardening and generally finding time for people you love will raise morale, and doing something different will appeal.

19 FEBRUARY

This is a lovely day for romance as you could deepen your understanding of someone, so be sure to organise a treat or get-together.

20 FEBRUARY

The new moon in Pisces signals a fresh chapter in your daily, health or work routine. This could be a healing time, including financially.

21 FEBRUARY

You're expressing yourself well at the moment but may need to be extra clear to avoid misunderstandings and delays.

22 FEBRUARY

You can make great progress with a work, health or personal matter, so be sure to take the initiative.

23 FEBRUARY

Developments may evolve rapidly, so be sure to be on your toes. A lovely teacher, colleague or expert may be super helpful.

24 FEBRUARY

This is a lovely day to reconnect with someone you love or admire. Be inspired. It's also a good day for self-development and study.

25 FEBRUARY

Be practical, and you can put wonderful plans in place that will broaden your horizons and may even be unexpected or out of the ordinary.

26 FEBRUARY

It's a good day for catching up on chores and improving your environment, and then to find time to relax.

27 FEBRUARY

Key talks and meetings are likely to go well. If you're looking for work it's a good day to circulate your résumé and make phone calls or have interviews.

28 FEBRUARY

The moon in Gemini will bring out your chatty side, making this a good time for work meetings and boosting your profile.

March

1 MARCH

Certain projects will require attention to detail, so be prepared to work that little bit extra for good results. For some, key financial and personal matters will need focus.

2 MARCH

Be prepared to think outside the box, especially as someone close has important news for you regarding shared duties, finances or projects.

3 MARCH

This is a good day for talks and to find the best way forward, especially if someone needs help or advice. Expert help will be available.

4 MARCH

You may be surprised by the support you receive, and a change of routine could be uplifting. You may receive invaluable news.

5 MARCH

A trip somewhere uplifting or a favourite activity will be refreshing. You may be surprised by developments now.

6 MARCH

A change in your usual routine or activities will be enjoyable, so be sure to organise something special.

7 MARCH

The full moon in Virgo spotlights a fresh chapter in your personal life. You may be prepared to make a commitment to a new work or personal circumstance.

8 MARCH

This is a lovely time to look for more peace and harmony in your personal life and within your collaborations.

9 MARCH

You may feel a little more sensitive to other people's circumstances, so be sure to retain perspective.

10 MARCH

A short trip and the chance to catch up with someone special will be revitalising. You may also experience a health or work boost.

11 MARCH

Being with people you love and engaging in your favourite activities will raise morale. This is likely to be an active weekend, so pace yourself.

12 MARCH

Someone close may reveal their sensitive side, which may mean changes for you.

13 MARCH

This is a sensitive time and a good time to focus on looking after yourself and others. Be prepared to take responsibility for your own actions. You may need to slow down.

14 MARCH

You'll feel proactive and wish to steam ahead at work but you must avoid making mistakes. Be particularly careful to avoid misunderstandings.

15 MARCH

This is a super romantic day, especially for Virgos born in mid-September. However, misunderstandings are possible, so be careful and avoid being misled.

16 MARCH

You'll receive news from someone close, and if it's unclear you must find out more. You may be easily distracted, so be prepared to focus.

17 MARCH

This is a good day for talks and negotiations and for making agreements, but you should avoid rushing. Focus on the facts and avoid making assumptions.

18 MARCH

You will appreciate the chance to do what makes your heart sing, even if it means changing some arrangements.

19 MARCH

You may confide in someone or someone may confide in you, which will enable you to deepen your relationship.

20 MARCH

This is a good day for collaborations and discussing important matters that can mean long-term change. You'll enjoy a reunion.

21 MARCH

The Aries new moon is a good time to start something new such as a fresh collaboration or personal or business partnership. Avoid making snap decisions.

22 MARCH

You or someone close may be feeling feistier than usual, and while this will be useful for getting ahead with projects you must avoid appearing bossy.

23 MARCH

This is a good time to enter fresh territory in your personal life, so be brave. Creative projects may take a new direction.

24 MARCH

A connection with your past circumstances is best clarified to avoid future discrepancies.

25 MARCH

You'll enjoy a lovely reunion with someone special. However, you must avoid thorny topics if you're looking for relaxation.

26 MARCH

It's a lovely day to truly relax and treat yourself. Your intuition is sparking on all cylinders, so you should trust it.

27 MARCH

Someone is likely to confide in you, and you may be surprised by news and developments. Your expertise will be in demand.

28 MARCH

A financial or personal commitment will be a focus. Research a large investment before making a commitment. It's a good day for talks and travel. Avoid rushing.

29 MARCH

Developments will move forward under their own steam. Trust your intuition.

30 MARCH

You can make great progress at work and with your projects. A surprise meeting or activity will be enjoyable.

31 MARCH

Your optimism and enthusiasm are infectious and you'll enjoy socialising and networking.

April

1 APRIL

This is a lovely day for romance and for deepening your relationships with those you love.

2 APRIL

A favourite activity or trip somewhere beautiful will draw your attention. You will enjoy get-togethers but must avoid misunderstandings.

3 APRIL

You'll feel more grounded in yourself by the end of the day, but during the day be careful to avoid intense conversations.

4 APRIL

You'll gain insight into whether you are seeing someone through rose-coloured glasses.

5 APRIL

If you're an expert or adviser you're likely to be busy. If you need advice it will be available. You may hear from an old friend or visit an old haunt.

6 APRIL

The full moon in Libra signals a new chapter in your personal life or financially. It's a good time to seek perspective and balance.

7 APRIL

You may be surprised by a chance encounter or unexpected development. You'll enjoy doing activities you love or the company of someone you love.

8 APRIL

An active, upbeat development will take you into new terrain. Just avoid impulsiveness.

9 APRIL

You're unafraid to express yourself and will enjoy being with fun people, but you must be tactful and avoid taking tactless comments personally.

10 APRIL

You'll appreciate the chance to collaborate and interact with upbeat and outgoing people. You may learn interesting news.

11 APRIL

Be prepared to enter new territory with your interests. Romance and creative projects can blossom now, so take the initiative.

12 APRIL

Your domestic life will provide a sense of stability and security. However, someone may need your help or extra attention.

13 APRIL

You won't always get on with everyone; a current disagreement needn't upset the apple cart. Be prepared to look at matters through someone else's eyes.

14 APRIL

You may need to negotiate and compromise at work or with a project. Luckily, an old friend or colleague will prove to be supportive.

15 APRIL

A change of routine or of place will feel refreshing and revitalising. You'll enjoy collaborating with someone fun.

16 APRIL

This is a lovely day for romance and for indulging in the arts, music and dance.

17 APRIL

Someone close may express their feelings. A practical yet inspired approach to work and collaborations will be successful.

18 APRIL

The moon in Aries for the next two days will bring out a partner or colleague's feistiness. Be prepared to collaborate but avoid feeling bossed around.

19 APRIL

This is a proactive time, and teamwork will be successful as long as you feel you're on the same page. If not, try to find common ground.

20 APRIL

The total solar eclipse in Aries will kick-start an important chapter, for many Virgos within shared duties, responsibilities and even space at home. Avoid a battle of egos.

21 APRIL

Developments will enable you to return to an old haunt or reunite with an old friend. Some Virgos will be able to review a project.

22 APRIL

Be prepared to enter new territory, as you will appreciate the chance to broaden your horizons.

23 APRIL

Fun and upbeat activities may be therapeutic in nature, so be sure to organise something entertaining.

24 APRIL

Meetings and activities are likely to progress well even if you feel you're going over old ground.

25 APRIL

This is a good time to discuss work, commitments and financial matters as you're likely to make progress.

26 APRIL

Trust your intuition during the day, then later be sure to be spontaneous with arrangements and avoid being stubborn.

27 APRIL

You'll enjoy an impromptu or unexpected get-together, and activities are likely to be refreshing.

28 APRIL

You'll enjoy socialising and networking over the next two days and focusing on your health and well-being.

29 APRIL

An unusual event will add a degree of spontaneity to your weekend as you meet a diverse group of people. It's a good day to be spontaneous.

30 APRIL

The secret to success lies in being practical and paying attention to details. Avoid being easily distracted and misled.

May

1 MAY

You may begin to look at your commitments in your personal life in a new light. Rest assured you will gain the time to review them over the coming weeks.

2 MAY

You'll enjoy a reunion and the chance to go over old ground. It's a good day for a trip and romance.

3 MAY

Someone may need your help, and if you feel sensitive avoid acting out.

4 MAY

You may need more information before you can take decisive action. Avoid giving mixed messages even if you are receiving them.

5 MAY

The lunar eclipse in Scorpio signals a fresh chapter in a key relationship. For some it will mean a new trip or study or even a work opportunity.

6 MAY

You're experiencing life in an intense and intuitive way, so take time out if you feel overwhelmed. This aside, it's a lovely day for get-togethers.

7 MAY

You'll gain perspective about how some other people see you. Avoid taking other people's comments personally, and if you work towards your goals you will attain them.

8 MAY

It's a great day to get on top of chores, especially those at home and in collaboration with others.

9 MAY

You will receive surprise news, which makes it a good time to broaden your horizons and find out more about your circumstances.

10 MAY

Be practical about domestic and personal matters and you will attain your goals.

11 MAY

Be prepared to look outside the box at your options, both domestically and with new activities. Draw on your creative abilities.

12 MAY

Discussions with someone you collaborate with or at work are likely to go well, so take the initiative. A partner may have news.

13 MAY

It's a great day for get-togethers and to review your finances. You may receive a health or financial boost.

14 MAY

This is a good time for romance or socialising. You'll enjoy a change of routine and boosting your health and appearance.

15 MAY

A collaboration or shared duty including a financial commitment is set to move forward. It's a good day for meetings and talks.

16 MAY

As Jupiter enters Taurus you're about to begin a more abundant phase in shared concerns including joint finances, so be optimistic.

17 MAY

This is a good time to discuss shared commitments but you must avoid being pressured and, in turn, pressuring others.

18 MAY

Your collaborations can blossom, but if you have major disagreements you must avoid pushing your agenda as conflict could escalate quickly.

19 MAY

The Taurus new moon signals a fresh chapter in your activities, interests and, for some, study or even legal matters. It's a good day to make a new agreement.

20 MAY

You will enjoy a lovely, light-hearted activity that brings you in touch with like-minded people.

21 MAY

You'll enjoy a get-together or outing with like-minded people, so organise a treat. Avoid entering into conflict, as it will escalate.

22 MAY

You're in a strong position to make a positive impression, so be optimistic about collaborations, work and activities.

23 MAY

This is a productive day but you must steer clear of butting heads with someone in a position of power.

24 MAY

This is another productive day but you must avoid allowing emotions to lead, as there are potential hurt feelings in the making.

25 MAY

You'll appreciate the opportunity to socialise and network but you must maintain a view to keeping the peace.

26 MAY

You're likely to be surprised by news or a change of circumstance. Be prepared to be adaptable.

27 MAY

The moon in your own sign this weekend will promote a more settled and contented few days, and you'll enjoy catching up with those you love.

28 MAY

While you'd much rather take things easy there are chores to be completed and duties to perform. You'll find time to relax once those are completed.

29 MAY

You may need to take the role of mediator or peacemaker, but rest assured you will manage to do so.

30 MAY

The key to success at the moment relies on being a team player, even if you're in charge. Avoid taking someone else's moods personally.

31 MAY

This is a good time to relax and regain a sense of peace and balance; you'll be glad you did.

June

1 JUNE

A work or social commitment may be challenging, but if you work hard at achieving your goals you will succeed.

2 JUNE

A trip, meeting or reunion will be memorable. This is a good day for travel, study and spiritual development.

3 JUNE

An adventurous and outgoing approach to others will be successful, as you'll enjoy the feeling of connectedness.

4 JUNE

The full moon in Sagittarius begins a new chapter in your home life or family. News may be unexpected in connection with travel or a meeting or project.

5 JUNE

This may be an intense day, as disagreements may bubble up. Nevertheless, this could also be a romantic or creative day.

6 JUNE

The Capricorn moon will put you in a practical frame of mind and therefore capable of dealing with personal matters and long-term plans.

7 JUNE

You may be feeling more emotional than usual so ensure you take breaks, especially if you feel your triggers have been set off.

8 JUNE

This is a good time to look at personal matters in a new light and to be more outgoing.

9 JUNE

A trip, meeting or visit is likely to be enjoyable. This is a good day for romance, so take the initiative!

10 JUNE

You are sensitive to other people's feelings and so may deepen your relationships, especially in your romantic life.

11 JUNE

You'll enjoy reminiscing, a reunion or returning to an old haunt.

12 JUNE

Be positive and you'll enjoy a productive day. If you're uncertain of your future you will gain the opportunity to review your options over the coming weeks.

13 JUNE

Be prepared to work hard towards your goals; even if a challenge arises you will attain them. You may need help from a group, friend or organisation.

14 JUNE

If difficulties have arisen, double-check you're on the same page as those you must collaborate with.

15 JUNE

You'll enjoy a trip or a meeting but you must avoid taking certain factors for granted, especially at work, as mistakes could be made.

16 JUNE

You're communicating well, which will enable you to enjoy your activities as you feel more light-hearted.

17 JUNE

This is a lovely weekend for socialising; however, you may have certain chores and responsibilities to look after first. It's a good day to improve your appearance.

18 JUNE

Make a wish at the new moon in Gemini, which signals a fresh phase in your career, general direction or status.

19 JUNE

This is a productive day and a good time to make a commitment, especially financially. However, you must ensure you have adequately researched the facts.

20 JUNE

Trust your instincts, especially at work and with bigger-picture decisions, but you must avoid impulsiveness as mistakes could be made.

21 JUNE

It's the solstice! You'll begin to see yourself and your status and general direction in a new light. Avoid feeling you're under pressure and give yourself room to move.

22 JUNE

You'll feel motivated to spend time with like-minded people. A collaborative effort may be rewarding, and you will receive or give help where it is needed.

23 JUNE

You'll enjoy therapeutic yet upbeat activities such as sport. You can make great headway with a personal or work collaboration.

24 JUNE

This is a good weekend to spend time with those whose company you love. It's a good time to make plans for the future.

25 JUNE

It's a lovely day to dream and for romance, but you must be clear with communications as there may be misunderstandings or delays. You may also be forgetful.

26 JUNE

Be prepared to be adaptable as a schedule or activity may be altered at the last minute. You may be surprised by developments.

27 JUNE

A key meeting or talk will provide you with perspective, so ensure you make the time for a chat or get-together.

28 JUNE

You are thinking intuitively but you may also tend to be emotional, so ensure you maintain perspective.

29 JUNE

There are therapeutic aspects to the day. It's a good day for a health or beauty appointment and also for work meetings, interviews and financial matters.

30 JUNE

This is an excellent day for work interviews, for enquiring about new work opportunities and for making financial and personal agreements.

July

1 JULY

You will enjoy a trip, socialising, a visit or a change of pace. A reunion will be memorable. If you're working you're likely to be busy.

2 JULY

A change of place or of pace may entail a surprise or the necessity to adapt to new circumstances.

3 JULY

The full moon in Capricorn shines a light on your personal life and, for many, home life. Aim for a secure and stable way forward.

4 JULY

You may be in the process of re-evaluating your priorities. If you are unsure, take the most reasonable and stable choice.

5 JULY

New ideas and influences will be impressive but you must avoid alienating those who have your back.

6 JULY

You will not always agree with everyone, so to avoid misunderstandings ensure you have the full details before making decisions.

7 JULY

This is a lovely day for being spontaneous, and you'll enjoy a fun event or get-together. A work meeting may entail a surprise.

8 JULY

This is a good time for catching up with friends and chores. You will enjoy socialising and improving your health and appearance.

9 JULY

You may hear news from the past or must overcome residual doubt or anxiety. Take a moment to focus on creating a calm environment.

10 JULY

Meetings and get-togethers will be inspiring and romance could blossom, so take the initiative!

11 JULY

As Mercury enters Leo you may need to increasingly focus on health and work and on being more proactive. A secret may be revealed.

12 JULY

Your help may be required, but rest assured you can provide it. If you need help it will be available from an expert. Avoid misunderstandings.

13 JULY

You may be required to be a little more outgoing or talkative, especially at work. You'll enjoy spending time in nature as it calms your nerves.

14 JULY

You'll enjoy being spontaneous and may receive good news to do with work, health or your status, but you must focus on communications to avoid mix-ups.

15 JULY

This is a good weekend to get ahead with your chores and to take a little extra time for someone close.

16 JULY

Make the time to try to understand someone, as they may be finding it difficult to express themselves. Avoid overindulgence, as you'll regret it!

17 JULY

The Cancer new moon signals a fresh interest in activities that bring your nurturing side out. Just be careful with some communications, as misunderstandings may arise.

18 JULY

Your involvement in certain groups and organisations will take much of your focus. You may revaluate your long-term plans.

19 JULY

Healing, self-development and generally helping others and yourself to feel more fulfilled will be a drawcard. Be inspired.

20 JULY

This is an excellent day for romance. However, you may need to focus at work as you could be easily distracted. The arts, music and creativity will all appeal.

21 JULY

A work, health or financial matter will require attention. You could make a valid commitment but you must avoid rushing into decisions.

22 JULY

Consider where your loyalties lie if you must make a tough call. Someone may confide their vulnerability in you and your help may be in demand. It's a good day to relax.

23 JULY

While you'll be feeling motivated by your activities you may experience a sudden change of plan that may lead you to slowly re-evaluate your interests.

24 JULY

Look for more balance in your relationships, especially if you feel that some aspects are simply not equal.

25 JULY

An expert's or adviser's support will be invaluable, especially if you're unsure of a major personal or work decision.

26 JULY

This is a good time to discuss your hopes and goals and to seek support and clarity about the best way forward.

27 JULY

It's another good day for meetings and to discuss shared projects, including finances. Your key to the right decision lies in collating facts.

28 JULY

Focus on good communication and negotiation skills. Double-check you're pursuing your own goals and are not being overly influenced by others.

29 JULY

You'll appreciate the chance to do something different, even if it involves a minor challenge. It's a good day to catch up on chores.

30 JULY

A change in your usual routine such as a social event may mean you must plan better, but your efforts will be rewarded.

31 JULY

The Capricorn moon will encourage you to be realistic about what you can and can't achieve, which will enable you to be productive.

August

1 AUGUST

The full moon supermoon in Aquarius spells a new chapter in your personal life or a creative project. Be prepared to leave your comfort zone.

2 AUGUST

You may reach a valid agreement, so this is an excellent day for negotiations and talks both at home and at work.

3 AUGUST

Be prepared to dream a little, but if you're at work you must focus more as your head is a little in the clouds.

4 AUGUST

While you have the drive to get things done others may be forgetful, so be prepared to negotiate delays or misunderstandings.

5 AUGUST

It's an active and upbeat weekend and you'll enjoy a trip or a fun activity that takes you somewhere new.

6 AUGUST

You'll feel more tuned in to someone close, so this is a good time to deepen your relationship but you must avoid taking their opinions personally.

7 AUGUST

Developments will gain their own momentum, but if you disagree with the direction you will need to voice your opinion without causing conflict.

8 AUGUST

You'll appreciate the chance to throw yourself into your activities.

9 AUGUST

An unexpected change of plan may arise and you may be surprised by developments. Be adaptable.

10 AUGUST

You'll enjoy a trip or meeting and communications will gather momentum, so be sure you agree with the direction circumstances now take.

11 AUGUST

Good communication skills are the key to success, so be sure to brush up your skills.

12 AUGUST

There is a therapeutic aspect to developments. Some may enjoy a health or beauty treat and others a social get-together that boosts morale.

13 AUGUST

You'll enjoy meeting like-minded, upbeat people. However, you may not agree with everyone so you must avoid touchy topics.

14 AUGUST

You'll be keen to avoid certain people, and focusing on your projects will enable you to do just that.

15 AUGUST

Be prepared to look outside the square at your various options and activities so you can maximise the positive opportunities that will arise now both at work and socially.

16 AUGUST

The new moon in Leo signals a fresh phase in your social life and the groups and organisations you belong to. You may be surprised by developments.

17 AUGUST

The moon in your sign for the next two days will enable you to be super organised and productive, so take the initiative.

18 AUGUST

This can be a successful time when you will feel more outgoing and self-confident, but you must avoid giving mixed messages.

19 AUGUST

Look for common ground with people you love, as you can make great personal progress and develop a sense of stability.

20 AUGUST

You may be drawn to nostalgia, the past or a reunion. Just avoid overindulging and resuming a bad habit.

21 AUGUST

You are in a powerful and influential position at the moment but you must avoid power struggles.

22 AUGUST

This is a good time to review shared finances and agreements, especially if these are unequal, but you must avoid arguments as they could become long term.

23 AUGUST

Try to get important paperwork completed to avoid having to review it over the coming weeks. You may hear key news.

24 AUGUST

Be adventurous with your projects but be tactful to avoid arguments.

25 AUGUST

Circumstances will gain their own momentum, which is great if you're on the right track. If you feel you're not, find ways to de-escalate matters.

26 AUGUST

You will gain a sense of more stability within your communications over the next two days, which will enable you to feel more relaxed.

27 AUGUST

It's a good time to reorganise your daily schedule and make a commitment at work or to someone special.

28 AUGUST

Be prepared to put your professional hat on to gain a sense of perspective about your goals. Your emotions may be intense, so take breaks when you can.

29 AUGUST

You'll gain fresh perspective about a personal or family matter, which will enable you to avoid a stalemate.

30 AUGUST

Be inspired, as your input will be appreciated at work and with your everyday activities.

31 AUGUST

The Pisces full moon supermoon spotlights a fresh daily, health or work routine, so look for inspired ways to improve your work/life balance.

September

1 SEPTEMBER

Be prepared to put in extra hard work as your efforts will be rewarded, even if chores seem challenging.

2 SEPTEMBER

This is a lovely weekend to be active with a group, partner or friends. A trip or hobby will be rewarding.

3 SEPTEMBER

A reunion or trip to an old haunt will be enjoyable; just avoid sensitive topics for the best results.

4 SEPTEMBER

You'll feel more inclined to let bygones be bygones and to move forward with your hopes, wishes and goals in a proactive and optimistic way.

5 SEPTEMBER

It's a great day to invest in yourself through a little beauty or health therapy. You'll enjoy romance or a meeting.

6 SEPTEMBER

You'll receive key news, and a meeting or trip may be successful. You may also experience an ego boost.

7 SEPTEMBER

You may repay a debt or have a debt repaid. You'll enjoy a reunion or news from the past.

8 SEPTEMBER

This is a lovely day to make progress with your interests. Self-development, spiritual matters, travel and even legal matters may appeal.

9 SEPTEMBER

You like to look after others and your caring approach will be in demand. Just be sure to look after yourself first to avoid tiredness.

10 SEPTEMBER

Take some time out for yourself or you'll find the demands of others take over. You'll enjoy an impromptu visit or trip.

11 SEPTEMBER

This is a good day for a health appointment or reunion and for getting on top of financial and personal matters.

12 SEPTEMBER

You have a strong support system from like-minded people but not everyone will agree with you, so a kind approach to them will be effective.

13 SEPTEMBER

You're productive and can get a great deal done at the moment but you must avoid overtiring yourself.

14 SEPTEMBER

Be prepared to review some health schedules and work matters to ensure you are as efficient as possible.

15 SEPTEMBER

The new moon in Virgo signals a fresh chapter within a personal arrangement, especially if it's your birthday. Romance can blossom.

16 SEPTEMBER

Unusual developments and activities that take you somewhere new will be enjoyable, so be spontaneous.

17 SEPTEMBER

You're a capable and outgoing character and sometimes people take it for granted that your time is theirs. You may need to remind them that you have your own interests.

18 SEPTEMBER

You'll feel passionate about and motivated by your chores and activities, and it's a good day to channel frustrations into hard work.

19 SEPTEMBER

This is a super romantic day but you must take nothing for granted. You'll discover whether you have over- or underestimated someone.

20 SEPTEMBER

You have the power of conviction on your side so you'll find it easier to communicate, but you must avoid alienating others through your intensity.

21 SEPTEMBER

This is a good time to make changes in your personal life and within your favourite activities. Be adventurous.

22 SEPTEMBER

This is a proactive day in which you can achieve so much but you must avoid rushing.

23 SEPTEMBER

The sun in Libra for the next month will encourage you to create more peace and harmony in your personal relationships. You may be drawn to improving your finances.

24 SEPTEMBER

You are proactive and productive but someone close may feel a little under the weather, so your attention will be well received.

25 SEPTEMBER

A reunion will raise morale and a trip will be enjoyable. You may need to concentrate extra hard to complete chores but you will.

26 SEPTEMBER

A pleasant activity or change in your usual routine will be enjoyable and you'll enjoy upbeat company.

27 SEPTEMBER

You're most effective in your activities when you combine your hard work ethic with empathy for others.

28 SEPTEMBER

The moon in Pisces will bring out your imaginative, spiritual side and you'll feel inspired by some of your activities.

29 SEPTEMBER

The Aries full moon signals a fresh phase in a key relationship. It's a good time to turn a corner but you must avoid making rash decisions.

30 SEPTEMBER

You'll gain a deeper understanding of someone close, which will help you to make changes at home or with family.

October

1 OCTOBER

It's an excellent day for a beauty or health treat and to catch up with someone special. Just avoid overspending.

2 OCTOBER

You're communicating well but others may be less precise, so double-check details and arrangements. Romance and artistic ventures will appeal.

3 OCTOBER

It's an excellent time to make plans, especially regarding long-term changes in your personal life and activities. You may receive good news. Double-check the facts.

4 OCTOBER

The Gemini moon is excellent for meetings and communications, especially at work, but you must be prepared to research details.

5 OCTOBER

This is another day when meetings and communications will be productive, but don't forget to research the details.

6 OCTOBER

Avoid making assumptions as misunderstandings can arise, especially at work and socially.

7 OCTOBER

Be prepared to accept a challenge and be diligent with your activities, as you will attain a positive outcome as a result.

8 OCTOBER

An optimistic attitude will help you get on with people, but you must avoid assuming they have the same aims as you do.

9 OCTOBER

This will be a busy or intense day. Arguments could flare up from nowhere, so be prepared to avoid a battle of wills and gambling.

10 OCTOBER

This is a good time to make an agreement or commitment as long as it's fair. Key work and health decisions may be made.

11 OCTOBER

Financial and personal matters are best approached carefully to avoid misunderstandings and losses. Someone may need your help.

12 OCTOBER

You'll feel more passionate about having a voice and being heard over the coming weeks. Keep an eye on financial transactions, communications and travel as there may be delays.

13 OCTOBER

This is a good time to make progress at work and financially. You may enjoy a change of routine.

14 OCTOBER

The solar eclipse represents a new chapter in your financial or personal life. You or someone close may feel sensitive, so be careful with communications. Avoid minor bumps and scrapes.

15 OCTOBER

A change of circumstances may come about unexpectedly. You may be drawn to a new environment or activity.

16 OCTOBER

Be prepared to express yourself and your values clearly so that someone close understands your decisions.

17 OCTOBER

Some activities may present as challenging, and the more you work towards your goals the better will be the outcome. An unpredictable situation is best navigated calmly.

18 OCTOBER

An outgoing and adventurous approach to your shared interests and collaborations will be effective, but you must avoid seeming to be blunt.

19 OCTOBER

Key financial matters must be reviewed. You may enjoy a reunion or the chance to return to an old haunt.

20 OCTOBER

Financial or personal news will enable you to gain more clarity about the best way ahead.

21 OCTOBER

News and developments are best handled carefully to avoid arguments and a battle of egos.

22 OCTOBER

This is a good day to plan ahead financially, work-wise and in your personal life. You may enjoy a compliment or ego boost.

23 OCTOBER

You'll feel motivated to prove yourself at work or in a financial capacity. If you're shopping avoid overspending, as you'll regret it.

24 OCTOBER

This is a good day to make agreements and commitments both at work and financially.

25 OCTOBER

Be inspired but also practical, as otherwise complexities may become a conundrum.

26 OCTOBER

You'll appreciate the help of a partner or someone close, so be sure to reach out if you need a hand.

27 OCTOBER

Be prepared to collaborate and cooperate and ask the same of those who could help you.

28 OCTOBER

The lunar eclipse in Taurus signals a fresh chapter in your shared duties. For some a new chapter in a relationship or regarding travel, spirituality or legal matters will begin now.

29 OCTOBER

Events will unfold swiftly. You'll be drawn to investing financially or emotionally, and while you could build a strong platform you must avoid making snap decisions.

30 OCTOBER

Take things one step at a time over the next two days to avoid impulsiveness. Financial or personal matters will be a focus.

31 OCTOBER

Happy Halloween! You may receive unexpected news at work or from the past.

November

1 NOVEMBER

This will be a busy day when your communication skill sets will be in demand, so be prepared.

2 NOVEMBER

This is a good day to discuss personal, travel, study and even legal matters, so take the initiative!

3 NOVEMBER

Key discussions and decisions to do with someone close, a trip or legal matters are best taken with good advice.

4 NOVEMBER

You may be surprised by an unusual visit or trip. News may be unexpected.

5 NOVEMBER

As developments are bringing swift change your way, be sure to double-check you're on the same page with your communications.

6 NOVEMBER

This is a good day for get-togethers with those you love and for making changes within your personal life. Romance could blossom.

7 NOVEMBER

This is a good time for romance, talks and meetings. You may receive good news from a personal or business partner.

8 NOVEMBER

You'll become more aware of the necessity for fair play at work, financially and in your personal life. Keep communications precise for the best results.

9 NOVEMBER

Be prepared to consider the opinion of another person. Someone may need your help or advice, and if you need help it will be available. It's a good day for a trip or change of environment.

10 NOVEMBER

You're likely to feel more outspoken, especially at home. However, some people may find this confronting so be sure to use tact.

11 NOVEMBER

Keep communications super clear to avoid misunderstandings, especially if you're working. A trip or meeting may be delayed, so be patient.

12 NOVEMBER

You'll feel passionate about your tasks and therefore will be productive, but you must avoid alienating those you associate with.

13 NOVEMBER

The Scorpio new moon signals a fresh chapter in a relationship. You may contemplate a fresh communications device, vehicle or trip. Unexpected news is on the way.

14 NOVEMBER

You'll feel more outgoing and adventurous about your circumstances and able to make the necessary changes.

15 NOVEMBER

This is a lovely day for a trip, visit or personal improvement such as a beauty treat. You may receive good news.

16 NOVEMBER

You're communicating well but you may need to work a little harder at one particular relationship. Rest assured that if you do you'll appreciate the outcome.

17 NOVEMBER

Romance, the arts and generally spending time with like-minded people will be a real joy, so make a date if you haven't already!

18 NOVEMBER

You'll enjoy being spontaneous, and a trip, meeting or favourite activity will raise morale. This is a good time for self-development.

19 NOVEMBER

You may learn a little more about someone close. A family member or a close friend will prove to be supportive.

20 NOVEMBER

This is a good time to make long-term changes, especially in your personal life and with creative projects. You'll enjoy a trip or meeting.

21 NOVEMBER

You may tend to dream a little, which is positive if you're engaged in creative projects, but you'll need to focus a little harder on details at work.

22 NOVEMBER

Someone may need your help, and if you need expert advice it will be available. Avoid taking the mood swings of others personally and be careful with money.

23 NOVEMBER

This is a good day to get things done, but a stubborn character may behave true to form. Rules and regulations will figure in your decision-making.

24 NOVEMBER

You're expressing yourself well but some circumstances may test your communication abilities, so avoid mix-ups.

25 NOVEMBER

You are both productive and fun-loving but must avoid getting too frustrated by delays, rules and restrictions.

26 NOVEMBER

Take a moment out of your day if constantly changing goal posts are becoming frustrating. Someone may surprise you.

27 NOVEMBER

The Gemini full moon signals a fresh phase in a relationship, venture, travel or study. Misunderstandings and delays are likely, so plan ahead.

28 NOVEMBER

This is a sociable, chatty time but you may need to be super tactful and diplomatic.

29 NOVEMBER

Your plans and projects will be successful even if you feel at times you're in challenging circumstances, so be diligent with your plans.

30 NOVEMBER

You can be successful with the changes you wish to make in your personal life and at home but you must be sensitive to someone else's feelings.

December

1 DECEMBER

You'll find communications easier, especially at home, over the coming weeks, which will enable you to express yourself better.

2 DECEMBER

This is a lovely day to get on top of chores at home and for working on your home and environment. You'll enjoy a get-together.

3 DECEMBER

Think before you speak, as words could be unintentionally hurtful. Approach a personal matter carefully to avoid a battle of wills.

4 DECEMBER

This is the beginning of a more passionate phase in your personal life over the next three weeks. Avoid overspending and overindulging – you'll regret it!

5 DECEMBER

This is a good time to review your finances and to work on a healthy budget. You may receive good news at work or financially.

6 DECEMBER

You'll be looking for fair play and a resolution to conflict, so be prepared to reach out.

7 DECEMBER

You or someone close may be feeling more sensitive than usual, so take things one step at a time.

8 DECEMBER

This is a therapeutic, healing time and you can make great inroads in your relationships, especially at home.

9 DECEMBER

You may feel a little more emotional than usual, and a meeting or get-together may be the catalyst.

10 DECEMBER

It's a good day for get-togethers, a trip and home improvements. Just avoid reigniting sensitive topics.

11 DECEMBER

A short trip or visit will be enjoyable as it's a good day for get-togethers.

12 DECEMBER

The Sagittarian new moon signals the start of a new chapter in your domestic, property or family circumstances. You may be surprised by developments.

13 DECEMBER

Important news to do with family or someone close and/or a property will provide food for thought. Try to get paperwork sorted out.

14 DECEMBER

Now that Mercury is retrograde you'll gain the opportunity to review your personal circumstances, including domestic matters.

15 DECEMBER

This is a good day to connect with those you love and deepen relationships, especially family circumstances.

16 DECEMBER

You'll enjoy diverse company and keeping interactions light-hearted to avoid intense discussions.

17 DECEMBER

Some talks and meetings may bring your sensitivities to the surface, so take things one step at a time. Someone close may need to alter their plans.

18 DECEMBER

This is a lovely day for a reunion or return to an old haunt. Family, property and domestic matters will be in focus.

19 DECEMBER

Outgoing and upbeat developments will demand that you sharpen your communication skills, especially in a domestic setting.

20 DECEMBER

This is a lovely day for a trip or visit and for talks and meetings.

21 DECEMBER

You'll enjoy improving your environment and may receive unexpected news or a visitor. A trip may take you somewhere new.

22 DECEMBER

You'll enjoy a change of environment and a reunion. You'll also enjoy visiting someone's house or receiving visitors.

23 DECEMBER

Be practical with travel and a change of environment and plan ahead for the best measure.

24 DECEMBER

This is a lovely day for spending time with friends and family. You'll enjoy a feeling of stability and belonging.

25 DECEMBER

Merry Christmas! There is a romantic atmosphere with music, dance and good company in your Christmas Day that you'll enjoy.

26 DECEMBER

You'll enjoy a reunion, upbeat news or a trip that puts you in a nostalgic frame of mind. Check details if you are travelling to avoid delays over the next two days.

27 DECEMBER

The Cancer full moon signals the start of a fresh chapter in your status, career or general direction. You may receive good news or enjoy a meeting.

28 DECEMBER

You'll be drawn to travelling, visits and making changes at home. Some plans may be delayed, so be patient.

29 DECEMBER

This is a lovely day for improving domestic dynamics and decor, and for trips somewhere beautiful and inspiring.

30 DECEMBER

The Leo moon will bring out your sociable and outgoing side. You'll enjoy being active.

31 DECEMBER

Happy New Year! A fun, active New Year's Eve will appeal. Your home life is a big drawcard and you'll enjoy a feeling of being settled.

♎

LIBRA

23 September - 23 October

FINANCES

This is an excellent year to bank on what you already have and to reach for more. The idea is that you do not risk what you already have in order to improve your finances; on the contrary, keep what you have safe. However, a business or personal partner is likely to wish to innovate and make tracks into new territory, so ensure you do your research financially and avoid risk-taking.

HEALTH

Chiron, the celestial body associated with healing and health, will be in your opposite sign for several years and offers the chance to truly focus on your well-being. It comes under a stressful aspect early in January, suggesting this is a time to take care of your health, so be careful to avoid over-indulging. Early March, early April and the month of May will be times to focus on health more than usual. July is likely to see some good news health-wise, and the rest of the year will involve careful lifestyle changes in order to engender better health.

LOVE LIFE

Two of this year's four eclipses will be in your partnership zones, so it's important to be ready to adapt to opportunities and, if you're single, to find someone compatible as a partner or companion. It's also important to adapt to life's relationship challenges if you're in a partnership. You'll gain the chance to deepen existing ties but you must be prepared to negotiate stressful periods such as those in April and October, when key decisions will be made regarding domestic and/or relationship matters.

CAREER

The full moon in your career zone on 6 January points to considerable changes already in your circumstances at the start of the year. It seems you are ready to move your career forward, as a fresh phase appeals to you. For some this will be due to considerable change in your domestic and/or health situation. Mars in your career sector in April will enable you to be more proactive about making change, but you must avoid making rash decisions as you may come to regret them.

HOME LIFE

You'll relish the opportunity to move forward from a domestic or family circumstance that you have outgrown. For some Librans this will literally mean a move is on the cards, while for others it will simply be a chance to change domestic or property circumstances so they suit you or your family or partner better. January will already present a good opportunity to make changes, then you'll have the chance again in May and early in 2024.

January

1 JANUARY

Happy New Year! Strong emotions may arise at home or with family. A trip or visit may bring intense feelings to the surface.

2 JANUARY

This is a good day for discussing family and shared concerns, but bear in mind that you or someone close may be feeling sensitive.

3 JANUARY

You'll be drawn to approaching your personal and home lives from a fresh perspective in an effort to find solutions to problems.

4 JANUARY

It's a good day to improve your health and vitality and also to boost domestic dynamics and decor.

5 JANUARY

A visitor or change in your environment will be unexpected but enjoyable.

6 JANUARY

The Cancer full moon suggests you are ready to turn a corner in relation to travel or within a favourite activity or project.

7 JANUARY

You'll enjoy a reunion and the opportunity to return to your home if you've been away or to reconnect with someone in your family. A trip or news could be pivotal.

8 JANUARY

You'll enjoy doing something different and may hear unexpectedly from a friend. You'll also enjoy a trip or visit.

9 JANUARY

This is a lovely day for improving your personal life and for creativity. You may be drawn to making changes at home or with family.

10 JANUARY

Your attention will turn to work or the chores ahead of you. You will adopt a more practical stance, which will enable you to get things done.

11 JANUARY

You may feel a little sensitive to undercurrents, so take a moment to ensure you have the right end of the stick to avoid misunderstandings. Plan ahead to avoid travel delays.

12 JANUARY

If you've felt tired recently prepare to experience improved energy levels over the next few weeks, starting today.

13 JANUARY

This is a good day to connect with people you love including friends and family. Romance could blossom.

14 JANUARY

You'll appreciate the results of your hard work at home. You may consider making a fresh commitment. You'll enjoy a trip or visit.

15 JANUARY

Someone who can be unpredictable will behave true to form. You may need to adjust your plans accordingly.

16 JANUARY

You'll feel drawn to expressing yourself passionately. If you feel angry, aim to channel excess energy into hard work otherwise you risk arguments.

17 JANUARY

This is a good day to be productive as you'll be motivated to achieve results. However, you must avoid rushing or you risk making mistakes.

18 JANUARY

Expect key news, for many to do with travel and for some finances or health. This may be an intense day, so pace yourself.

19 JANUARY

You will feel driven to achieve your best outcomes and will appreciate the opportunity to relax later in the day.

20 JANUARY

The next four weeks will be ideal to gain fresh insight into your personal life, so be prepared to look outside the box.

21 JANUARY

The new moon supermoon in Aquarius signals a fresh chapter in your personal life or property. A trip, new vehicle or communications device may appeal.

22 JANUARY

This is a good time to consider a commitment at home or with a family member. You may receive unexpected news.

23 JANUARY

You'll find out whether you've over- or underestimated a domestic or personal circumstance and will gain the opportunity to correct your expectations.

24 JANUARY

It's a good time to improve relationships so take the initiative, but if you've been seeing circumstances through rose-coloured glasses you will find out now.

25 JANUARY

It's a good day for get-togethers and a short trip, so make a plan!

26 JANUARY

The moon in Aries will encourage you to be busy, so make the most of this productive energy.

27 JANUARY

Take extra time with your communications and travel to avoid delays and misunderstandings.

28 JANUARY

You'll appreciate the sense that certain relationships are becoming more settled, and you'll appreciate the opportunity to slow down.

29 JANUARY

This is a lovely day to relax with someone special. A plan may need to be altered at the last minute.

30 JANUARY

This is a proactive day that will bring about positive results. You may need to alter your plans to suit someone else's.

31 JANUARY

It's a romantic day, especially for September-born Librans, and October-born Librans will be super productive and enjoy creative projects.

February

1 FEBRUARY

There are healing attributes to the day. A partner, work or health circumstance will be helpful.

2 FEBRUARY

Trust your instincts and find the time for someone special or a favourite activity as you'll be glad you did.

3 FEBRUARY

You may wear your heart on your sleeve, so if you have important work matters to attend to be sure to keep your professional hat on.

4 FEBRUARY

You may receive unexpected news from someone close and may benefit from re-organising some of your shared duties.

5 FEBRUARY

The Leo full moon signals a fresh chapter in your social life and, for some, regarding family and the people you associate with at work. Be prepared to discuss options.

6 FEBRUARY

This is a lovely day to improve your environment at work or at home. A visit, health or beauty appointment will be productive.

7 FEBRUARY

You'll enjoy finding the time for someone special, as this will provide a sense of belonging and perspective.

8 FEBRUARY

Be prepared to be spontaneous and outgoing, as you will enjoy a lovely get-together or change of routine.

9 FEBRUARY

It's a good day for talks with someone special at home, in your family or regarding property. You may make a commitment or financial decision.

10 FEBRUARY

Key meetings and news will signal changes to come at home or with family. Intense emotions may arise, so pace yourself.

11 FEBRUARY

You'll enjoy a lovely reunion although you may feel emotional, so take time out when you can.

12 FEBRUARY

It's a lovely day for self-development, spiritual pursuits, romance and the arts.

13 FEBRUARY

Feeling motivated by work and your daily activities will propel you towards taking positive action, so you'll be productive.

14 FEBRUARY

Happy St Valentine's Day! This is a good day to improve your health and appearance, and you'll appreciate being with someone you love.

15 FEBRUARY

This is a good day for a health or beauty treat. Working Librans will receive key news at work.

16 FEBRUARY

It's a good day to make a commitment to someone special, for example in your personal life or family, but you must avoid making assumptions.

17 FEBRUARY

A practical stance to someone special will reap rewards and enable you to progress despite uncertainty.

18 FEBRUARY

It's a lovely day for romance and relaxing with someone you love. You may enjoy a visit or a trip.

19 FEBRUARY

This is a good day for making changes at home or to your usual routine. You may enjoy improving domestic dynamics or decor.

20 FEBRUARY

The new moon in Pisces signals a fresh chapter in your personal life and/or with a creative project. There are healing aspects to the day.

21 FEBRUARY

Someone who can be unpredictable will behave true to form. Look outside the box for new ways to communicate with them.

22 FEBRUARY

Communications are better so it's a good time to broach sensitive topics. It's also a good time for changes at home or with family.

23 FEBRUARY

You'll enjoy being more spontaneous, and someone close may wish to be more dynamic in the relationship but you must avoid arguments.

24 FEBRUARY

This is a lovely day to reconnect with someone you love or admire such as a partner or family member.

25 FEBRUARY

You'll enjoy creature comforts but may need to deal with an obstinate character, so tact and diplomacy will be invaluable.

26 FEBRUARY

You'll appreciate the opportunity to feel more relaxed and recharge your batteries. Activities such as sport will boost your energy levels.

27 FEBRUARY

Key talks and meetings are likely to go well. Communications at home are likely to improve.

28 FEBRUARY

The moon in Gemini will bring out your chatty, upbeat side, making this a good time for your favourite activities and being productive.

March

1 MARCH

Trust your intuition when you're making key decisions. Take other people's opinions into account, but ultimately you must be happy with your choices.

2 MARCH

You'll receive key news from someone close at home or at work. Health news will require special attention from October Librans.

3 MARCH

You'll appreciate the opportunity to talk to an expert about work or health matters. This is a good day for health and beauty appointments.

4 MARCH

A friend, group or organisation will be super helpful and you'll enjoy touching base with them to create an uplifting mood.

5 MARCH

Someone special will raise morale or surprise you. You may bump into an old friend and will enjoy being spontaneous.

6 MARCH

A change in your usual routine or activities will be enjoyable, so be sure to organise something special. You may receive surprisingly good news or bump into an old friend.

7 MARCH

The full moon in Virgo spotlights a fresh chapter in your daily or health routine. Be inspired but also practical about your personal life and projects.

8 MARCH

This is a good time to work towards configuring more work/life balance and achieving the kind of daily routine you want.

9 MARCH

The moon in your sign will encourage you to find more peace and harmony, especially in your personal life and at work.

10 MARCH

You'll enjoy doing something fun and upbeat. It's a good day for meetings, health appointments, self-development and trips.

11 MARCH

A lovely activity will catch your eye and you'll enjoy spending time with like-minded people. Romance could blossom, so organise a treat!

12 MARCH

Someone close may reveal their sensitive side. You may receive delicate news from an expert and may be asked for help.

13 MARCH

This is a sensitive time, especially if you were born in early October. You may need to make a tough call, yet you can look on the bright side.

14 MARCH

This is an excellent time to gain expert advice and direction, especially in areas you're uncertain about. Mistakes can be made, so avoid rushing.

15 MARCH

This is a super romantic day, so take the initiative and organise a lovely event. You may simply be drawn to the arts and music.

16 MARCH

This may be an intense day. News will deserve research, so avoid making a snap decision. Avoid conflict, as you may not have the facts.

17 MARCH

Information will come your way that will enable you to make clear choices. This is a good day for romance but you must avoid giving mixed messages.

18 MARCH

Be prepared to look outside the box at your domestic circumstances to avoid being stuck in one mindset.

19 MARCH

You may confide in someone, which will deepen your relationship. You'll enjoy a change of atmosphere or a visit or trip.

20 MARCH

This is a lovely day for get-togethers and talks and for being spontaneous as you'll enjoy the company of someone special.

21 MARCH

The Aries new moon is a good time to start something different such as a fresh routine in your daily or health schedule.

22 MARCH

You or someone close may be feeling feistier than usual, and while this will be useful for getting ahead with projects you must avoid appearing bossy.

23 MARCH

This is a good time to enter fresh territory in your personal life. You may contemplate travel, as this will broaden your horizons.

24 MARCH

The more practical you are about making changes in your personal life and at work the better will be the outcome. Be prepared for hard work.

25 MARCH

A goal and favourite activity can be achieved but you will need to focus and work hard. Someone special will be super helpful.

26 MARCH

You'll enjoy a reunion if you didn't already yesterday. Just avoid impatience, especially with chores.

27 MARCH

News from a business or personal relationship may come as a surprise. This is a good day for a health appointment.

28 MARCH

A partner or close business colleague may wish to confide in you. It's a good day for talks, financial discussions and travel plans.

29 MARCH

You may wish to hurry several matters along but will need to be patient, as others have their own timeframes.

30 MARCH

You'll enjoy a spontaneous get-together and news may be unexpected. You can make a great deal of progress with a favourite activity or interest.

31 MARCH

You're connecting well with colleagues, groups and organisations and can make a positive impression.

April

1 APRIL

This is a good day to improve your health and well-being and for research, especially finding out more about shared finances.

2 APRIL

You'll enjoy being with like-minded people, so organise a treat! Romance could blossom. If you're shopping, avoid overspending.

3 APRIL

Take things one step at a time as you may experience some delays or mix-ups, especially regarding finances and your home.

4 APRIL

Trust your intuition, especially with regard to a health matter and someone close.

5 APRIL

If you are an expert or adviser you'll be in demand. If you need advice it will be available. You may hear from an old friend or visit an old haunt.

6 APRIL

The full moon in Libra signals a new chapter in your personal life, especially if it's your birthday in early October or before. If you were born later, a fresh chapter will begin in a health or daily routine such as work.

7 APRIL

You may experience a surprise or change of schedule. You may also receive a compliment, and an improvement in a relationship is possible.

8 APRIL

Be prepared to initiate talks and meetings, especially those that can improve your finances, relationships and status.

9 APRIL

You may wear your heart on your sleeve and emotions will bubble up, so if you're at work ensure you have your professional hat on.

10 APRIL

Be optimistic with talks and meetings as a positive outlook and demeanour will speak volumes about your integrity.

11 APRIL

It's a good time to make changes at home or with family and property. A key talk or meeting will be significant.

12 APRIL

Be grounded and practical, especially concerning personal matters and important decisions about shared concerns.

13 APRIL

You won't always agree with everyone, so be prepared to consider another person's point of view. However, be prepared to stick to your principles.

14 APRIL

The key to making agreements is to cooperate and, if necessary, compromise. Avoid a Mexican stand-off.

15 APRIL

Willingness to see personal matters from a fresh perspective will enable you to find common ground, especially if you have recently argued.

16 APRIL

This is a good day to make positive changes to your daily and health schedule to include more relaxation, music and love.

17 APRIL

You're inspired and your imagination is sparking on all cylinders but you must avoid forgetfulness and appearing vague, especially at work.

18 APRIL

The Aries moon will bring out your feistiness or that of someone close. Avoid arguments, as they could spiral into conflict.

19 APRIL

An active and outgoing time will be enjoyable but also potentially tiring, so ensure you give yourself the space to relax.

20 APRIL

The total solar eclipse in Aries will kick-start an important chapter, for many within a personal or business relationship. Avoid a battle of egos.

21 APRIL

You may receive key news. Try to get important paperwork and legal matters tied up before the end of the day.

22 APRIL

This is a good weekend to tie up loose ends, especially to do with shared interests and projects and your home life.

23 APRIL

Fun and upbeat activities will have a therapeutic effect, so be sure to organise something enjoyable.

24 APRIL

Enjoy being outgoing and active. A reunion or return to an old haunt will appeal.

25 APRIL

This is a good day for negotiations and for being practical with shared concerns such as joint finances and duties.

26 APRIL

It's a good day for collaborations, but if someone is feeling sensitive avoid pushing them. Avoid rushing.

27 APRIL

You may hear unexpectedly good news to do with a legal matter, favourite pastime or get-together.

28 APRIL

You'll enjoy socialising with the people you love and doing activities you like but will be selective.

29 APRIL

A fun or unexpected invitation or development will be enjoyable, so aim to be spontaneous. Just avoid making rash decisions.

30 APRIL

This is an excellent day to catch up with chores. However, you may prefer to catch up with old friends.

May

1 MAY

You may begin to look at your home life, property or family in a new light over the coming weeks and will gain the chance to review circumstances.

2 MAY

You'll enjoy a reunion and the chance to review finances, legal matters and paperwork. It's a good day for romance.

3 MAY

Find ways to channel excess energy into favourite activities; you'll avoid overanalysing your circumstances as a result.

4 MAY

You'll find out whether you've over- or underestimated circumstances. You may be easily distracted, so focus more if you're at work.

5 MAY

The lunar eclipse in Scorpio signals a fresh chapter in a key relationship or financially. A fun event will boost morale.

6 MAY

Life gains its own momentum. Use your instincts to guide you through a fast-paced situation.

7 MAY

You'll gain perspective about your domestic circumstances and where they lead. Work hard at attaining your goals and you will succeed.

8 MAY

It's a great day for research and meetings. However, there may be travel delays and misunderstandings, so be patient.

9 MAY

You'll receive surprising news that will clarify your situation with regard to shared duties and responsibilities and, for some, financially.

10 MAY

Be practical about developments in your personal and domestic life to attain your goals.

11 MAY

Be prepared to look outside the box at your options domestically and in your relationships.

12 MAY

This is a good day for discussions with a personal or business partner and for making agreements. You may enjoy a reunion.

13 MAY

It's a great day for get-togethers and reunions. You may enjoy a trip somewhere beautiful, and a favourite activity will raise morale.

14 MAY

This is a creative day and you'll love the arts, dance and music. Romance could also blossom.

15 MAY

Key news or a get-together will be memorable as you turn a corner in a key project or relationship.

16 MAY

You're about to begin a more abundant phase in a close relationship. However, you may need to overcome a difference of opinion first.

17 MAY

Be prepared to be flexible with arrangements and discussions, otherwise circumstances may feel stuck.

18 MAY

Many of your activities can succeed. This could be an intense day regarding someone close or your home.

19 MAY

The Taurus new moon signals a fresh chapter in a shared circumstance or relationship. Be prepared to negotiate and come to mutually agreeable arrangements.

20 MAY

You'll enjoy the chance to free your mind of many of your worries and will enjoy a lovely improvement at home or with someone special.

21 MAY

You'll enjoy relaxing and spending time at home with someone you love. However, changes may feel intense, so ensure you take breaks.

22 MAY

You'll adapt to a change at home or at work. This is a productive day and you'll enjoy working collaboratively.

23 MAY

You can achieve a great deal now; however, someone close may express strong emotions. Avoid conflict, as it will quickly escalate.

24 MAY

The key to success lies in being able to adapt to new circumstances. Avoid clinging to the past; embrace the new.

25 MAY

You'll appreciate the chance to look after your health and well-being and may be called upon to demonstrate your expertise at work.

26 MAY

Be prepared to be spontaneous, as you'll enjoy an impromptu event or get-together. You may be pleasantly surprised by developments.

27 MAY

A friend, group or organisation will be supportive, especially if you find some developments intense. Romance could blossom.

28 MAY

You will appreciate the opportunity to complete chores around the house but you must avoid sensitive topics with someone who can be stubborn.

29 MAY

You may prefer to play your cards close to your chest, especially if you know your views are not supported by those in your environment.

30 MAY

You'll feel more self-confident about expressing your ideas and opinions. A friend or family member will prove to be supportive.

31 MAY

While you're striving to find more balance and peace in your life emotions may get the better of you, so pace yourself and take breaks.

June

1 JUNE

Prepare to work hard towards your goals and you will succeed, even if you feel a challenge has arisen.

2 JUNE

A key talk or meeting will help you gain perspective with someone close either at work or in your personal life.

3 JUNE

In the lead-up to the full moon you may experience life intensely. Be optimistic but avoid arguments.

4 JUNE

The full moon in Sagittarius begins a new chapter in a relationship and, for some, financially. You may update a communications device or vehicle. News may be unexpected.

5 JUNE

This may be an intense day, as feelings will bubble up. Changes at work or at home are likely.

6 JUNE

The Capricorn moon will put you in a practical frame of mind and make you capable of dealing with personal matters and long-term plans.

7 JUNE

Aim to think laterally about developments, especially those that signal long-term change.

8 JUNE

This is a good time to look at personal matters in a new light and to be more outgoing.

9 JUNE

It's a good day for get-togethers to discuss mutual agreements. You may receive beneficial financial, personal or health news.

10 JUNE

You're thinking creatively and imaginatively and will enjoy music, the arts and daydreaming. Enjoy relaxing! Therapeutic or sports events will be enjoyable.

11 JUNE

You may return to an old haunt or will enjoy a get-together.

12 JUNE

You'll be productive and could attain your goals at work, so be positive and outgoing.

13 JUNE

You're being noticed for your likeability. However, sometimes challenges arise, as they will today. Work towards your goals and you will attain them.

14 JUNE

A stubborn character may behave true to form. Avoid disputes and look for a positive way forward.

15 JUNE

This is a good day for negotiating, especially financially; however, some matters may not be smooth sailing so be cautious.

16 JUNE

The Gemini moon will help you to communicate well so aim to find common ground, especially in negotiations if they stall.

17 JUNE

If you're working you'll be busy. You'll appreciate the chance to catch up with someone special. Avoid allowing disputes to linger if possible.

18 JUNE

Make a wish at the new moon in Gemini, which signals a fresh activity or even relationship. You may be drawn to travelling or studying and to broadening your horizons.

19 JUNE

It's a good time for self-development and research. You may be drawn to making a personal or financial commitment. Avoid forgetfulness.

20 JUNE

Be patient with travel and collaborations, as changes will take place in your usual schedule.

21 JUNE

It's the solstice! Rise to challenges in your domestic or personal life. If you consider another person's point of view you will overcome obstacles.

22 JUNE

Work and activities that truly interest you will be motivating and even therapeutic.

23 JUNE

You may receive good news at work or experience a strong connection with someone you find inspiring.

24 JUNE

This is a good weekend for boosting your health, vitality and feel-good factor and that of someone close.

25 JUNE

A trip and activity this weekend will be inspiring; however, you may experience delays or misunderstandings.

26 JUNE

You're likely to be surprised by a change of circumstance or unexpected development, for some at work and for others with a partner.

27 JUNE

You'll enjoy deepening your relationship with someone you find inspiring.

28 JUNE

A favourite activity or interest will be motivating. Trust your intuition, as it is spot on.

29 JUNE

There are therapeutic aspects to the day. It's a good day to enjoy your favourite pastimes and look deep into your relationship with someone special. You may receive good news at work.

30 JUNE

A trip, study or self-developmental curve will be productive and inspiring. You may receive key news to do with legal matters.

July

1 JULY

A trip or get-together will be significant. You may enjoy a favourite activity and deepening your connection with someone special.

2 JULY

Someone unpredictable will behave true to form. Expect a surprise and be prepared to adapt to prevailing circumstances.

3 JULY

The full moon in Capricorn shines a light on certain relationships. You may be drawn to travelling and broadening your horizons in other ways.

4 JULY

A practical approach to an unpredictable person or circumstance will reap rewards.

5 JULY

Consider looking outside the box at spiritual, domestic and family matters.

6 JULY

A trip and communications will merit a patient approach, as there may be delays and mix-ups. Be prepared to research a complex matter.

7 JULY

This is a lovely day for being spontaneous, and you'll enjoy a fun event or get-together. A work meeting may entail a surprise.

8 JULY

You'll enjoy entering fresh territory and will boost certain relationships in the process.

9 JULY

A friend, group or association may be very helpful but you will need to first overcome a challenge.

10 JULY

You can make a great deal of progress at work and with a beauty or health matter, so take the initiative!

11 JULY

As Mercury enters Leo you'll be expressing yourself more, especially at work and regarding your general direction and hopes.

12 JULY

Someone close will need help, and you'll benefit from looking at a personal or work circumstance in a new light. Help is available if you need it.

13 JULY

This is a good time to deepen your understanding of yourself or of someone close, so be prepared to dive deep.

14 JULY

You'll enjoy collaborating with someone fun, visiting a lovely place and enjoying favourite activities. However, work and chores may come first.

15 JULY

Be guided by your intuition and take things slowly, as you'll enjoy spending a relaxing day with those you love.

16 JULY

Make the time to try to understand someone, as they may be finding it difficult to express themselves.

17 JULY

The Cancer new moon signals a fresh interest in activities that bring out your nurturing side. You may begin to see yourself and your family in a new light.

18 JULY

Be prepared to shine, as you may need to prove yourself. Rest assured you will.

19 JULY

You can make great progress both at work and health-wise, so take the initiative. A change of routine will be enjoyable.

20 JULY

This is an excellent day for romance. Take the time to enjoy your environment, the arts, music and self-development.

21 JULY

It's a good day to come to an agreement in a personal situation, but you must avoid making rash decisions.

22 JULY

Be prepared to communicate clearly as otherwise a battle of wills or intense circumstance could prevail.

23 JULY

The sun at the zenith of your chart will encourage you to be more outgoing, but you must be super clear to avoid misunderstandings. Be adaptable.

24 JULY

Your vulnerabilities may surface, so take extra time for yourself to unwind and gain perspective.

25 JULY

This is a good time to look for ways to improve your daily routine and work life, as your efforts will be successful.

26 JULY

Someone else's emotions may seem exaggerated so find ways to balance circumstances, especially at work.

27 JULY

Key news to do with your status, work or general direction will arise. If it's unclear, ensure you research it. You'll enjoy a reunion.

28 JULY

This is a good time to move conversations along as you enter fresh territory.

29 JULY

You'll succeed with your activities and goals even if a minor challenge arises. It's a good day to catch up on chores.

30 JULY

You can't second guess other people's true feelings, so aim to find out the truth instead and avoid giving mixed messages.

31 JULY

Be practical with an unpredictable circumstance or person for the best results.

August

1 AUGUST

The full moon supermoon in Aquarius spells a new chapter in your home life or with family or property. You'll enjoy a get-together.

2 AUGUST

It's a good day to reach an agreement with a friend, group or organisation and, for some, to make changes at home or work.

3 AUGUST

Combine an inspired approach to personal matters with the facts to gain a sense of progress. Avoid seeing circumstances through rose-coloured glasses.

4 AUGUST

Enjoy time spent with your favourite people and the arts, music and film and generally relaxing this evening.

5 AUGUST

An active and outgoing day will prove successful. You may enjoy boosting your health and appearance through a new look or wardrobe item.

6 AUGUST

Activities that boost morale such as sports and outdoors events will prove successful.

7 AUGUST

A personal or business partner may not agree with you over key matters. Try to honour their opinion while honouring your own.

8 AUGUST

The help of an organisation or friend will be invaluable. Avoid contributing to a stubborn situation by showing willingness to achieve common ground.

9 AUGUST

An unusual change of circumstance will arise. You may be surprised by developments and wish to review your position.

10 AUGUST

This is a good day for meetings and get-togethers both socially and at work, so take the initiative.

11 AUGUST

Good communication skills are the key to success, so be sure to brush up on your skills.

12 AUGUST

There are healing aspects to the day. It's a good time to overcome hurdles and mend bridges, and for beauty and health appointments.

13 AUGUST

News or changes to do with work or your general status and direction in life will be enlightening. You'll enjoy socialising.

14 AUGUST

Be prepared to be outgoing and active. However, you may need to be super tactful to avoid arguments.

15 AUGUST

Changes may occur swiftly, so be prepared to think on your toes and especially with a friend, group or organisation. Avoid misunderstandings.

16 AUGUST

The new moon in Leo signals a fresh phase in your status, career or general direction in life. You may be surprised by developments.

17 AUGUST

Pay attention to details, especially in important communications and work matters, to avoid mistakes.

18 AUGUST

You can set in motion successful and practical plans, especially to do with your home, relationships and family.

19 AUGUST

Look for a fair go in your work and personal plans, and if you work with practical plans you will be successful.

20 AUGUST

Prepare to research facts and details, especially if you are making key decisions, or you could make mistakes.

21 AUGUST

Be prepared to gather information from groups and organisations as you could boost your personal circumstances.

22 AUGUST

An uncertain situation requires you to be proactive, so ensure you're clear about your options. Avoid daydreaming and forgetfulness.

23 AUGUST

Try to get important paperwork completed now to avoid having to review it over the coming weeks. You may receive key news.

24 AUGUST

Be optimistic about your circumstances. If you're shopping you must avoid overspending and overindulging as you'll regret it!

25 AUGUST

A return to an old haunt for a reunion will be enjoyable. Circumstances will gain their own momentum, so be sure you're happy with them.

26 AUGUST

Check your itinerary and travel arrangements and give yourself plenty of time, as delays may be possible.

27 AUGUST

It's a good day for family get-togethers and socialising and for making long-term commitments.

28 AUGUST

Be prepared to step into fresh circumstances in your personal life even if they seem to rock the boat.

29 AUGUST

Starting now, you'll feel driven over the coming weeks to find more peace and balance in your life, especially at home.

30 AUGUST

Be inspired, as your input will be appreciated at home and with family.

31 AUGUST

The Pisces full moon supermoon spotlights a fresh chapter in your personal life. A health or work situation will have a bearing on circumstances.

September

1 SEPTEMBER

Be prepared to put in a big effort in your personal life and at work, as your endeavours will be rewarded.

2 SEPTEMBER

You'll appreciate the opportunity to improve your health, well-being and appearance.

3 SEPTEMBER

Certain interactions will be enjoyable but others, as you already know, will be tense, so choose your activities carefully.

4 SEPTEMBER

Your career, direction and activities will move forward more easily over the coming weeks. You may already have received news of developments.

5 SEPTEMBER

A social or work event will be enjoyable and you may receive good news.

6 SEPTEMBER

You'll receive key news and a meeting or trip may be successful. You may also experience an ego boost.

7 SEPTEMBER

A social or work meeting may involve a nostalgic element. You may return to an old haunt.

8 SEPTEMBER

This is a lovely day for socialising and networking, so take the initiative. A partner may have good news for you.

9 SEPTEMBER

This is a good day to look after yourself and others and for self-development.

10 SEPTEMBER

You will appreciate a sense of belonging, so find ways to feather your nest as you'll be glad you did.

11 SEPTEMBER

You may resume a particular schedule or routine or return to an old haunt. It's a good day for a health appointment.

12 SEPTEMBER

This is a proactive and outgoing day when you can be productive and feel fulfilled as a result. Just avoid arguments.

13 SEPTEMBER

You're productive and can get a great deal done at the moment but you must avoid overtiring yourself.

14 SEPTEMBER

A more focused and detailed approach to your chores and health will be productive. Avoid being overly analytical.

15 SEPTEMBER

The new moon in Virgo signals a fresh chapter in your career, status or general direction in life. A strong relationship may be formed.

16 SEPTEMBER

Unusual developments and activities that take you somewhere new will be enjoyable, so be spontaneous. A partner may surprise you.

17 SEPTEMBER

You prefer peace at all costs, however, someone stubborn may behave true to form. Avoid giving in to their demands but avoid arguments if possible. Find common ground instead.

18 SEPTEMBER

You'll feel passionate about your goals but not everyone will feel the same, so be patient.

19 SEPTEMBER

You may experience a change in your usual routine. It's a good day for a health or beauty appointment. One relationship may be difficult, but if you're constant you'll overcome difficulties.

20 SEPTEMBER

Be motivated by your interests. Freedom and adventure will appeal but you must keep those who rely on you in the loop.

21 SEPTEMBER

This is a good time to make changes both at home and at work. Be adventurous.

22 SEPTEMBER

This is a productive day in which you can achieve so much, but you must avoid rushing. Enjoy a fun or therapeutic get-together.

23 SEPTEMBER

The sun in your sign for the next month will encourage you to create more peace and harmony in your life. Your efforts are likely to be successful.

24 SEPTEMBER

You'll feel active and outgoing but someone close may not feel the same. You or they may need expert help, and rest assured it will be available.

25 SEPTEMBER

Be prepared to work hard to overcome differences with someone stubborn or in authority. You'll enjoy a reunion or good news at work or regarding your health.

26 SEPTEMBER

An upbeat activity or group of fun people will raise morale. You'll appreciate the opportunity to blow off some steam.

27 SEPTEMBER

Your creativity will emerge and you'll enjoy being imaginative along with music, dance and romance. You must, however, avoid forgetfulness and daydreaming.

28 SEPTEMBER

You may discover you've had excessively high expectations. If so, rest assured your discovery will lead to a better outcome.

29 SEPTEMBER

The Aries full moon signals a fresh phase in a key relationship for September Librans and a fresh work or health chapter for October Librans. Avoid making rash decisions.

30 SEPTEMBER

Someone close may be super active or even feisty. Find clever ways to channel excess energy and avoid arguments.

October

1 OCTOBER

You'll enjoy finding time for yourself and also a reunion, but you won't be inclined to go out of your way for anyone.

2 OCTOBER

It's a good day for a health or beauty appointment. Meetings may be inspiring, but you must avoid forgetfulness.

3 OCTOBER

You'll enjoy a reunion and sprucing up your domestic decor and interpersonal dynamics at home. If you're making decisions, double-check the facts.

4 OCTOBER

The Gemini moon will bring your restlessness to the surface and you'll enjoy sports, meetings and a short trip. It's a good day for research.

5 OCTOBER

Keep an eye on the facts and on your goals, as you may be easily distracted.

6 OCTOBER

Double-check you're on the same page as someone important as you may be speaking at cross purposes.

7 OCTOBER

You prefer to maintain peace and balance in your life but sometimes stresses arise. Rest assured you'll overcome a difference of opinion.

8 OCTOBER

An optimistic attitude will help you get on with people but you must keep them in the loop to avoid any fallout.

9 OCTOBER

You're keen to get on, and while this will be a productive approach you must avoid arguments, especially at home.

10 OCTOBER

Serious discussions will take your focus. It's a good time to make a commitment but you must have the facts.

11 OCTOBER

Your help and expertise are in demand. If you require expert advice it will be available. Avoid taking the random opinions of other people personally.

12 OCTOBER

You'll feel more passionate about your projects. Avoid crossing swords with someone you must collaborate with.

13 OCTOBER

This is a good time to make progress with your chores and to establish a sense of security and stability at home.

14 OCTOBER

The solar eclipse represents a new chapter in your personal life and at work and, for some, regarding health.

15 OCTOBER

Be prepared to consider your circumstances from a fresh perspective. Someone close may have unexpected news.

16 OCTOBER

Your emotions may be intense, so find ways to channel them into constructive pursuits for the best results.

17 OCTOBER

This is a good time to improve your communication skills as some news may be difficult to convey or understand. Someone close will be supportive.

18 OCTOBER

An outgoing and adventurous approach to your finances and personal situation will be effective.

19 OCTOBER

This is a good day to find out more about your true choices. You may enjoy a reunion or the chance to return to an old haunt.

20 OCTOBER

Key news or a trip or meeting will provide you with invaluable insight into your best way forward.

21 OCTOBER

Discussions and meetings may become intense, especially those at home or regarding someone close. Avoid arguments and a battle of egos.

22 OCTOBER

This is a better day for discussions and meetings. You may enjoy socialising and romance could blossom.

23 OCTOBER

This is a good day for making a commitment to a plan that is practical and realistic.

24 OCTOBER

News, meetings and developments will provide a sense of stability. You'll appreciate the chance to move forward from a stalemate.

25 OCTOBER

Be inspired but also practical, as otherwise complexities may become a conundrum.

26 OCTOBER

Be prepared to dream a little and infuse your life with the arts and music where possible to lighten your mood.

27 OCTOBER

You or someone close may feel a little sensitive, so be sure to give yourselves extra space and nurturance.

28 OCTOBER

The lunar eclipse in Taurus signals a fresh chapter in a key agreement or partnership. For some a key financial decision will be on the table.

29 OCTOBER

Events will unfold swiftly. You may tend to make snap decisions but you must avoid impulsiveness. A trip or meeting will bring out your passionate side.

30 OCTOBER

It's a good day to try to slow down the pace if possible, as otherwise you may tend to be swept along by developments.

31 OCTOBER

Happy Halloween! It's a good day for socialising. You may hear good news from a friend, group or organisation. This day is more treat than trick.

November

1 NOVEMBER

This is a good day for research and getting down to brass tacks with personal and financial matters.

2 NOVEMBER

You can make progress with personal, travel, study and even legal matters, so take the initiative!

3 NOVEMBER

Key discussions and decisions to do with someone close, work, a trip or legal matters is best taken with expert advice.

4 NOVEMBER

Unexpected news or a visit will require you to be adaptable. A financial matter is best approached carefully. Avoid overspending.

5 NOVEMBER

Be prepared to consider someone else's point of view. Avoid rushing and minor bumps and scrapes.

6 NOVEMBER

This is a good day for a reunion and for making changes at home and work.

7 NOVEMBER

You may receive a compliment or financial boost. If you're shopping avoid overspending, especially if you're already in debt.

8 NOVEMBER

You may need to review some of your values and principles, especially if someone close disagrees with you.

9 NOVEMBER

Be prepared to consider another person's opinion. It's a good day for discussions, especially regarding finances and your home, and a talk could be transformative.

10 NOVEMBER

You may be drawn to retail therapy but you must avoid overspending. Be careful with some discussions, as someone may be feeling sensitive.

11 NOVEMBER

You'll enjoy getting together with someone whose company you enjoy and may need to alter some of your plans accordingly. You'll receive unexpected news.

12 NOVEMBER

You'll feel passionate about your activities and the people you associate with. Romance could blossom.

13 NOVEMBER

The Scorpio new moon signals a fresh chapter in a relationship and, for some, financially. Unexpected news is on the way.

14 NOVEMBER

An outgoing and adventurous approach to someone who can be unpredictable will be productive but you must avoid reacting erratically.

15 NOVEMBER

You'll enjoy a reunion. This is a good day for a health or beauty appointment. You may repay a debt or have one repaid.

16 NOVEMBER

You'll appreciate a get-together, although someone may not be as relaxed as you.

17 NOVEMBER

It's a lovely day for the arts and romance and improving your finances, looks and wardrobe. Avoid gambling.

18 NOVEMBER

A favourite activity, friend or family member will take your focus. Romance could blossom, so be sure to organise a date if you haven't already. Avoid overspending and gambling.

19 NOVEMBER

The comfort of your home will appeal and you'll appreciate the opportunity to improve domestic dynamics and decor.

20 NOVEMBER

It's an excellent day to kick off changes you've been meaning to make for a while, especially financially and at home.

21 NOVEMBER

You may have your head in the clouds a little so be sure to focus extra hard at work to avoid making mistakes.

22 NOVEMBER

It's a good day for a health or beauty treat. Avoid rushing so there are no minor accidents. Someone may need your help and an expert will prove to be useful.

23 NOVEMBER

This is a good day to get things done, but a stubborn character at home may behave true to form. You may need to follow certain rules.

24 NOVEMBER

It's a good time for a mini financial review. You're communicating well, but some circumstances may test your communication skills. Avoid mix-ups.

25 NOVEMBER

You are productive but must avoid being too frustrated by delays, rules and restrictions, especially at home or concerning property or family.

26 NOVEMBER

Someone who can be unpredictable will behave true to form. Try to see things from their point of view to find common ground.

27 NOVEMBER

The Gemini full moon signals a fresh phase in a relationship or agreement. Misunderstandings and delays are likely, so plan ahead.

28 NOVEMBER

It's a good day to reach out to someone who may need help or a friendly chat.

29 NOVEMBER

Some communications may be challenging or difficult, but rest assured that if you aim for your goals you can overcome obstacles.

30 NOVEMBER

A change of pace or of place will be enjoyable. You'll enjoy a get-together but you must avoid misunderstandings.

December

1 DECEMBER

Communications will gain a more even keel over the next few weeks but you must avoid stubbornness in yourself and others.

2 DECEMBER

This is a lovely day to find the time to relax at home. You may enjoy spending money on improving decor and family relationships.

3 DECEMBER

Meetings and communications will be enjoyable but you must avoid sensitive topics if you don't want a battle of egos.

4 DECEMBER

This is the beginning of a more passionate phase in your personal life, but you may be inclined to overspend and overindulge – starting today!

5 DECEMBER

This is a good time to review your finances and work on a healthy budget. You may receive good news concerning a friend, family or creative project.

6 DECEMBER

A practical and down-to-earth approach to your work, chores, health and home will reap rewards.

7 DECEMBER

You'll enjoy the opportunity to spend time with someone you love in a relaxed environment, as this will boost the relationship.

8 DECEMBER

A close friendship or relationship will prove to be therapeutic. It's a good time for get-togethers, meetings and a trip.

9 DECEMBER

This will be a passionate weekend ideal for getting closer to someone you love. However, arguments may arise over finances or minor disagreements so be careful.

10 DECEMBER

It's a good day for get-togethers, financial planning and a short trip. Romance could flourish but you must avoid arguments.

11 DECEMBER

A short trip or visit will be enjoyable as it's a good day for get-togethers. You may receive a compliment or financial boost.

12 DECEMBER

The Sagittarian new moon signals the start of a new relationship chapter. You may be drawn to update a vehicle or communications device and may be surprised by news.

13 DECEMBER

Important news to do with a trip or agreement will arrive. It's a good time for a financial review. Try to get paperwork sorted out now.

14 DECEMBER

Now that Mercury is retrograde it's a good time to be practical with travel arrangements and communications to avoid mistakes.

15 DECEMBER

Your help may be required, and if you need help or expert advice it will be available.
Avoid rushing.

16 DECEMBER

It's a lovely weekend to make changes at home but you must keep others in the loop to avoid misunderstandings. Plan your travel so you can avoid delays.

17 DECEMBER

Some talks and meetings may bring your sensitivities to the surface or those of someone else, so take things carefully. Avoid travel delays and mix-ups.

18 DECEMBER

Key news and a fun meeting or trip will be enjoyable. You'll enjoy a reunion.

19 DECEMBER

You may wish to dream a little. You'll enjoy the arts, music and romance. Give yourself time to adjust to a fresh schedule.

20 DECEMBER

A little retail therapy will be enjoyable. Last-minute Christmas shopping will appeal but you must avoid impulse buys. You may receive a compliment or gift.

21 DECEMBER

It's a good day for altering your environment at home or via a trip. You may he surprised by developments or a chance encounter.

22 DECEMBER

You'll enjoy a reunion or a return to an old haunt. This is a lovely time for get-togethers.

23 DECEMBER

The more practical you can be with arrangements the better will be the outcome. Keep your feet on the ground.

24 DECEMBER

This is a lovely day for spending time with friends and family. A trip or event will provide a feeling of belonging and stability; just avoid misunderstandings and delays.

25 DECEMBER

Merry Christmas! A lovely change of routine will prompt you to fill your day with a little luxury and indulgence. Romance will flourish.

26 DECEMBER

You'll enjoy a little retail therapy but you must avoid spending all your Christmas money in one go.

27 DECEMBER

The Cancer full moon signals the start of a fresh interest, hobby or activity. You'll enjoy travelling and reconnecting with someone special but you must plan ahead to avoid delays.

28 DECEMBER

A return to an old haunt and the chance to travel will bring out your romantic side. Avoid being too frustrated by delays and mix-ups.

29 DECEMBER

There are many aspects of the day you'll relish, not least being with people you love. This is an expensive time but you must avoid speculation.

30 DECEMBER

The Leo moon highlights your outgoing side. You'll enjoy being active and improving your health and well-being.

31 DECEMBER

Happy New Year! A fun atmosphere will prevail and you'll make the effort to meet friends and celebrate.

♏ SCORPIO

23 October - 22 November

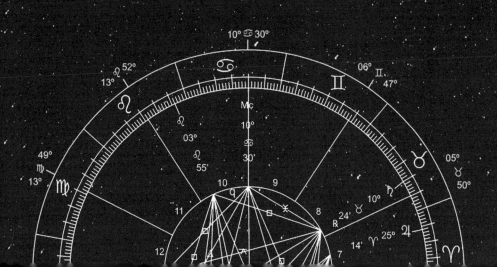

FINANCES

While Mars, Venus and the sun transit your eighth house of money during the first six months of the year and also during October, managing shared finances such as a mortgage, pension and taxes will be particularly important. The new moon in Sagittarius on 12 December will be an ideal time to consider a fresh financial investment or even kick-start a new cycle in your own finances.

HEALTH

Your sign's ruler Pluto makes a brave step out of Capricorn and into Aquarius this year, and with it will bring momentous change to your daily life. Be prepared to consider new and courageous ways to look after yourself and those you love, as developments this year will stretch your self-development and experiences and ask that you be innovative.

LOVE LIFE

Be prepared to reinvent the wheel in 2023. You'll be drawn to invest in your love life, with the eclipses in May and October bringing key turning points and being times when you could make great changes that have a long-term effect. An existing relationship will step into new territory. Singles may meet someone in unusual circumstances or will fall in love with someone you wouldn't usually consider a match.

CAREER

You'll need to make serious work decisions this year. You'll be aware that changing work scenarios will impact on your personal life, so your decisions need to be the correct ones. From April until September you'll gain the chance to improve your career, although it may seem the decisions are not your own in October. Be prepared to forge new agreements and collaborations, as that's where you'll find the key to moving forward.

HOME LIFE

You're set for considerable changes at home; for November-born Scorpios more immediately due to domestic developments and for October Scorpios due to travel and changes in your daily routine. Find the time to decide very carefully how you envisage the next five to 10 years, as Pluto's entry into innovative Aquarius will help you to put advantageous and long-term plans into action.

January

1 JANUARY

Happy New Year! A trip, conversation or visit may bring intense feelings to the surface. It's a good day for romance.

2 JANUARY

This is a good day for a trip, family and shared concerns, but bear in mind that you or someone close may be feeling sensitive.

3 JANUARY

You'll appreciate the opportunity to go somewhere new and deepen your understanding of someone close.

4 JANUARY

A friend, family member or neighbour will prove particularly helpful. A trip will be exciting.

5 JANUARY

You may hear unexpected news or enjoy being more spontaneous. If you're shopping you must avoid overspending. Your usual schedule may change.

6 JANUARY

The Cancer full moon suggests you're ready to turn a corner in relation to travel or within a favourite activity or project. Some Scorpios will be prepared to re-organise shared duties.

7 JANUARY

You'll enjoy a reunion and returning to an old haunt. A trip or news could be pivotal. It's a good time to review your finances.

8 JANUARY

A change of pace or of place will be enjoyable. You may be surprised by developments.

9 JANUARY

This is a lovely day to be outgoing, proactive and sociable. A meeting will be productive.

10 JANUARY

You'll appreciate the opportunity to plan ahead and slow the pace down later in the day.

11 JANUARY

You'll discover whether you've overspent during the festive season and need to review your finances. Be prepared to discuss circumstances to avoid arguments.

12 JANUARY

A collaboration or shared venture will move forward rapidly over the coming days and weeks, so be prepared to collaborate.

13 JANUARY

Friday the 13th! This is a good day to improve your environment both at home and at work and to boost domestic dynamics.

14 JANUARY

Be practical, as you could come to a solid agreement with someone special and regarding finances.

15 JANUARY

Someone who can be unpredictable will behave true to form. You may enjoy a change of routine, so be spontaneous.

16 JANUARY

You may experience a slight case of Mondayitis, but rest assured that once you get going things will fall into place.

17 JANUARY

You'll appreciate the chance to get things done, however, a financial or personal agreement will deserve a little more focus to avoid disputes.

18 JANUARY

Discussions to do with finances, your personal life, a vehicle, a communications device or a trip will be intense but will produce results.

19 JANUARY

A positive, upbeat attitude will reap rewards. Just ensure you have all the details if you are making domestic decisions.

20 JANUARY

The next four weeks will be an ideal time to enter fresh territory and see yourself and key relationships in a new light.

21 JANUARY

The new moon supermoon in Aquarius signals a fresh chapter in your relationships or travel. A trip, new vehicle or communications device may appeal. Avoid mix-ups.

22 JANUARY

Over the coming weeks you'll begin to see your work and daily life become more dynamic. This is a good day for meetings and making a commitment.

23 JANUARY

Trust your instincts, as you will be on the mark. A change of schedule or circumstance will merit an adventurous approach.

24 JANUARY

While you're keen to embrace the new year some are not as enthusiastic as you. Be positive but sensitive to the feelings of other people.

25 JANUARY

Financial developments will benefit from a careful approach to avoid mistakes. It's a good day for shopping, get-togethers and a short trip, so make a plan!

26 JANUARY

The moon in Aries will encourage you to be productive and dynamic. However, some people may find your approach overbearing, so maintain perspective.

27 JANUARY

It's a good day for a financial review and to take extra time with your communications and travel to avoid delays and misunderstandings. Avoid gambling.

28 JANUARY

You'll appreciate the opportunity to slow down and enjoy the simple pleasures in life. Good news is on the way.

29 JANUARY

This is a lovely day to spend doing something you love and being in the company of someone fun. Be spontaneous.

30 JANUARY

Meetings will be productive, and you may be pleasantly surprised by a change in your work or financial circumstance.

31 JANUARY

It's a romantic day and you'll enjoy cocooning at home at the end of the day or a short trip to somewhere beautiful.

February

1 FEBRUARY

There are healing attributes to the day. It's a good day for conversations, especially those concerning family and creative projects.

2 FEBRUARY

A lovely relationship can deepen, so it's a good day to take the initiative romantically. A work meeting is likely to go well if you trust your instincts.

3 FEBRUARY

A collaboration can succeed. You'll enjoy a reunion and the chance to catch up with someone special.

4 FEBRUARY

An unusual change of circumstance will benefit from a spontaneous but practical approach. Avoid taking unexpected news personally.

5 FEBRUARY

The Leo full moon signals a fresh chapter in your activities and general outlook, especially regarding travel, study and, for some, legal matters.

6 FEBRUARY

You may find some conversations a little difficult yet others will progress very straightforwardly. It's a good day to improve domestic dynamics.

7 FEBRUARY

The Virgo moon will bring out your practical side, which you will appreciate as it's likely to be a busy time.

8 FEBRUARY

A change in your usual schedule or a surprise get-together will raise morale.

9 FEBRUARY

It's a good day for talks with someone special at home, in your family or regarding property. You may make a commitment or financial decision.

10 FEBRUARY

Talks and meetings will be intense. A trip may invoke strong feelings.

11 FEBRUARY

It's a good day to get on top of chores at home and also for a reunion.

12 FEBRUARY

It's a lovely day for romance, time spent with the family, self-development, spiritual pursuits, romance and the arts.

13 FEBRUARY

The Scorpio moon will motivate you to be productive and proactive. Domestic matters can improve.

14 FEBRUARY

Happy St Valentine's Day! You'll appreciate the opportunity to spend time in a domestic environment. Romance can blossom.

15 FEBRUARY

This is a good day to improve domestic dynamics and decor. You'll also enjoy the arts, music and film.

16 FEBRUARY

It's a good day to make a commitment to someone special, for example in your personal life or family, but you must avoid making assumptions.

17 FEBRUARY

Be practical above all else with arrangements as you'll manage to accommodate developments.

18 FEBRUARY

You'll enjoy a visit or trip and a fun activity will raise morale. It's a good time for making domestic improvements. A friend or partner may surprise you.

19 FEBRUARY

This is a good day for making changes at home and in your environment such as your garden as your efforts will provide a sense of comfort and security.

20 FEBRUARY

The new moon in Pisces signals a fresh chapter in your personal life and/or at home or with family. A trip or news will be therapeutic.

21 FEBRUARY

A change of circumstance regarding travel, someone special or in a usual schedule will merit a patient approach to avoid frustration.

22 FEBRUARY

This is a good day for meetings and get-togethers. A colleague or partner may have good news for you.

23 FEBRUARY

The Aries moon will bring out your feisty, passionate side, which will be useful for getting things done but you must avoid arguments.

24 FEBRUARY

A reunion or get-together may be more significant than meets the eye, so be sure to reach out.

25 FEBRUARY

It's a lovely weekend to focus on your priorities and find time for a little luxury or a treat. You may enjoy boosting your health or appearance.

26 FEBRUARY

You'll appreciate getting together with someone special and it's in your interest to avoid sensitive topics.

27 FEBRUARY

Key talks, a trip and meetings are likely to go well. Communications at home are likely to improve.

28 FEBRUARY

Stay on your toes, as someone you must collaborate with may be a little changeable or unpredictable.

March

1 MARCH

Trust your intuition with key decisions. It's a good day to research and listen to other people's opinions so you can gauge where you stand.

2 MARCH

Developments at home will require focus and facts. It's a good day for some do-it-yourself projects.

3 MARCH

A surprise guest or improvement at home will raise spirits. You may enjoy a fun trip or meeting. A therapeutic time is on the cards.

4 MARCH

You know just what to do with domestic developments, family or someone special, so be proactive and enjoy improving your home life.

5 MARCH

An unexpected change in your usual routine will be enjoyable. Someone close may surprise you.

6 MARCH

You'll enjoy a change in your usual routine or activities, so be adaptable. You may receive surprisingly good news or bump into an old friend.

7 MARCH

The full moon in Virgo spotlights a fresh chapter in your interests such as your favourite activities, studies or even travel.

8 MARCH

You may be wearing your heart on your sleeve, so keep your professional hat on when you are at work and aim to fully relax at home. Take short breaks if necessary.

9 MARCH

Trust your instincts at work and with key financial or personal decisions and back your intuition up with research.

10 MARCH

You'll enjoy doing something fun. It's a good day for a short trip or a visitor at home and for improving your environment.

11 MARCH

This is a romantic and active weekend. You may be surprised by a change in your usual routine or a visitor. Organise a date!

12 MARCH

Someone close may be feeling sensitive. If it's you, take time out to gain a sense of nurturance. This is a good time for self-development.

13 MARCH

This may be a moody start to the week, but as the day goes by you'll feel more dynamic and productive.

14 MARCH

Someone close may wish to pressure you into certain ideas or viewpoints. If you are making a long-term decision ensure you research the facts first.

15 MARCH

It's another good day to make changes at home, with family or property but you must avoid gambling and making rash decisions. Romance could blossom.

16 MARCH

You won't always agree with everyone and today is a case in point. A change of routine or of place may be stressful, so pace yourself.

17 MARCH

Important discussions are best approached calmly. Luckily, a constructive change of routine will help take some of the pressure off you.

18 MARCH

Be prepared to look outside the box at your circumstances to avoid being stuck in one mindset.

19 MARCH

You can make the changes you wish to make, especially at home and regarding a change of environment, but you must avoid making rash decisions.

20 MARCH

A change of atmosphere at home or in your environment will be pleasant. You'll enjoy a reunion or will hear good news at work or from someone close.

21 MARCH

The Aries new moon is a good time to start something new in your personal life or at home. Creative projects could bring a change of environment your way.

22 MARCH

You're more known for your passionate side yet you can be as feisty as Aries, as Mars is both signs' ruler. Avoid arguments and look for practical solutions.

23 MARCH

You're ready to enter fresh territory, either literally or metaphorically. You may see yourself and your work in a new light.

24 MARCH

A reunion, work meeting or return to an old haunt may be complex, but if you face circumstances head on you will succeed.

25 MARCH

It's a lovely time to deepen your ties with someone special with a favourite activity, even if you feel a little like a fish out of water.

26 MARCH

You'll enjoy a reunion if you didn't already yesterday. Be prepared to dream a little, but if you have important chores they will not wait!

27 MARCH

Some conversations may be sensitive and you'll need to be diplomatic. You may experience a surprise get-together or news.

28 MARCH

A creative, musical or artistic project will catch your attention. A trip or visit will be important. Avoid both financial and emotional gambling.

29 MARCH

This is a good day to read the room and consider the most practical way ahead, especially with personal or family matters.

30 MARCH

A personal or business partner may have surprising news. This is a good day to commit to a business or personal agreement and/or property.

31 MARCH

This will be a proactive, outgoing day when taking the time for your favourite activities and people will be rewarding.

April

1 APRIL

Chores both at home and in the garden may turn out to be enjoyable. Someone will prove helpful. It's a lovely weekend for romance, so organise a date!

2 APRIL

You'll enjoy a fun and upbeat activity with someone you love. It's also a good time to plan ahead financially.

3 APRIL

The key to success lies in good communication skills. However, good planning will be a key factor as there may be traffic delays and misunderstandings.

4 APRIL

Developments at work or regarding your health will benefit from a practical point of view. It's another day to be patient with travel delays and mix-ups.

5 APRIL

Your expertise may be in demand, especially at work and if you work in property. However, you may feel sensitive so be sure to take breaks and avoid minor accidents.

6 APRIL

The full moon in Libra signals a new chapter in a health or daily routine such as work.

7 APRIL

You may experience a surprise or a change of schedule. It's a good day to be spontaneous. You'll enjoy romance and the arts and relaxing later in the day.

8 APRIL

A fun outing, trip or activity will bring you together with like-minded people, which you'll enjoy.

9 APRIL

You'll feel motivated to bring more stability, happiness and security to your personal life. It's a good day for personal development and spirituality.

10 APRIL

Be optimistic with talks and meetings, as a positive outlook and demeanour will speak volumes about your abilities and productivity.

11 APRIL

Key news and meetings are likely to be upbeat. You can deepen your relationship with someone special and romance will blossom. You may hear good news at work or health-wise.

12 APRIL

You'll be drawn to planning ahead but you must avoid putting the cart before the horse. Be practical.

13 APRIL

You won't always agree with everyone, so be prepared to consider another person's point of view and look for new ways to approach old themes.

14 APRIL

It's a good day to co-operate and, if necessary, compromise. Avoid a Mexican stand-off. You'll enjoy the chance to relax at home.

15 APRIL

Be prepared to innovate and look outside the box, especially if some matters seem to be stuck.

16 APRIL

You'll enjoy infusing your day with romance, the arts, music and dance. A friend or family get-together will be enjoyable.

17 APRIL

Trust your instincts with a personal, family or property matter. Just avoid allowing your imagination to run away with you.

18 APRIL

It's a good time to research facts, especially to do with your personal and financial planning to avoid mistakes.

19 APRIL

You'll gain an increased sense of motivation both at work and in your personal life, so plan to incorporate more of what you love in your life.

20 APRIL

The total solar eclipse in Aries will kick-start a new chapter, for many at work or health-wise and for some in a personal context. Avoid a battle of egos.

21 APRIL

You may receive key news, especially if you were born in early November. Try to get important paperwork and key talks agreed upon before the end of the day.

22 APRIL

A practical approach to your activities will reap rewards and bring you closer to your goals. It's a good time to share chores or delegate.

23 APRIL

A fast-talking and fun person will be lovely to have around but may also be distracting, so focus on your priorities.

24 APRIL

This is going to be a chatty, busy day that will be productive. Work and research projects are likely to go well.

25 APRIL

If you're looking for a commitment from someone this could be your day. You will at least come to a mutually agreeable outcome.

26 APRIL

Take a moment out of your day to catch your breath and recalibrate, especially if some developments are stressful.

27 APRIL

You may hear unexpectedly good news from someone you love or admire and you'll enjoy being spontaneous.

28 APRIL

You'll enjoy the excitement of the coming weekend. This is certainly a good time to plan something fun and active.

29 APRIL

An unexpected invitation or development will be enjoyable, so be sure to take the initiative and be spontaneous. Just avoid making rash decisions.

30 APRIL

A little planning will help you achieve a happy and calm day, and your efforts will be worthwhile.

May

1 MAY

This is a good time to review some of your paperwork, projects and collaborations with a view to finding better ways to move ahead.

2 MAY

You'll receive news at work regarding health or an improvement in your daily routine. The arts, music and romance will appeal.

3 MAY

You may experience an introspective phase as you consider your work and health schedules in the light of finding more balance.

4 MAY

This is a good time to research your projects and find common ground with someone you tend to disagree with. Avoid misunderstandings.

5 MAY

The lunar eclipse in Scorpio signals a fresh chapter in your personal life, especially if it's your birthday in early November. It's a good day to plan a fun event.

6 MAY

Use your instincts to go with the flow and avoid thorny topics that could lead to conflict.

7 MAY

You'll gain perspective into how someone feels about some shared matters such as finances. Work hard at attaining your goals and you will succeed.

8 MAY

You'll appreciate the opportunity to be productive at work and enjoy some of your favourite activities.

9 MAY

You'll receive surprise news from someone close. A personal or business partner may surprise you and you could experience a change in your usual routine.

10 MAY

The more down to earth you are with communications, projects and travel the better will be the outcome.

11 MAY

Be prepared to look outside the box at your options at work, health-wise and with your commitments and important decisions.

12 MAY

You'll appreciate the opportunity to get down to brass tacks with a work, domestic or health circumstance. You can come to mutually agreeable arrangements.

13 MAY

It's a great day for improving your home life and close relationships. You may also be drawn to boosting your health and appearance.

14 MAY

There is a dreamy quality to your day. You'll enjoy relaxing at home and the arts, dance and music.

15 MAY

Key news or a get-together will be memorable as you turn a corner in a key project or relationship. Developments at home will be uplifting.

16 MAY

You're about to begin a more abundant phase at work and, for some, in a close relationship.

17 MAY

Be flexible with arrangements and discussions as otherwise circumstances may feel stuck and a business or personal partner may seem stubborn.

18 MAY

If you like a challenge you'll enjoy current circumstances, but if not prepare for an intense day and avoid arguments.

19 MAY

The Taurus new moon signals a fresh chapter in a personal or business relationship. Be prepared to negotiate and come to mutually agreeable arrangements.

20 MAY

You will enjoy a lighter feel to the day and the company of someone fun.

21 MAY

This is a good time to enjoy being active and outgoing through activities such as sports and being with like-minded people. Just avoid tense topics and rushing.

22 MAY

Be confident, as your activities and projects can succeed. Aim to collaborate for the best results. Avoid entertaining unrealistic expectations.

23 MAY

You have a lot of energy, and unless you express it constructively you may feel frustrated by events. Aim to channel impatience into productivity and avoid conflict.

24 MAY

The Leo moon later in the day will contribute to an upbeat attitude, but you may be impatient with those who do not share your views so maintain perspective.

25 MAY

It's another good day to be proactive with your many goals and projects but also to avoid arguments with those you find to be slow or obstinate.

26 MAY

Be prepared to be spontaneous as you'll enjoy an impromptu event or get-together. You may be pleasantly surprised by developments.

27 MAY

You'll appreciate a slower pace this weekend and being able to touch base with activities you find grounding and relaxing.

28 MAY

You will appreciate the opportunity to make future plans and be practical about your home life and family but you must avoid sensitive topics with someone who can be stubborn.

29 MAY

Finding more balance in your work and personal life will appeal over the next two days and enable you to pace yourself.

30 MAY

You'll enjoy a social get-together and spending time with someone you love this evening. Some communications may be more intense than they need to be, so aim to de-escalate tension.

31 MAY

A key get-together or reunion over the coming days will provide you with more perspective regarding work and health.

June

1 JUNE

Paperwork and communications will deserve a little extra focus so you can proceed with your ventures and plans.

2 JUNE

Key news will be significant and provide insight into your best path ahead.

3 JUNE

In the lead-up to the full moon you may experience life intensely. Be optimistic, avoid arguments and gain the information you need.

4 JUNE

The full moon in Sagittarius begins a new chapter in your personal life and, for some, financially. Someone close has unexpected news for you.

5 JUNE

This may be an intense day, as feelings will bubble up. Take things carefully, especially if you are travelling and have important communications. It could be a passionate time.

6 JUNE

The Capricorn moon will promote a practical approach to dealing with personal matters, work, health and long-term plans.

7 JUNE

Think laterally about developments, especially those that signal long-term change or fresh ways to communicate when matters seem to be stuck.

8 JUNE

You're likely to be drawn to a fresh environment as you don't want to be bogged down by stubborn circumstances.

9 JUNE

It's a good day for creative projects and the arts, and also for romance and discussing mutual agreements.

10 JUNE

You're thinking creatively and imaginatively but you must avoid forgetfulness and daydreaming, especially if you have sports activities and domestic chores.

11 JUNE

It's a lovely day for a trip or meeting and to make changes in your environment. You may enjoy a reunion.

12 JUNE

You'll be productive and could attain your goals at work, so be positive and outgoing.

13 JUNE

Your favourite activities will be a big drawcard yet there are domestic and family-related duties that may lead to conflicting priorities.

14 JUNE

It's a good day to aim for collaboration, especially as a stubborn character may behave true to form and you'll need to avoid disputes.

15 JUNE

This is a better day for communications but you may still need to negotiate and be patient with someone close.

16 JUNE

The Gemini moon will bring out the chatty, talkative aspects of a colleague or partner, which will enable you to make more light-hearted plans.

17 JUNE

Developments at home will merit careful focus. This is a good day to plan collaborative efforts and enjoy mutually enjoyable activities such as sport.

18 JUNE

Make a wish at the new moon in Gemini, which signals that a fresh agreement is possible; however, you must ensure you have the full facts to avoid making mistakes.

19 JUNE

It's a good time to organise a fresh schedule at home or at work. You may be drawn to making a personal or financial commitment. Avoid forgetfulness.

20 JUNE

You or someone close may feel a little sensitive, so take time out and organise a treat during the day or at home.

21 JUNE

It's the solstice! Celebrate life and its many positive aspects but be careful with communications and avoid travel delays by planning ahead.

22 JUNE

You'll feel outgoing and upbeat with your activities and at work and can be productive, but you must avoid rushing and getting involved in arguments.

23 JUNE

A meeting, news or personal development will be uplifting. There are healing attributes to the day that you'll appreciate.

24 JUNE

This is a good weekend for getting things shipshape at home and for the working week ahead. It's an excellent weekend for boosting your health.

25 JUNE

It's an excellent day to dream a little and be creative. However, you may be forgetful and must avoid misunderstandings.

26 JUNE

A sudden or unexpected development will mean a change of plan. Avoid making rash decisions but, nevertheless, try to be spontaneous.

27 JUNE

You'll enjoy deepening your relationship with someone inspiring. This is a good day for a health or beauty appointment. You may receive positive work or financial news.

28 JUNE

You'll enjoy getting together with like-minded people and will appreciate a relaxing atmosphere at home. Trust your intuition, as it is spot on.

29 JUNE

You may receive good news at work or regarding your health and enjoy a favourite activity. Developments at home will provide a sense of stability.

30 JUNE

It's a good day to make a financial commitment, especially to do with your home, family or a property. You'll enjoy a reunion.

July

1 JULY

You'll enjoy a change of pace or of place. If you're making an investment, avoid overspending. You'll enjoy deepening a special relationship.

2 JULY

Someone unpredictable will behave true to form. Expect a surprise and be prepared to adapt to prevailing circumstances.

3 JULY

The full moon in Capricorn shines a light on finances and certain relationships. Avoid both financial and emotional gambling.

4 JULY

You may feel more serious about certain matters, making this a good time for introspection. A practical attitude will reap rewards.

5 JULY

Consider a fresh approach to communications, especially those that seem to be stuck or difficult.

6 JULY

A personal or financial matter, including work, is best approached with a sensitive but well-informed attitude to avoid mix-ups.

7 JULY

This is a lovely day for a spontaneous get-together. You may be pleasantly surprised by news from someone close.

8 JULY

A favourite activity such as sport or a hobby will be super relaxing, and you'll enjoy connecting with like-minded people.

9 JULY

It's a passionate day, so find ways to channel excess energy into productive activities as otherwise tension in the air could be destructive.

10 JULY

You can make a great deal of progress at work or home and with favourite projects, so take the initiative!

11 JULY

As Mercury enters Leo you'll express yourself more passionately and will inspire others, but you must avoid putting people offside.

12 JULY

Someone close may need your help, and if you need advice it will be available. Avoid taking the comments of other people personally.

13 JULY

This is a good time to deepen your understanding of someone close, so try to find time for chats and a get-together.

14 JULY

You'll enjoy an impromptu meeting with someone you collaborate with. It's a good time to make a commitment or agreement but you must be prepared to negotiate.

15 JULY

You're more sensitive to someone's feelings than usual, so avoid taking any random comments personally. It's a good time for self-development.

16 JULY

It's your day off, so make the time and space to relax as otherwise activities and people's demands will take precedence.

17 JULY

The Cancer new moon signals a fresh chapter in a shared circumstance such as a domestic arrangement. Some discussions may surprise you.

18 JULY

You may be more assertive than usual, which will benefit your projects, but you must avoid appearing overbearing.

19 JULY

You are productive at the moment and can achieve a great deal but you must avoid taking on too much at once.

20 JULY

This is an excellent day for taking time out with someone you love and for improving your domestic circumstances, including decor.

21 JULY

It's a good day to come to an agreement in an activity or project and in your personal life. A trip or negotiation will be significant.

22 JULY

A key meeting or trip may be intense, so pace yourself. Nevertheless, there are therapeutic aspects to the day, which is perfect for self-development.

23 JULY

You'll feel clearer and more motivated about your activities and loyalties but you must be super clear to avoid misunderstandings. Be adaptable.

24 JULY

Your vulnerabilities or those of someone else may surface, so be patient and focus on the tasks at hand such as work.

25 JULY

You'll be looking for more peace, harmony and balance in your daily life, which will be reflected in your attempts to smooth over disagreements.

26 JULY

The moon in Scorpio will bring out your best side as you engage more deeply with projects and those you love.

27 JULY

You'll appreciate the opportunity to review a work project, activity or decision. If matters are unclear, ensure you do your research.

28 JULY

You'll appreciate the opportunity to gain more insight into your position in your career, status or personal life. Avoid being overly analytical and trust your gut.

29 JULY

Your hard work will pay off, especially at home and with your favourite activities and hobbies, so be positive.

30 JULY

You can't second guess people's true feelings, so aim to trust your intuition and avoid giving mixed messages yourself. It's a good day to beautify your home.

31 JULY

A practical attitude to moving goal posts will be productive. Someone close will provide an upbeat feeling to the day.

August

1 AUGUST

The full moon supermoon in Aquarius spells a new chapter in a relationship or a change of environment. You may consider a fresh communications device or vehicle repair.

2 AUGUST

It's a good day for serious discussions, especially to do with work and domestic duties.

3 AUGUST

Combine an inspired approach with the facts to gain a sense of progress with domestic or property matters.

4 AUGUST

This is a good day for the arts and music and enjoying the company of someone special, so organise a date!

5 AUGUST

An active and outgoing day will prove to be successful. Sports, the outdoors and taking the initiative with your favourite activities will appeal.

6 AUGUST

You'll enjoy the therapeutic aspects of the day, especially in relation to upbeat people whose company you enjoy. Avoid intense topics.

7 AUGUST

You may experience a slight case of Mondayitis so you must be super careful with communications to avoid appearing gruff. You'll need to be attentive in your collaborations.

8 AUGUST

A patient and understanding approach to someone who can be stubborn will be successful, especially if developments take you by surprise.

9 AUGUST

It's another day when your negotiation skills will be invaluable. Avoid contributing to arguments by looking for common ground.

10 AUGUST

This is a better day for meetings and get-togethers, especially at work and regarding someone you must collaborate with.

11 AUGUST

Good communication skills are the key to success again, plus the willingness to be a mediator or go-between.

12 AUGUST

There are healing aspects to the day, especially in relation to your favourite activities, hobbies and, for some, travel.

13 AUGUST

You'll enjoy a visit to somewhere beautiful or a meeting with someone you admire. This is a good day for self-development.

14 AUGUST

A bold and upbeat approach will be effective, especially if some relationships are still a little rocky. Just avoid appearing flippant.

15 AUGUST

Meetings, news and developments will boost your self-esteem and potentially also status at work or in your favourite activities.

16 AUGUST

The new moon in Leo signals a fresh phase for some Scorpios in your status, career or general direction in life and, for others, within a bold venture or activity.

17 AUGUST

Be prepared to enter fresh territory and pay attention to details, especially in important communications and work matters, to avoid mistakes.

18 AUGUST

Your ability to bring people together in friendly and innovative ways will be appreciated, and you'll enjoy socialising and networking.

19 AUGUST

You're looking for some peace, harmony and balance this weekend and you'll find it in romance, the arts, music and people you love.

20 AUGUST

The key to a smoothly running day lies in careful preparation and research. Avoid delays and misunderstandings.

 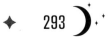

21 AUGUST

You are in a proactive and dynamic phase and will shine. However, you must avoid putting someone in a position of power offside.

22 AUGUST

You have a wonderful ability to be productive but you must focus a little harder to avoid needless errors and unnecessary disputes.

23 AUGUST

Try to get important paperwork completed now to avoid having to review it over the coming weeks, especially in relation to work and a special project or interest.

24 AUGUST

A dynamic approach to your day will reap rewards. Just avoid minor arguments through careful negotiation skills.

25 AUGUST

Important talks at work and, for some, regarding finances will be productive but you must avoid giving in to pressure.

26 AUGUST

A change of pace or of place may lead to a restless feeling, so ensure you blow off excess steam in productive ways through fun activities or sports.

27 AUGUST

It's a good day to boost relationships and make the intention to find more peace and balance in your life. You may be drawn to making a commitment.

28 AUGUST

You'll appreciate the opportunity to consider your circumstances in a new light, especially those to do with the people closest to you.

29 AUGUST

There is a nostalgic feeling in the air and you may be drawn to revisiting old haunts and reconnecting with people you admire.

30 AUGUST

Be inspired, as your input will be appreciated at home and at work. You may be easily distracted, so focus that little bit more at work.

31 AUGUST

The Pisces full moon supermoon spotlights a fresh chapter in your domestic life that may come about due to decisions made at work.

September

1 SEPTEMBER

Certain conversations and interactions may be more difficult than they need to be, but if you're diligent you will succeed with your projects.

2 SEPTEMBER

For an uplifting day, focus on what and who makes you happy and pour your energy into your favourite activities.

3 SEPTEMBER

Approach chores dynamically in the morning as this will provide the opportunity in the afternoon to enjoy a relaxed time. Avoid tense topics for the best results.

4 SEPTEMBER

A key interest, activity or project will proceed with less obstruction over the coming weeks and you may have already received encouraging news.

5 SEPTEMBER

It's a good day for meetings and to obtain expert advice if necessary regarding your plans and projects.

6 SEPTEMBER

Important news, a meeting or development at work will provide perspective for you moving forwards.

7 SEPTEMBER

It's a good day for a reunion, work meeting or favourite activity, so take the initiative.

8 SEPTEMBER

This is a lovely day for socialising and networking. A partner or colleague may have good news for you. You may receive positive health news.

9 SEPTEMBER

You may be drawn to investing in yourself and those you love a little more. A shopping trip or change of environment will be uplifting but you must avoid overspending.

10 SEPTEMBER

This is an excellent day to relax and take the pressure off yourself and those you love. Avoid intense topics and focus on bringing a sense of relaxation into being.

11 SEPTEMBER

You may resume a particular project or will need to review a previous decision. You'll enjoy a social get-together.

12 SEPTEMBER

The more proactive you are about enjoying life the more you will enjoy it. However, someone unpredictable may behave true to form so find ways to be patient.

13 SEPTEMBER

You may be inclined to be overly analytical, and while this will be useful at work you risk being seen as super critical.

14 SEPTEMBER

This is a productive day, so be practical and take positive steps towards your goals as you are likely to achieve them.

15 SEPTEMBER

The new moon in Virgo signals a fresh chapter in your career, status or general direction in life. You may turn a corner in a key relationship or financially.

16 SEPTEMBER

It's a lovely day to be spontaneous and enjoy doing something new. A partner or someone in your family may be instrumental in raising your mood.

17 SEPTEMBER

Certain arrangements may need to be thought out to avoid a clash of priorities. Work out what is most important and allow this to take precedence.

18 SEPTEMBER

The Scorpio moon for the next two days will enable you to communicate well but you must avoid allowing your emotions to rule your head.

19 SEPTEMBER

You prefer to go full steam ahead with your various goals but you may encounter delays, especially if you haven't adequately planned ahead.

20 SEPTEMBER

Trust your instincts as they are spot on now. A work and personal matter can stride ahead, so take the initiative with your plans.

21 SEPTEMBER

Socialising and networking will appeal and you can make great headway with your various relationships.

22 SEPTEMBER

There's a go-ahead flavour to the day that you'll enjoy. Just avoid rushing so there are no minor accidents or mistakes.

23 SEPTEMBER

The sun in Libra for the next month will encourage you to create more peace and harmony in your work and health and to improve your appearance.

24 SEPTEMBER

Take a little extra time with communications and interactions so there are no hurt feelings. Avoid rushing to prevent minor accidents.

25 SEPTEMBER

Meetings and get-togethers are likely to gain their own momentum. Some talks may be more productive than others, so choose your words wisely.

26 SEPTEMBER

Consider adopting a fresh approach to domestic matters as you'll benefit from a fresh perspective.

27 SEPTEMBER

A creative and upbeat approach to developing better dynamics at home or with family will be fruitful.

28 SEPTEMBER

At work, be prepared to think outside the box as your creative and inspired insight will be appreciated. At home, music, romance and film will all be relaxing.

29 SEPTEMBER

The Aries full moon signals a fresh phase in your personal life, and if you're a creative Scorpio in a project. Avoid making rash decisions.

30 SEPTEMBER

This is an excellent day to clear a backlog of chores at home and in your environment and for a health or beauty treat.

October

1 OCTOBER

A fun trip or activity will be enjoyable. It's an excellent day to relax at home. You may be forgetful, so keep an eye on the house keys.

2 OCTOBER

You'll discover whether your expectations at home or at work have been unrealistic, enabling you to adjust them. Avoid forgetfulness.

3 OCTOBER

Developments will gain their own momentum, so ensure you double-check facts and details to avoid making mistakes. You'll enjoy a trip or get-together.

4 OCTOBER

The Gemini moon will enable you to communicate so much better with those you must collaborate with, so take the initiative.

5 OCTOBER

A project or activity you value is worth investing in even if you must overcome some challenges. Rest assured your hard work will succeed.

6 OCTOBER

Be prepared to aim for your goals and stick with your principles, as your efforts will pay off.

7 OCTOBER

The key to success now rests in being super clear and practical about your activities and intentions. You'll find ways to overcome a hurdle.

8 OCTOBER

This is an excellent weekend to find ways to nurture yourself and those you love. Romance can blossom if you invest in the language of love: music, relaxation and beauty.

9 OCTOBER

You won't always agree with everyone, and this is one day when choosing words carefully will avoid conflict.

10 OCTOBER

It's a good day to find a little balance in your environment and also to make a long-term commitment to a person or plan.

11 OCTOBER

Personal circumstances may bring out your vulnerabilities, and you may need to help someone in your family or immediate peer group.

12 OCTOBER

You'll enjoy renewed vitality over the next few weeks. You must avoid speaking out of turn as you could be easily misunderstood.

13 OCTOBER

This is a good time to make progress at work and create the sense of stability and security you like. Avoid rushing.

14 OCTOBER

The solar eclipse represents a new chapter in your personal life. You may be called upon to help out a family member and improve harmony in your domestic or daily life.

15 OCTOBER

The key to success and happiness lies in good communication skills and avoiding taking someone's unpredictability personally.

16 OCTOBER

You'll feel motivated to be productive and could achieve a great deal but you must avoid perceiving life too intensely. Take breaks when you can.

17 OCTOBER

This is a good time to improve your communication skills as you may receive or inadvertently give mixed messages.

18 OCTOBER

It's a good time to plan a lovely social get-together. Domestic matters may require additional focus as you may be forgetful.

19 OCTOBER

You'll enjoy a reunion or may need to review a work project or plan. Keep domestic logistics simple and practical to avoid mix-ups and making mistakes.

20 OCTOBER

This is a good day for a health or beauty appointment and for a lovely social reunion.

21 OCTOBER

You are known for your intensity and current developments may bring this aspect out, so to avoid arguments be tactful for the best measure.

22 OCTOBER

While this is a better day for discussions and meetings, you may discover or reveal a secret. Discretion may be necessary.

23 OCTOBER

As the sun enters your sign you'll appreciate the sense of feeling more energetic over the coming weeks. Just avoid getting involved in arguments.

24 OCTOBER

This is a good day to make work plans, and if you'd like to revisit an old haunt or make domestic repairs this is the day to do it!

25 OCTOBER

Be inspired and creative, especially at home and in your personal life, as your efforts will be appreciated.

26 OCTOBER

You may be easily distracted, so if you're working be sure to take breaks so you can remain focused. You'll enjoy relaxing at home this evening.

27 OCTOBER

Take time out to look after yourself and those you love. An active, fun event will catch your eye and you'll need to choose your activities wisely.

28 OCTOBER

The lunar eclipse in Taurus signals a fresh chapter in your daily routine such as your work life or health schedule. It's a good day for a get-together or trip.

29 OCTOBER

Be prepared to take the initiative, especially with sports and fun events. Just avoid minor bumps and scrapes and conflict, as it will quickly escalate.

30 OCTOBER

Someone close may need a little attention and care, so be prepared to alter your plans to accommodate their needs.

31 OCTOBER

Happy Halloween! Changes you wish to see in your life are going to be easier to implement over the coming days as long as you're practical and plan ahead.

November

1 NOVEMBER

Developments will gain their own momentum and you'll manage to stay on top of things. Be adaptable for the best results.

2 NOVEMBER

You'll gain insight into someone close and your intuition is spot on, so trust your instincts.

3 NOVEMBER

Key discussions and decisions with someone close will take a great deal of focus, so be prepared to discuss matters creatively and realistically.

4 NOVEMBER

You may be surprised by news at work, regarding your health or from someone close. You may bump into someone unexpectedly.

5 NOVEMBER

Be prepared to consider someone else's point of view, as a tense topic or situation will move forward with a sensitive approach.

6 NOVEMBER

This is a good day for making the changes you would like to see in your life. You'll enjoy a trip or meeting. Some Scorpios will receive a boost at work or financially.

7 NOVEMBER

This is a good day to enjoy the company of someone you love and to indulge in romance, the arts and music.

8 NOVEMBER

It will be to your benefit to look at a domestic matter from a new perspective and to consult a friend or organisation if matters are challenging.

9 NOVEMBER

Be prepared to consider another person's opinion. It's a good day for discussions, especially regarding your home life or family, and a talk could be transformative.

10 NOVEMBER

Take the time to choose your words carefully as an ill-chosen word could do more harm than no words at all.

11 NOVEMBER

An unpredictable person may behave true to form. You'll experience a surprise or sudden development that means you must change your plans. Be spontaneous and avoid making rash decisions.

12 NOVEMBER

You'll appreciate the opportunity to spend time with those you love and at home. This is a good time for self-development.

13 NOVEMBER

The Scorpio new moon signals a fresh chapter in a relationship and, for some, at work or health-wise. Unexpected news is on the way.

14 NOVEMBER

Be prepared to leave your comfort zone, especially in talks and negotiations. Just avoid appearing blunt.

15 NOVEMBER

This is a good time for socialising and networking. Some Scorpios will receive a financial or ego boost.

16 NOVEMBER

You're communicating well but, still, not everyone will get on with you. You'll overcome obstacles but you must be tactful. Plan ahead to avoid travel delays.

17 NOVEMBER

You will enjoy being dynamic and productive and also spending energy investing in your personal and domestic life. It's a good time to improve decor.

18 NOVEMBER

Being active and outgoing will help you work off excess energy. Sports and focus on your home life and family will be rewarding.

19 NOVEMBER

The comfort of your home will appeal and you'll appreciate the opportunity to improve domestic dynamics and decor.

20 NOVEMBER

Unusual meetings or a visit somewhere different will raise morale, so why not organise a treat?

21 NOVEMBER

You may have your head in the clouds a little, so be sure to focus extra hard on travel and communications to avoid making mistakes.

22 NOVEMBER

Someone close may be feeling super vulnerable. If it's you, a friend or organisation will be supportive. Avoid both financial and emotional gambling.

23 NOVEMBER

Your adventurous approach to life will be rewarding but, nevertheless, there will be delays or people who are simply not moving at your speed.

24 NOVEMBER

You have a lot of excess energy, so be prepared to channel it into constructive activities to avoid feeling frustrated. Be patient with someone unpredictable.

25 NOVEMBER

You may need to rethink some plans, meetings or communications. Avoid being too frustrated by delays, rules and restrictions.

26 NOVEMBER

It's a good day to sharpen your communication skills to manage an unpredictable person or circumstance well.

27 NOVEMBER

The Gemini full moon signals a fresh phase in a relationship or agreement. Mix-ups and delays are likely, so plan ahead to avoid misplacing valuables such as house keys.

28 NOVEMBER

It's a chatty, fun day, although someone close may require a little more attention and focus to avoid difficulties.

29 NOVEMBER

A change in your usual routine or an overload of work will require patience and diligence. Rest assured you will achieve your goals.

30 NOVEMBER

You'll enjoy a short trip or meeting. If you're shopping, avoid overspending. Check you're on the same page as someone at home to avoid misunderstandings.

December

1 DECEMBER

Key financial matters will deserve careful scrutiny. If you've been prone to overspending, the following few weeks may see you reverse the trend.

2 DECEMBER

A financial negotiation or transaction could provide more security. Be practical above all else. You may enjoy a trip or meeting.

3 DECEMBER

You'll appreciate the opportunity to connect with someone close but you must avoid arguments, especially to do with money.

4 DECEMBER

This is the beginning of a more passionate phase as you'll feel drawn to expressing yourself more and in increasingly creative ways.

5 DECEMBER

This is a good time for get-togethers and discussing key domestic matters. You may need to focus on a work or health matter.

6 DECEMBER

A practical and down-to-earth approach to those you share duties and space with at home will reap rewards.

7 DECEMBER

You'll look for balance and may see only the lack of it, so ensure you maintain perspective especially with respect to an unpredictable character.

8 DECEMBER

It's a lovely day for a short trip or get-together and for key discussions, both at work and regarding finances. You'll enjoy a health boost.

9 DECEMBER

This will be a passionate weekend ideal for getting closer to someone you love. However, disagreements may arise so be careful.

10 DECEMBER

It's a good day for get-togethers, financial planning and relaxing. Romance could flourish but you must avoid arguments, as it's a passionate time.

11 DECEMBER

You'll enjoy a short trip or visit. It's an excellent day for meetings. You may receive a compliment or financial boost and will also appreciate a health or beauty boost.

12 DECEMBER

The Sagittarian new moon signals the start of a new chapter financially or in your personal life. You may be surprised by news.

13 DECEMBER

Try to get key paperwork and discussions sorted out now, especially financially, to avoid having to review your decisions in the coming weeks. Important news will arrive.

14 DECEMBER

Now that Mercury is retrograde it's a good time to be practical with travel, financial and personal arrangements and communications to avoid making mistakes.

15 DECEMBER

It's a lovely day for a get-together, and a healing or therapeutic event will be uplifting. Your help may be required. Avoid rushing.

16 DECEMBER

It's a busy weekend when you'll enjoy doing something different but you must plan ahead to avoid travel delays and miscommunications.

17 DECEMBER

Your sensitivities or those of someone close may come to the surface, so take things one step at a time. Avoid travel delays and mix-ups and overspending if you're shopping.

18 DECEMBER

News, a reunion or a fun activity will be enjoyable. It's a good time to review your budget, especially if you're in debt.

19 DECEMBER

Your domestic life, family and generally improving your home environment will appeal. You may also enjoy a beauty treat.

20 DECEMBER

You'll enjoy a little retail therapy, a beauty or health treat and a reunion but you must avoid impulse buys you'll regret.

21 DECEMBER

A get-together, compliment or financial boost will raise your mood. You'll enjoy improving your environment. Someone unpredictable may behave true to form.

22 DECEMBER

Last-minute Christmas shopping will appeal but you must avoid overspending. Important news, financial matters and a reunion will capture your attention.

23 DECEMBER

This is a sensual, enjoyable day when you'll prefer to relax. However, certain duties may need to be attended to beforehand.

24 DECEMBER

A practical approach to your arrangements will be most effective, including last-minute shopping and organising domestic matters.

25 DECEMBER

Merry Christmas! Romance will flourish and your connection with friends and family will be super enjoyable.

26 DECEMBER

Being with people you love and reconnecting is the most important aspect of your day. You'll also enjoy a little retail therapy.

27 DECEMBER

The Cancer full moon signals the start of a fresh chapter in a shared situation such as joint finances. Back up your choices with facts.

28 DECEMBER

You'll be drawn to living life in the fast lane but you must take into account those whose pace is slower than yours.

29 DECEMBER

You're in a celebratory mood and will enjoy being outgoing and upbeat. Meetings will take you somewhere new and raise morale.

30 DECEMBER

The Leo moon highlights your outgoing side. You'll enjoy favourite activities and spending time with friends and family.

31 DECEMBER

Happy New Year! You'll enjoy celebrating and will need to take into account the circumstances of someone at home or in your family.

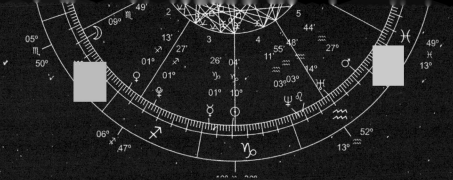

SAGITTARIUS

22 November - 21 December

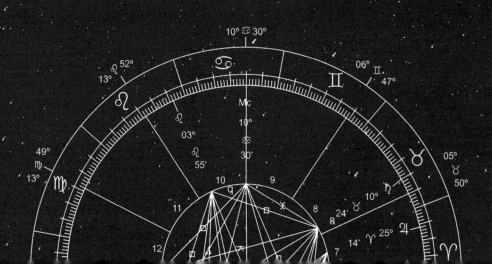

FINANCES

This is your year financially, as you'll gain the chance to change the way you earn money and prospectively how you work. In the process you will need to evaluate who and what is most important to you as you may have a conflict of interest on your hands, especially in April and May. Luckily, you'll gain the chance to step into new territory and make a financial improvement as a result. It's important, however, to avoid gambling this year, as it could be your real undoing.

HEALTH

Uranus brings its usual share of quirky complaints, aches and sniffles, but this year it will also bring the chance to reboot your health and well-being schedule so it better suits you and your need to keep up with your daily demands and chores. Prime periods to make positive changes in your health regime will be at the end of March until the end of April, and you will subsequently get the chance to review your health choices until December so there's no pressure to get it right the first time around!

LOVE LIFE

This is an excellent year to be creative and innovative in your love life, as the stars will support your efforts. If your love life has been lacklustre of late, this is the year to spice things up! You'll certainly gain the chance to do so, especially from the end of March and during April if not before. The end of October is also a good time to make changes in your love life and family circumstances, so be prepared to take the initiative in your relationships.

CAREER

Once Mars hits your work zone at the end of May, expect life to get busy until at least mid-October. If you've been considering making changes in your career it will be a good idea to set ideas in motion in March and April so you're ready to make the most of the opportunity to change things at mid-year. Be open to new ideas and being creative. The new moons in your career sector in August and September further spell the chance to take part in fresh projects you'll enjoy.

HOME LIFE

January and February will be particularly productive months for making changes at home, and you may receive visitors or visit someone yourself during these times. Travel will be inspiring and may create the need to make domestic changes as a result. Do-it-yourself projects and potentially a move in the early months could be productive if you plan ahead in advance. Saturn in your home sector will bring fresh responsibilities to bear at home from mid-March. You'll feel better equipped and on top of duties by the year's end, so ensure you pace yourself to avoid feeling restricted by domestic considerations.

January

1 JANUARY

Happy New Year! Strong feelings will arise, so take things carefully. If you like the new year sales you'll love shopping, but you must avoid overspending.

2 JANUARY

It's a lovely day to reconnect with someone special and to review paperwork and finances.

3 JANUARY

A fresh approach to someone special and also to a personal and financial matter will reap rewards. Someone may need your help, and if you need support it will be available.

4 JANUARY

A trip will be exciting and could take you somewhere new. It's a good day to overcome financial conundrums.

5 JANUARY

You may hear unexpected news and will enjoy being spontaneous. A fun activity will appeal.

6 JANUARY

The Cancer full moon will bring a fresh chapter in a personal relationship where being more caring of each other will succeed.

7 JANUARY

Key financial developments or discussions will enable you to review or even rectify a past matter.

8 JANUARY

An impromptu event will be fun and you'll enjoy a reunion or returning to an old haunt. Someone may surprise you.

9 JANUARY

You'll gain the opportunity to improve both your personal and work lives, so take the initiative. You may enjoy a beauty treat and a shopping trip.

10 JANUARY

While you are a fun-loving person, sometimes it's important to be serious about matters such as finances and career and this is one such a day.

11 JANUARY

You'll appreciate the opportunity to see important matters from someone else's point of view but you must avoid taking unwarranted criticism personally.

12 JANUARY

Your daily life is about to become busier, and if you're returning to work you'll catch up on projects.

13 JANUARY

Friday the 13th! You may discover your expectations have been unrealistic, providing you with the opportunity to set things right. A meeting could be ideal.

14 JANUARY

You will enjoy being with like-minded people. It's also a good day to review finances and put a steady budget in place.

15 JANUARY

A surprise change of plan or circumstance needn't derail your plans. Avoid gambling and be practical instead.

16 JANUARY

You may experience a slight case of Mondayitis and will need to brush up your communication skills, especially with people you find difficult.

17 JANUARY

Find the time to express yourself well as you may be prone to getting the wrong end of the stick. You'll enjoy a reunion.

18 JANUARY

News to do with finances or your personal life will be intense, but careful negotiations and discussions will produce results.

19 JANUARY

A positive and upbeat attitude will reap rewards. Ensure you research important matters to avoid making mistakes.

20 JANUARY

The next four weeks will be ideal to find a fresh approach, not only to someone special in your life but also to money management.

21 JANUARY

The new moon supermoon in Aquarius signals a fresh perspective on values and how you express these in your daily life, so consider your priorities and follow them.

22 JANUARY

Over the coming weeks you'll begin to see your finances and personal commitments in a new light. Consider how your personal life impacts these areas.

23 JANUARY

Key developments in your personal or financial life will ask that you consider a fresh approach to these important aspects of your life.

24 JANUARY

You are thinking creatively and ingenuously but may also be prone to forgetfulness, so be sure to focus a little bit extra.

25 JANUARY

It's a good day for a get-together and romance could blossom. It's also a good day to alter the terms of some of your personal or financial commitments.

26 JANUARY

The moon in Aries will encourage you to be outgoing and discuss important matters with experts and advisers. Seek support if necessary as it will be available.

27 JANUARY

Take a little extra time with your communications and travel as these may be prone to mix-ups and delays.

28 JANUARY

Be practical with personal, financial and domestic matters as you will gain the opportunity as a result to enjoy being spontaneous and do something different.

29 JANUARY

The Taurus moon will bring out your love of comfort and of like-minded people, friends and family.

30 JANUARY

This is a productive day on which you'll appreciate doing something different and the company of an upbeat group of people.

31 JANUARY

You'll enjoy a short trip or a shopping spree but you must avoid overspending and overindulging, which you will regret.

February

1 FEBRUARY

It's a good day to invest in your home. Someone in your family or close by may need your help. An expert's advice will be useful at home.

2 FEBRUARY

Trust your intuition, as it is spot on. It's a good day to invest time in someone you love.

3 FEBRUARY

You are communicating well yet someone may get the wrong end of the stick. Aim to be super clear to avoid misunderstandings.

4 FEBRUARY

Be prepared to be spontaneous, as you may be surprised by a development or someone's news. Avoid both financial and emotional gambling.

5 FEBRUARY

The Leo full moon signals a fresh chapter in the way you share some of your duties, space at home or finances and, for some, legal matters. Avoid making snap decisions.

6 FEBRUARY

It's a better day for discussions and you could overcome differences, so take the initiative. A trip or visit will be fun.

7 FEBRUARY

The Virgo moon will bring out your ability to focus on details, which will enable you to be particularly effective at work and with your projects.

8 FEBRUARY

You'll enjoy an impromptu get-together and news may be positive concerning a personal matter.

9 FEBRUARY

It's a good day for talks to do with finances. You may make an important commitment now.

10 FEBRUARY

Talks and meetings will be intense. You may reveal your deeper feelings for someone. If you're investing, avoid being easily influenced.

11 FEBRUARY

You'll appreciate the opportunity to invest in yourself and someone you love. A purchase or commitment could provide you with more stability but you must choose wisely.

12 FEBRUARY

A meeting or short trip could be ideal. It's a lovely day for romance, self-development, spiritual pursuits and the arts.

13 FEBRUARY

The Scorpio moon will motivate you to look beyond the obvious. You'll enjoy a social or work meeting.

14 FEBRUARY

Happy St Valentine's Day! The moon in Sagittarius for the next two days will encourage you to be outgoing and expressive. Enjoy the romance.

15 FEBRUARY

A lovely romantic or arts-oriented get-together will be enjoyable; just avoid forgetfulness. You'll also enjoy music and film.

16 FEBRUARY

It's a good day to make a commitment to someone special in your personal life and also financially.

17 FEBRUARY

Be practical, as you'll manage to be productive and can make the changes you wish to see, especially in your personal life. Just avoid appearing pushy.

18 FEBRUARY

You're communicating well with those close to you and can make some wonderful agreements that bring defining changes into your daily life.

19 FEBRUARY

It's another good day for putting changes in motion, especially in your environment and neighbourhood and through travel.

20 FEBRUARY

The new moon in Pisces signals a fresh chapter financially or in your personal life. You may experience a therapeutic trip or meeting. A debt may be repaid.

21 FEBRUARY

Be prepared to consider new arrangements and try to see matters from someone else's point of view. Avoid misunderstandings and gambling.

22 FEBRUARY

This is a good day for meetings and get-togethers. You may receive beneficial work or financial news.

23 FEBRUARY

The Aries moon will encourage you to voice your opinions and discuss important work matters with those they concern.

24 FEBRUARY

A reunion or get-together may be more significant than meets the eye so be sure to reach out, especially regarding family, finances and self-development.

25 FEBRUARY

You'll appreciate the opportunity to cocoon and spend time on your home life, family and property.

26 FEBRUARY

You'll enjoy treating yourself and those close to you to a little luxury but you must avoid overspending and overindulging, which you'll regret.

27 FEBRUARY

A lovely get-together with someone you find inspiring will be uplifting. Avoid forgetfulness.

28 FEBRUARY

It's a varied and busy day ideal for getting things done but you must avoid being easily distracted and subsequently making mistakes.

March

1 MARCH

You'll gain insight into someone's feelings, so be prepared to listen carefully and trust your impressions.

2 MARCH

Developments at home will require focus and a little fact finding. It's a good day for do-it-yourself projects, and if you're moving this promises to be a good start. Just avoid minor bumps and scrapes.

3 MARCH

You'll enjoy a short trip or visit but you must keep an eye on the road more than usual. A little do-it-yourself may appeal but be careful to avoid minor accidents. Someone may need your help.

4 MARCH

Be proactive and enjoy improving your home life. Some Sagittarians will find a trip and meeting require thought. Avoid erratic drivers.

5 MARCH

Someone close may surprise you, so be prepared to be spontaneous and enjoy doing something different.

6 MARCH

You'll enjoy a change in your usual activities, so be adaptable. You may receive surprisingly good news or bump into an old friend.

7 MARCH

The full moon in Virgo spotlights a fresh chapter in your interests such as your favourite activities, studies or even travel.

8 MARCH

You may be drawn to reconfiguring how you share duties, finances or space.

9 MARCH

You'll be drawn to looking for balance in particular arrangements including certain agreements, so be prepared to make changes.

10 MARCH

You will enjoy doing something fun, such as a get-together, shopping spree or trip somewhere lovely.

11 MARCH

This is an active, outgoing weekend. You may enjoy a change of environment or a visit. Organise a date! Be careful with travel and avoid erratic drivers and mix-ups.

12 MARCH

Someone close may be feeling sensitive. If it's you, take time out to gain a sense of nurturance. This is a good time for self-development and clearing the air if you have argued.

13 MARCH

This may be a moody start to the week, but as the day goes by you'll feel more dynamic and productive. Look at mending bridges if possible.

14 MARCH

Take the time to consider someone else's point of view but avoid being pressured. You'll appreciate the arts, music and romance.

15 MARCH

Romance could blossom and you'll be drawn to investing in yourself and someone special. A trip will be romantic but you must avoid delays and erratic drivers.

16 MARCH

Double-check details of plans and schedules to avoid delays. Misunderstandings are possible so be super clear.

17 MARCH

Financial and personal matters are best approached carefully. You must avoid impulsiveness. When you do you could make great strides.

18 MARCH

Consider looking outside the box at your circumstances to avoid being stuck in one mindset, especially regarding someone special.

19 MARCH

This is a good day to be bold and express yourself, making noteworthy changes in your environment and improving relationships.

20 MARCH

It's a good time for a financial review and to improve your environment. You'll enjoy a reunion or will hear good news at work or from someone close.

21 MARCH

The Aries new moon is a good time to start something new in your personal life. You may be drawn to travelling and to developing your writing and speaking abilities.

22 MARCH

It's a good time to improve communications and domestic circumstances. You may need to update a communications device or vehicle.

23 MARCH

You're ready to enter fresh territory, especially financially. You're also ready to view yourself and someone special in a new light.

24 MARCH

A reunion, work meeting or social event may be complex, but if you face circumstances head on you will succeed.

25 MARCH

You'll appreciate the opportunity to unwind and spend time with favourite people. However, some interactions may be more intense than others, so organise meetings wisely.

26 MARCH

You'll enjoy a reunion if you didn't already yesterday. You'll gain a deep insight into someone special.

27 MARCH

Developments at home and, for some, at work will merit a careful approach to avoid misunderstandings, so you'll need to be on your toes.

28 MARCH

Key developments in your personal life, family or at home will grab your focus. Be practical for the best results.

29 MARCH

The moon in Cancer will bring out your intuitive side, so be sure to trust your instincts. Avoid taking people's random comments personally.

30 MARCH

A surprise change of pace will be refreshing. A personal or business partner may have good news or wish to make a commitment.

31 MARCH

It's a good day to be proactive and outgoing and put some of your plans in motion, even if this seems challenging.

April

1 APRIL

It's a lovely day to improve domestic dynamics and decor. You'll enjoy a visit or a trip somewhere beautiful.

2 APRIL

A change in your usual routine will be refreshing. You'll appreciate the opportunity to beautify your home, family or yourself.

3 APRIL

Key discussions are best handled carefully and tactfully as misunderstandings may arise, especially in connection with family, home and money.

4 APRIL

Focus on the details both at work and in your projects for the best results and to avoid making unnecessary mistakes.

5 APRIL

Your help will be needed, especially at home, with family and for some in relation to a short trip. If you need help it will be available. It's a good day for self-development.

6 APRIL

The full moon in Libra signals a new chapter in your general direction such as with your career or status. For some this will be due to changes at home or in your environment.

7 APRIL

You may experience a surprise. It's a good day to be spontaneous and beautify your environment. It's also a good day for a beauty treatment or a trip somewhere beautiful.

8 APRIL

Meetings, get-togethers and romance will be drawcards. It's a good day to take the initiative but you must avoid impulsiveness.

9 APRIL

You'll feel passionate about your activities and will be drawn to improving your environment and completing outstanding chores. Just avoid arguments.

10 APRIL

The moon in your sign for the next two days will be motivating and productive. However, you must avoid appearing overbearing for the best results.

11 APRIL

Expect key news and meetings at home. Work developments are likely to be upbeat. It's a good time to make changes both at home and work.

12 APRIL

Be practical with developments at work as you are likely to be busy, and also be cooperative.

13 APRIL

Be prepared to consider another person's point of view and look for new ways to approach old themes to avoid arguments.

14 APRIL

It's a good day to aim to co-operate and, if necessary, to compromise. Avoid a Mexican stand-off. A reunion will be enjoyable.

15 APRIL

This is a lovely day to make improvements at home and enjoy the company of someone you love. It's also a good day to review your finances and make a commitment.

16 APRIL

A trip or visit will be enjoyable. Romance can flourish. It's another good day to improve your home or environment.

17 APRIL

Double-check you're not seeing circumstances through rose-coloured glasses and find ways to communicate your wonderful ideas and plans.

18 APRIL

A busy or chatty day will keep you on your toes. Your secret to success lies in using tact and diplomacy.

19 APRIL

The lead-up to an eclipse can be intense, so take things one step at a time. Avoid feeling pressured into making decisions if possible by being tactful.

20 APRIL

The total solar eclipse in Aries will kick-start a new chapter at home or with family or a property. Be prepared for hard work and avoid a battle of egos.

21 APRIL

You may receive key news. Try to get important paperwork and key talks agreed upon before the end of the day to avoid having to review them at a later date.

22 APRIL

Be practical, as you can achieve a great deal and enjoy fun and upbeat developments. Just avoid a battle of egos and rushing.

23 APRIL

Another busy or chatty day will bring entertaining developments your way, so take the initiative and plan something fun if you haven't already.

24 APRIL

This is a lovely day for meetings and get-togethers. A great deal can be achieved, so be positive. It's a good day for a health or beauty appointment.

25 APRIL

If you're looking for a commitment from someone this could be the day. It's a good day to make financial decisions and for self-development.

26 APRIL

Someone close such as a colleague or partner may have news for you. If they are a little moody avoid taking it personally.

27 APRIL

An unexpected change of plans is best navigated spontaneously as you may enjoy doing something different.

28 APRIL

Certain aspects of your life may seem stuck, making this an excellent time to plan something fun and upbeat.

29 APRIL

Someone close may surprise you. You'll enjoy being spontaneous and going outside your comfort zone if necessary. Just avoid making rash decisions.

30 APRIL

A little planning will achieve a happy and calm day and your efforts will be worthwhile.

May

1 MAY

It's a good time to review finances and personal investments with a view to finding better ways to move ahead.

2 MAY

You'll enjoy a reunion and the chance to invest time in your home and someone special. A personal project may need to be reviewed.

3 MAY

You're looking for balance above all else and this will be a good measure for conversations to avoid them becoming difficult.

4 MAY

Take a little extra time to get on with people as it's likely there will be misunderstandings. Travel may be delayed. Avoid distractions.

5 MAY

The lunar eclipse in Scorpio signals a fresh chapter in your social circle and loyalty to groups and organisations. You may be drawn to spending time with someone special.

6 MAY

You'll appreciate a return of your characteristic energy levels as the weekend progresses. You may enjoy a reunion or a return to an old haunt.

7 MAY

Trust your instincts as they are spot on. It's a lovely day for get-togethers and to self-nurture and nurture others. Avoid taking someone else's moods personally.

8 MAY

This is a productive day but not everyone will be operating at your speed. Just avoid delays and misunderstandings.

9 MAY

You will receive surprise news. For some this will be at work and for others in your personal life.

10 MAY

A serious matter deserves a serious approach. You will manage to make important changes by looking outside the box.

11 MAY

Be prepared to gain fresh perspective regarding your options financially and in your personal life.

12 MAY

A domestic matter will progress with a patient and dedicated attitude. You may enjoy a reunion and repay a debt.

13 MAY

It's a great day for deepening your relationship with those you care about and also for making a personal or financial commitment.

14 MAY

There is a dreamy quality to the day that makes it ideal for self-development and get-togethers or a trip somewhere beautiful.

15 MAY

Key news or a get-together will be memorable as you turn a corner in a domestic or shared circumstance.

16 MAY

You're about to begin a more abundant phase at home, with family or in a personal relationship.

17 MAY

An upbeat and productive day will enable you to reach many of your goals but you must avoid being stubborn about changes that are inevitable.

18 MAY

This is a good time to reconsider some of your principles and values, especially if they no longer suit your personal or domestic circumstances.

19 MAY

The Taurus new moon signals a fresh chapter in a personal relationship or creative project. It's a good day to discuss finances, especially those concerning your home.

20 MAY

This is going to be a busy day so ensure you plan activities and projects you love.

21 MAY

Your favourite activities and fun events will appeal. However, emotions will run deep so you must avoid allowing disagreements to escalate to conflict.

22 MAY

It's a great day for improving relationships and mending bridges, especially if you've recently argued with someone. It's also a good day for romance.

23 MAY

Past disagreements could resurface, so if you sense tension in the air avoid adding to it and instead find ways to collaborate.

24 MAY

You're extremely perceptive and sensitive to other people's moods, so if people are happy or sad then so will you be! Try to maintain perspective.

25 MAY

You're productive and can achieve a great deal, but again you must avoid being drawn into arguments or intrigue.

26 MAY

Someone close may surprise you with pleasant and unexpected news. You'll enjoy being spontaneous and doing something different.

27 MAY

It's a great day for spending time at home and with those you love in your favourite activities, so be sure to invest in a little comfort and relaxation.

28 MAY

There are chores and work that must be completed and, luckily, it's a good time to dig in. Avoid both financial and emotional gambling.

29 MAY

A perceptive and light-hearted approach to the day will be productive. It's a good time to organise a get-together.

30 MAY

Your chatty, outgoing nature will be appreciated, especially at work and in your general activities.

31 MAY

Look for balance both at work and home to avoid overtiring yourself and having unrealistic expectations.

June

1 JUNE

A diligent and careful approach to your plans and financial situation will pay off. Avoid feeling pressured by others and take breaks when you can.

2 JUNE

A lovely reunion or news from someone from your past may be more significant than meets the eye. Changes at home could provide more security.

3 JUNE

In the lead-up to the full moon life may become more intense. Avoid taking other people's feelings personally.

4 JUNE

The full moon in Sagittarius signals a fresh chapter in your personal life and, for some, at work or in your health situation. Someone close has unanticipated news or will arrive unexpectedly.

5 JUNE

Someone close or you yourself may have intense feelings that must be expressed. Just avoid arguments as they will escalate quickly.

6 JUNE

You finances will benefit from close scrutiny. An expert's help may be useful.

7 JUNE

Think laterally about developments, especially those to do with finances and your personal life.

8 JUNE

A talk with someone who has original viewpoints will be insightful, so ensure you touch base with someone whose ideas you value.

9 JUNE

It's a good day for meetings and a short trip somewhere beautiful. It's also a good day for health and beauty treats.

10 JUNE

You'll enjoy dreaming a little and indulging in the arts, film and music. Just avoid absent-mindedness.

11 JUNE

A mini financial review may appeal to you as a way to get on top of your finances. You'll also enjoy a reunion or return to an old haunt.

12 JUNE

It's a productive day, and meetings and a short trip may be enjoyable.

13 JUNE

Keep an eye on financial transactions and avoid making assumptions in communications to avoid misunderstandings.

14 JUNE

A stubborn character may behave true to form so you'll need to avoid disputes by being willing to negotiate and collaborate.

15 JUNE

Some communications and meetings will proceed very smoothly but others may create tension. Avoid delays and mix-ups.

16 JUNE

The Gemini moon will help you to negotiate and communicate with those you must collaborate with, so it's a good day to forge agreements.

17 JUNE

Communications and transactions will merit careful focus as you may need to rethink some of your plans.

18 JUNE

Make a wish at the new moon in Gemini, which signals a fresh chapter in a close relationship such as a romantic partnership or business alliance.

19 JUNE

It will be important to establish common ground because otherwise a lack of clarity could cause disagreements.

20 JUNE

You or someone close may feel a little sensitive, so take time out and organise a treat during the day or at home.

21 JUNE

It's the solstice! Celebrate life and its many positive aspects but be careful with communications, as some matters may otherwise cause needless tension.

22 JUNE

You'll enjoy being outgoing and upbeat with your activities and communications. A short trip or meeting may be therapeutic.

23 JUNE

A meeting or trip will be uplifting. There are healing attributes to the day that you'll appreciate.

24 JUNE

This is a good weekend for mending bridges with anyone you have argued with. It's also a good time to get ahead with chores.

25 JUNE

It's an excellent day to dream a little. However, you may be forgetful and must avoid misunderstandings and delays by planning travel carefully.

26 JUNE

A sudden or unexpected development will mean a change of plan. You may receive unexpected news from someone. Avoid making rash decisions if possible.

27 JUNE

It's a good day for meetings and to discuss important domestic and personal matters.

28 JUNE

Your intuition is spot on, so trust your instincts. However, you may feel intense emotions and must check these to avoid making rash decisions.

29 JUNE

There are healing and therapeutic aspects to the day. Someone close may need your help. It's a good day to make a commitment to someone.

30 JUNE

It's a good day to make a financial commitment, especially with someone close. You'll enjoy a reunion.

July

1 JULY

You'll appreciate spending time with someone special and on favourite interests. You'll also enjoy deepening a special relationship. A trip or visit will be fun.

2 JULY

Expect a surprise and be prepared to adapt to prevailing circumstances or to an abrupt change of plan.

3 JULY

The full moon in Capricorn shines a light on shared concerns such as joint finances and duties, especially those at home or with family.

4 JULY

Be prepared to be practical with your long-term decisions, especially those that concern personal and financial matters.

5 JULY

It's a good day to be outgoing and research your options, especially at work and with your favourite plans and activities.

6 JULY

It's a good day for research about long-term plans, especially financially. A personal or domestic expense must be carefully weighed up.

7 JULY

This is a lovely day for a spontaneous get-together. You may be pleasantly surprised by news at work or from someone close.

8 JULY

You may receive positive news from someone close and shared efforts will be productive. It's a good day to sort out communal finances and duties.

9 JULY

Strong feelings are likely to emerge, and while romance thrives on a little tension all-out stress is a passion killer. Avoid arguments.

10 JULY

You'll enjoy meeting like-minded people and discussing plans. It's a good day to focus on details but you must avoid being overly analytical.

11 JULY

As Mercury enters Leo you'll express yourself more passionately and will inspire others, but you must avoid putting people offside.

12 JULY

Someone close may need your help, and if you need advice it will be available. Avoid taking other people's comments personally and also avoid minor bumps and scrapes.

13 JULY

A chatty, upbeat couple of days will bring out your sunny side, so be yourself as you'll see great results from taking the initiative.

14 JULY

You'll enjoy an impromptu meeting with someone fun. If you are making long-term commitments, ensure you have all the facts.

15 JULY

Your empathic sensitive side will come out and will be ideal for reading the room, but you must avoid taking other people's comments personally.

16 JULY

You'll enjoy using pleasant relaxation techniques such as meditation. It's a lovely day for self-development.

17 JULY

The Cancer new moon signals a fresh chapter in a shared circumstance such as a domestic or financial arrangement. Avoid arguments, as they will escalate.

18 JULY

You may be more assertive than usual, which will benefit your projects, but you must avoid appearing overbearing.

19 JULY

You are productive right now and can achieve a great deal but you must avoid taking on too much at once and appearing rash.

20 JULY

This is an excellent day for taking time out with someone you love and for a trip somewhere beautiful such as the ocean, and also to indulge in the arts, romance and music.

21 JULY

It's a good day to reach an agreement financially and to make a commitment. Just avoid feeling pressured and do your research first.

22 JULY

You or someone close may have very strong feelings, so check your own feelings aren't running away with your better sense. This could be a therapeutic time.

23 JULY

Someone close has an upbeat and energetic effect. If you find this empowering you'll enjoy the situation but you may experience a surprise.

24 JULY

You'll be looking for balance and a fair go in your activities and conversations and may ask for this from someone in return.

25 JULY

You're motivated to see the results you want now but not everyone has the same viewpoint, so ensure you maintain perspective.

26 JULY

The moon in Scorpio will bring out your passionate side and you'll engage more deeply with your projects and those you love.

27 JULY

Key financial circumstances merit careful thought. If you are making large investments ensure you have done adequate research.

28 JULY

This is a good day for research, especially with a project or decision you already know will have profound repercussions.

29 JULY

It's a good weekend to combine healthy, outdoors activities with the need to be disciplined, especially financially and with your interpersonal dynamics.

30 JULY

Romance, relaxation and generally treating yourself and others to a little luxury will appeal. Avoid overspending, as you'll regret it.

31 JULY

In the lead-up to the supermoon some matters may appear more intense, so be sure to pace yourself.

August

1 AUGUST

The full moon supermoon in Aquarius spells a new chapter in which you may reconsider your main priorities and values. It's a good day for a favourite project or activity.

2 AUGUST

It's a good day for serious discussions, especially to do with the finances, study, travel and commitments.

3 AUGUST

Trust your gut instincts, especially where an agreement or arrangements must be made. The more precise and factual you are the better it will be.

4 AUGUST

You'll enjoy the arts and music and the company of someone special, but you must focus a little more on details to avoid making mistakes.

5 AUGUST

An active and outgoing day will prove successful. You'll enjoy sprucing up your home and a short, revitalising trip.

6 AUGUST

Your home, family or a property will take your focus as you visit someone or receive guests and enjoy an upbeat or even therapeutic time.

7 AUGUST

You may experience a slight case of Mondayitis so you must be super meticulous with arrangements and communications. You'll need to collaborate carefully.

8 AUGUST

A patient and understanding approach to someone who can be stubborn will be successful, especially if developments take you by surprise.

9 AUGUST

Be prepared to be spontaneous, especially with collaborations, as you may be surprised by someone's news or developments.

10 AUGUST

This is a better day for meetings and get-togethers, especially regarding your favourite activities and with like-minded people. A trip could be fun.

11 AUGUST

A versatile and upbeat outlook will grease the wheels of communications and collaborations. Just avoid forgetfulness.

12 AUGUST

There are healing aspects to the day, especially at home and regarding shared ventures, duties and responsibilities. It's a good day for collaboration.

13 AUGUST

Romance and your appreciation of beauty and love will blossom. If you're shopping avoid overspending, as you may regret it.

14 AUGUST

It's a perfect day to spend with someone you care about and to mutually support and nurture each other's plans, projects and ideas.

15 AUGUST

You'll gain traction with a favourite project or venture and a trip will be enjoyable. It's a good day to plan travel and review your finances.

16 AUGUST

The new moon in Leo signals a fresh phase in a shared venture that promises to be active and upbeat. You must avoid making rash decisions.

17 AUGUST

Be positive about your plans as they have a chance to succeed. The key to success lies in taking care with research.

18 AUGUST

Your communication skills are on form so be confident, especially if you must push into fresh territory.

19 AUGUST

You're looking for some peace, harmony and balance this weekend and you'll find it in your favourite hobbies such as sport, the arts and adventure.

20 AUGUST

Double-check you're on the same page as someone close as decisions that concern you both will be the correct ones.

 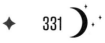

21 AUGUST

You're in a proactive and dynamic phase and will shine. Be prepared to discuss your projects with someone close. Avoid power struggles.

22 AUGUST

While you're keen to plan and put projects in motion you must avoid making assumptions, so double-check that everyone is on the same page.

23 AUGUST

It's a good time to look at the feasibility of your plans. Try to get important paperwork completed now to avoid having to review it over the coming weeks.

24 AUGUST

Certain limits or restrictions may cause delays, so be patient and avoid minor arguments by using careful negotiation skills.

25 AUGUST

It's all systems go, so take the initiative with your carefully made plans as you could be super productive.

26 AUGUST

While you prefer a fast-paced life sometimes there are benefits to slowing down, such as this weekend. Nevertheless, being active and outgoing will appeal.

27 AUGUST

A meeting, get-together or news will provide a solid framework for you moving forward. A commitment or financial transaction may be significant.

28 AUGUST

You'll gain a sense of appreciation for how hard you're working to reap rewards, as things begin to fall into place.

29 AUGUST

It's a good day to discuss sensitive topics with someone close as you're likely to come to a solid agreement.

30 AUGUST

Be inspired and imaginative but also prepared to work hard towards your goals.

31 AUGUST

The Pisces full moon supermoon spotlights a fresh chapter in your personal life. For some this will involve travel and for others be due to financial developments.

September

1 SEPTEMBER

Be prepared to consider another person's point of view as their values may be very different from yours. Avoid making rash decisions.

2 SEPTEMBER

You're communicating well but you may be prone to speaking before thinking things through, which will be counterproductive.

3 SEPTEMBER

Your key to success relies on good collaborative and communication skills, so be prepared to listen and co-operate for the best results.

4 SEPTEMBER

A key interest, collaboration, relationship or project will proceed with less obstruction over the coming weeks, and you may already receive encouraging news today.

5 SEPTEMBER

You'll enjoy improving your immediate environment such as your office and a meeting will be enjoyable. Romance could blossom.

6 SEPTEMBER

A reunion will bring you back up to date with someone important. For some, today's events will revolve around a financial review or trip to an old haunt.

7 SEPTEMBER

It's a good day for talks, a financial review and discussing collaborations.

8 SEPTEMBER

There's a fortunate aspect to the day's proceedings. You'll enjoy music, your favourite activities, fun and laughter, so plan an event if you haven't already.

9 SEPTEMBER

You may feel more emotional than usual, making this a good time to channel excess energy into fun activities and finding time to nurture yourself and someone you love.

10 SEPTEMBER

It's a great day to deepen your relationships and go over common ground to validate that you're on the same page.

11 SEPTEMBER

You have a wonderful chance to review or repair plans and relationships, so take the initiative with talks. Just avoid being stubborn.

12 SEPTEMBER

You're productive and efficient, so put your energy into your plans as your efforts will succeed.

13 SEPTEMBER

It's a good day to focus on the details and nitty-gritty of financial and personal commitments to ensure you're on the right track.

14 SEPTEMBER

It's an excellent time to get paperwork shipshape, especially if you're planning a fresh commitment or venture.

15 SEPTEMBER

The new moon in Virgo signals a fresh chapter in a favourite project, relationship or activity. For some this will involve careful planning and financial expertise.

16 SEPTEMBER

You'll enjoy a fun get-together, trip or domestic development. You may be surprised by an impromptu event.

17 SEPTEMBER

Take time out to enjoy some rest and recuperation, as you or someone close may feel frustrated or antagonistic.

18 SEPTEMBER

The Scorpio moon for the next two days will motivate you to be productive and effective, especially at work and financially, so take the initiative.

19 SEPTEMBER

You may be easily influenced and prone to daydreaming, so avoid delays and misunderstandings. A meeting will be enjoyable and romance and the arts could thrive.

20 SEPTEMBER

You are super productive, so be sure to work hard as your efforts will be rewarded. Avoid overspending and overindulging, which you'll regret.

21 SEPTEMBER

You'll derive a great deal of satisfaction from your work and projects but you must avoid overtiring yourself.

22 SEPTEMBER

Good organisational skills will provide great results in the activities you undertake. Avoid making rash decisions.

23 SEPTEMBER

The sun in Libra for the next month at the zenith of your chart will encourage you to create more balance in your life through the activities you undertake.

24 SEPTEMBER

It's possible someone will have hurt feelings, either at work or at home. Avoid rushing and you will prevent minor accidents.

25 SEPTEMBER

Meetings and get-togethers will gain their own momentum. A go-ahead attitude will reap rewards but you must keep an eye on maintaining perspective.

26 SEPTEMBER

Think clearly about the repercussions of your decisions as this will enable you to work out the best path for you to take.

27 SEPTEMBER

This is a good time to work towards your career and financial goals by being practical and methodical.

28 SEPTEMBER

You'll feel inspired by some of your projects and activities and, if not, this is a good time to look for more exciting projects.

29 SEPTEMBER

The Aries full moon signals a fresh phase in your commitments, activities and, for some, regarding travel. Avoid making rash decisions.

30 SEPTEMBER

You'll feel motivated to get things done and clear a backlog of chores at home. A fun and upbeat reunion will appeal.

October

1 OCTOBER

You can't please everyone all the time, so bear in mind that some activities may not go as well as you would like but that others will be a treat.

2 OCTOBER

This is a good time for reviewing your finances and projects to ensure you're still on track. Travel and some meetings may be delayed. Avoid distractions.

3 OCTOBER

Developments will gain their own momentum, so ensure you double-check facts and details to avoid making mistakes. Be practical and avoid excessive expectations.

4 OCTOBER

The Gemini moon will bring out someone's chatty side, making this a great time to gauge where you stand with them. Avoid assuming you're on the same page.

5 OCTOBER

You'll find out whether you've over- or underestimated a circumstance, which will enable you to get back on track.

6 OCTOBER

Your ideas and opinions may differ from someone else's, but if you work towards a common goal you will succeed.

7 OCTOBER

You can obtain your hopes and goals even if you feel under pressure or tense. You'll find ways to overcome a minor hurdle.

8 OCTOBER

Be positive and find ways to enjoy your downtime with someone special. Avoid arguments, as these are likely to escalate quickly.

9 OCTOBER

A dynamic approach to your working day will work wonders but you must avoid appearing bossy, as arguments could flare up out of nowhere.

 336

10 OCTOBER

It's a good day to find a little balance in your environment and also to make a long-term commitment to a person or financial plan.

11 OCTOBER

Personal circumstances may bring out your vulnerabilities or those of someone close and you may need to help someone. If you need support it will be available.

12 OCTOBER

The next few weeks are ideal for improving your well-being. Focus on communications as mix-ups could occur.

13 OCTOBER

This is a good time to focus on work and create the stability and security you like. You may receive positive personal, work or financial news. Avoid rushing.

14 OCTOBER

The solar eclipse signals a fresh chapter in your status, career or general direction. Someone may feel vulnerable at home or in your family. It's a good time to consider a fresh communication device or travel options.

15 OCTOBER

This is a good time to look for support in your situation as you may be in an unusual circumstance.

16 OCTOBER

The Scorpio moon will bring your inner feelings to the surface, so be sure to take breaks and avoid making rash decisions.

17 OCTOBER

Unexpected news at work or a change of routine will merit a careful approach to avoid making mistakes.

18 OCTOBER

Look at life philosophically, especially if you're feeling out of sorts. You'll enjoy a lovely reunion or good news in the next two days.

19 OCTOBER

You'll enjoy a reunion or may need to review a work project. Be prepared to listen to another person's point of view to avoid misunderstandings. Travel may be delayed so plan ahead.

20 OCTOBER

It's a good day to look for peace and balance in your communications and relationships. Avoid arguments, as these will escalate quickly.

21 OCTOBER

Intense feelings are likely to surface. Despite this it's a good time to make a fresh commitment to your own happiness. Avoid misunderstandings and delays by planning ahead.

22 OCTOBER

You'll enjoy spending time doing something you love and improving your self-esteem and status. If you're shopping avoid overspending, as you'll regret it.

23 OCTOBER

Key work meetings are best approached even-handedly. Aim to channel your energy into productive work and avoid intrigue.

24 OCTOBER

You may enjoy a work, career or financial improvement and a debt may be repaid. It's a good day to make a fresh commitment.

25 OCTOBER

You'll enjoy being inspired and creative but you must avoid having your head in the clouds, as mistakes could be made.

26 OCTOBER

Find the time to plan your goals as you may otherwise be easily distracted, leaving little time for the things you'd rather be doing.

27 OCTOBER

In the lead-up to the lunar eclipse developments can be intense so find ways to de-stress, especially if your home life has been strained. Avoid arguments.

28 OCTOBER

The lunar eclipse in Taurus signals a fresh chapter in your home life or family. It's a good day for a fun get-together but you must avoid making snap decisions.

29 OCTOBER

Events will gather their own momentum and a visitor at home has news. You may enjoy a trip but you must avoid rushing.

30 OCTOBER

A slight case of Mondayitis will encourage you to take time out to self-nurture this evening. Take breaks during the day if possible.

31 OCTOBER

Happy Halloween! You'll enjoy doing something different, and changes at home or with family and your activities will be fun.

November

1 NOVEMBER

A busy, chatty day will add a light-hearted feeling to your work. You'll enjoy a short trip and getting ahead with domestic chores.

2 NOVEMBER

Trust your intuition with someone close, financially and with work projects. It's a good day to focus on people who need you.

3 NOVEMBER

Key discussions and decisions with someone at work or at home will take your focus. You'll enjoy shopping but you must avoid overspending. Romance could blossom.

4 NOVEMBER

You may be surprised by an unexpected visitor or news. You'll enjoy socialising and going somewhere different.

5 NOVEMBER

It's an excellent day to look after your health and improve your domestic circumstances through some do-it-yourself projects and repairs and improving domestic dynamics.

6 NOVEMBER

This is a good day for making the changes you'd like to see in your life, especially financially and with your favourite activities.

7 NOVEMBER

This is a good day for health or beauty appointments and a reunion. Music, the arts and romance will appeal.

8 NOVEMBER

Look for ways to establish more balance in your relationships and environment, even if doing so means you need to overcome an obstacle.

9 NOVEMBER

It's a lovely day for a reunion. You may receive a financial or ego boost. Avoid taking people's random comments personally.

10 NOVEMBER

Take the time to choose your words carefully as an ill-chosen word could do harm. It's a good day for a mini financial review.

11 NOVEMBER

You'll experience a surprise or impromptu invitation that takes you into new territory. Be spontaneous and avoid making rash decisions.

12 NOVEMBER

Strong focus on your past may arouse nostalgic feelings. It's a good time to improve your health and well-being and for self-development.

13 NOVEMBER

The Scorpio new moon signals a fresh chapter in a work or health schedule. You may receive unexpected news from a friend, family member or organisation.

14 NOVEMBER

The moon in your sign for the next two days will promote an optimistic outlook. Just avoid being unrealistic or you may come back down to earth with a bump.

15 NOVEMBER

It's a good day for work and personal get-togethers, so be sure to take the initiative.

16 NOVEMBER

An obstinate character may behave true to form, but rest assured that you will overcome obstacles with charm and diligence.

17 NOVEMBER

This is a lovely day for meetings, a trip somewhere beautiful and socialising. Romance can flourish, so if you're single keep an eye out!

18 NOVEMBER

A get-together will be enjoyable. It's an excellent day for socialising; just avoid making snap decisions.

19 NOVEMBER

Your usual outgoing and upbeat qualities will promote an optimistic outlook, especially regarding refreshing activities such as sport.

20 NOVEMBER

This is a good day to make long-term changes, especially within your social circle and with your appearance.

21 NOVEMBER

Be inspired but maintain a practical approach, especially at work and regarding finances, to avoid making mistakes.

22 NOVEMBER

Your sensitivities may arise, so take things one step at a time and avoid taking random comments personally. Your help may be required.

23 NOVEMBER

This is a good day to seek expert advice, especially in relation to finances and your duties and responsibilities.

24 NOVEMBER

Your energy levels are set to rise over the coming weeks, so find ways to channel excessive energy into fun or productive activities. You may receive unexpected news.

25 NOVEMBER

As a productive, energetic person you don't like delays, so patience will be a virtue. You may need to rethink a plan or financial matter.

26 NOVEMBER

Be prepared to think on your toes as you may be surprised by developments or news.

27 NOVEMBER

The Gemini full moon signals a fresh phase in your daily schedule such as at work or health-wise. For some a fresh personal circumstance is in the making. Avoid misunderstandings and delays by planning ahead.

28 NOVEMBER

Someone close will be feeling chatty, so this is a good day to find out a little more about how they feel.

29 NOVEMBER

A change in your usual routine or a plethora of work and activities will require patience and diligence. Rest assured you will achieve your goals.

30 NOVEMBER

Take aim at your goals as you can achieve them. Just be super clear and avoid mix-ups.

December

1 DECEMBER

Communications are going to become less rushed and more grounded over the coming weeks but you must avoid obstinacy in yourself and others.

2 DECEMBER

A financial negotiation or transaction could provide more security. This is a good day for being practical about commitments.

3 DECEMBER

Someone you find difficult to get along with may voice viewpoints that are contrary to yours. Avoid allowing disagreements to escalate as they will rapidly turn into conflict.

4 DECEMBER

This is the beginning of a more passionate phase as you'll feel drawn to expressing yourself more, but you must avoid disagreements.

5 DECEMBER

This is a good day to make great progress at work and financially, so be sure to take the initiative.

6 DECEMBER

The key to a successful day lies in attention to detail and avoiding being distracted by delays and mix-ups.

7 DECEMBER

The next two days are good for seeking agreement, especially in areas where disagreements have arisen.

8 DECEMBER

It's a lovely day to improve domestic dynamics and decor. You may enjoy a trip somewhere beautiful and the opportunity to mend bridges.

9 DECEMBER

This will be a passionate weekend ideal for getting chores done and preparing for the festive season. Just avoid impulse buys if you're shopping.

10 DECEMBER

A get-together and the chance to improve your relationships will appeal. Romance could flourish but you must avoid arguments, as it's a feisty time.

11 DECEMBER

This is an excellent day to get ahead with paperwork and for meetings at work. If you're looking for a job it's a good day to circulate your résumé.

12 DECEMBER

The Sagittarian new moon signals the chance to turn a corner at work and in your personal life and to improve your health, appearance and well-being.

13 DECEMBER

Try to get key paperwork and discussions sorted out now, especially regarding plans at Christmas or regarding travel, to avoid having to review things at a later date.

14 DECEMBER

Important news will arrive if it didn't already yesterday. Now that Mercury is retrograde it's a good time to be practical with travel and financial and personal arrangements and also with communications to avoid making mistakes.

15 DECEMBER

There is a therapeutic quality to the day that is ideal for a health or beauty treat and for a reunion.

16 DECEMBER

A trip will be therapeutic. Someone may need your help, and if you need expert advice it will be available.

17 DECEMBER

Be prepared to discuss your plans and hopes with someone close to ensure you're on the same page. Plan ahead to avoid delays and mix-ups.

18 DECEMBER

You'll enjoy a reunion at your home or someone else's. It's a good time to improve domestic decor and dynamics.

19 DECEMBER

A slight case of Mondayitis may lead you to be easily distracted, so ensure you keep an eye on clear communications to avoid making mistakes.

20 DECEMBER

You'll enjoy a reunion, beauty or health treat and the chance to prove yourself at work.

21 DECEMBER

You'll enjoy a personal or financial improvement. A get-together may come from out of the blue. Be prepared to adapt to new circumstances.

22 DECEMBER

A reunion or return to an old haunt will be enjoyable. You may experience travel or communication delays, so be patient.

23 DECEMBER

You'll appreciate the opportunity to slow down and enjoy a little comfort and luxury. Romance could flourish but you must avoid giving mixed messages.

24 DECEMBER

The more practical you are with arrangements the more smoothly your weekend will proceed. You'll appreciate a sense of security and stability and even an ego or financial boost.

25 DECEMBER

Merry Christmas! It's a lovely day for a reunion and return to an old haunt. Just avoid overindulgence, which you'll regret.

26 DECEMBER

A reunion will make your heart sing. It's a good day for improving your health, well-being and appearance.

27 DECEMBER

The Cancer full moon signals the start of a fresh chapter in a key relationship. You'll enjoy domestic developments but you must avoid misunderstandings and travel delays.

28 DECEMBER

You are a proactive and dynamic character, and when everyone else is operating at a slower pace you can find this frustrating. Avoid rushing and erratic drivers.

29 DECEMBER

Venus, the planet of love and money, enters your sign, bringing focus to these qualities. You may enjoy an ego or financial boost and a lovely get-together.

30 DECEMBER

The Leo moon will bring out your upbeat and dynamic side and you'll wish to be active, so be sure to find activities in which you can blow off steam.

31 DECEMBER

Happy New Year! You'll enjoy celebrating with like-minded people but you must avoid overspending and overindulging as you'll regret it on New Year's Day.

CAPRICORN

21 December - 20 January

FINANCES

As Pluto enters Aquarius, the sign that rules your finances, at the end of March and again in January 2024 (where it will be for the next 20 years) you are on track for major financial changes. You will discover new ways to earn, save and invest money. Developments in 2023 will presage important options that will see you through the next two decades, so be sure to carefully plan money management. You may be particularly drawn to innovative investment options and potentially even digital currencies, but you must be super careful to research your options to avoid making costly mistakes.

HEALTH

As you will be forging a fresh path for yourself in 2023 it's vital you look after your own well-being, as you may otherwise find yourself feeling overwhelmed or ambushed by developments. Luckily, you will have Mars in your sixth house of health for the first quarter, making this an ideal time to self-nurture and put in place a valid health schedule that supports your mind, body and soul for the entire year. Just be sure to pace yourself at the end of August and December, as you may be liable to overdo things then.

LOVE LIFE

This year you'll be inclined to try something new either within your existing relationship or, if you're single, in your pursuit of a companion/partner – and even in your approach to love itself. You're ready to let go of an outmoded model or concept of love and embrace new ways to love someone and be loved yourself. The times when considerable change is likely to occur, and therefore the times to embrace change, will be at the end of March, during the months of April and May and then in late October and during December. You may even be surprised by the circumstances that arise.

CAREER

Change right across the board is on the cards for you in 2023, so if you've already been undergoing career and personal developments you'll be a master of many skills by now! If you've miraculously avoided considerable change in your personal life and career it will be more difficult to continue doing so this year, so be prepared to navigate new options and especially during the two eclipse seasons at the end of April/early May and during October. You are in the process of metamorphosis and your career is a vital aspect of who you are, so be prepared to spread your wings!

HOME LIFE

This is an excellent year to make changes at home, especially in the first quarter of the year. The end of March and the month of April are likely to see considerable developments in your personal life and/or family. If you're particularly creative this will be an excellent time for do-it-yourself projects and home improvement. You may also be ready to up- or downsize, depending on your circumstances. You'll appreciate the chance to reflect your personality and self in your surroundings and domestic circumstances and thus feel more at home, both literally at home and in yourself.

January

1 JANUARY

Happy New Year! Strong feelings will arise due to developments in your personal life, so take things carefully.

2 JANUARY

It's a lovely day to reconnect with someone special and also for shopping and a financial review. However, you must avoid overspending and may need to settle a debt first.

3 JANUARY

A fresh approach to someone special and to a personal and financial matter will reap rewards.

4 JANUARY

It's an excellent day to embrace a new attitude to your personal life, someone special and your finances, wealth and abundance.

5 JANUARY

You may hear unexpected news and will enjoy being spontaneous. You'll make changes at home or within your environment that you'll appreciate.

6 JANUARY

The Cancer full moon will bring a fresh chapter in a personal relationship for December Capricorns and a fresh daily routine for January Capricorns.

7 JANUARY

You'll appreciate the opportunity to review paperwork and enjoy a lovely reunion or short trip.

8 JANUARY

An unexpected development will keep you on your toes and you'll enjoy entering new territory or doing something different.

9 JANUARY

It's a lovely day to enjoy close family relationships and friendships and to improve domestic decor and dynamics.

10 JANUARY

You prefer life to be at an even pace, so even though you find dynamic developments thrilling be sure to pace yourself.

11 JANUARY

It's a good day for a mini financial review as a debt may need repaying. Take the time to listen to someone else's viewpoint to avoid mix-ups.

12 JANUARY

Your home life is about to become busier, so be prepared for dynamic change in your personal and domestic lives.

13 JANUARY

Friday the 13th! You may discover your expectations have been unrealistic, which will provide you with the opportunity to set things right. A meeting could be ideal.

14 JANUARY

It's a good day to review financial and personal commitments. You'll enjoy a get-together and romance could thrive.

15 JANUARY

Be prepared to reorganise a plan or activity at short notice as someone may be unpredictable or your situation may change. Avoid misunderstandings.

16 JANUARY

You'll feel passionate about getting things done but not everyone has the same drive as you, so be patient.

17 JANUARY

It's a good time to review some of your projects to ensure you're happy with them and to make changes if you're not.

18 JANUARY

News in your personal life will be poignant. Avoid having knee-jerk reactions and find the time to research your options.

19 JANUARY

Many emotions will be bubbling up to the surface so be sure to take breaks when you can to avoid them bubbling over, especially at work.

20 JANUARY

The next four weeks will be an ideal time to find a fresh approach to someone special in your life and also to money management.

21 JANUARY

The new moon supermoon in Aquarius signals a fresh chapter that will present you with different options in your personal life and financially. Consider your priorities carefully.

22 JANUARY

You may hear unexpected news at home or undertake an unusual trip. You may begin to see your finances and personal commitments in a new light.

23 JANUARY

This year it's in your interest to find fresh ways to approach important areas of your life, and there's no time like the present.

24 JANUARY

You're thinking creatively and imaginatively but you may also be prone to high expectations, so be sure to maintain perspective.

25 JANUARY

It's a good day to alter the terms of some of your personal or financial commitments. You'll enjoy sprucing up your appearance.

26 JANUARY

The moon in Aries will encourage you to be outgoing but you must avoid appearing bossy, especially at work.

27 JANUARY

You may be prone to seeing life through rose-coloured glasses, so be realistic. Take a little extra time with your communications and travel as there may be mix-ups and delays.

28 JANUARY

Be practical and plan ahead with communications and travel. You'll enjoy doing something a little different this weekend, so take the initiative!

29 JANUARY

The Taurus moon will bring out your love of comfort and of like-minded people, friends and family. Romance could blossom.

30 JANUARY

This is a lovely day for meetings as you will be productive and efficient. Be prepared to be spontaneous.

31 JANUARY

Financial and personal discussions may take your focus. It's a good day for negotiations and making agreements.

 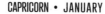

February

1 FEBRUARY

Your expertise will be in demand, and if you need expert advice such as financial or personal guidance it will be available.

2 FEBRUARY

Trust your intuition as it is spot on, especially regarding your work, finances and health.

3 FEBRUARY

You have natural empathy with someone close and your help may be needed. Romance could blossom.

4 FEBRUARY

You may experience unexpected developments. Unanticipated delays with travel and computer glitches may arise, so be sure to back up devices.

5 FEBRUARY

The Leo full moon signals a fresh chapter in a relationship. You may discover you have different points of view and values. Avoid making snap decisions.

6 FEBRUARY

It's a better day for discussions and you could overcome differences, so take the initiative with talks. It's a good day to improve your appearance. Avoid overspending.

7 FEBRUARY

The Virgo moon will bring out your practical side, so focus on how to attain your goals in the most realistic way.

8 FEBRUARY

You'll enjoy an impromptu get-together and may receive unexpected news or a financial or ego boost.

9 FEBRUARY

It's a good day for talks at work, in your personal life and to do with finances, as you could come to an important agreement.

 350

10 FEBRUARY

Talks and meetings will be important and you could make a great deal of changes now. You may reveal your deeper feelings for someone.

11 FEBRUARY

You'll appreciate your free time and will enjoy spending it with someone special, so make a date if you haven't already!

12 FEBRUARY

This is a lovely day to relax and indulge in the arts, romance, music and film.

13 FEBRUARY

The Scorpio moon will motivate you to engage fully in your activities. However, you may be seeing life through rose-coloured glasses so be practical.

14 FEBRUARY

Happy St Valentine's Day! You'll be feeling outgoing and expressive, so enjoy romance. Key financial decisions or a commitment may be made.

15 FEBRUARY

It's one of the most romantic days of the year for you. You'll enjoy a get-together, music, the arts and film. Avoid forgetfulness.

16 FEBRUARY

Finances will deserve attention. It's a good day to make a commitment to someone special or to yourself if you feel you've strayed off the path.

17 FEBRUARY

The Capricorn moon will bring out your sensible, reasonable side but you must avoid being stubborn and seeing only the negatives.

18 FEBRUARY

This is a good day to be spontaneous and embrace all that is working well for you, as developments show progress. You may be pleasantly surprised at home.

19 FEBRUARY

It's a good day for putting changes in motion, especially in your personal life and financially. You may embrace a new look or approach to someone close.

20 FEBRUARY

The new moon in Pisces signals a fresh chapter in your personal life. You may experience a healing development that indicates positive progress.

21 FEBRUARY

An unexpected development is likely. Be prepared to see matters from someone else's point of view. Avoid misunderstandings and travel delays by planning ahead.

22 FEBRUARY

You'll enjoy meetings and get-togethers. You may receive good news from a friend or family member.

23 FEBRUARY

The Aries moon will bring out your talkative side and you'll wish to discuss your plans and projects with those they concern.

24 FEBRUARY

You'll enjoy getting together with someone you admire. It's a good day for romance and for improving your self-esteem and appearance.

25 FEBRUARY

Make the time to enjoy the company of someone special. A short trip or meeting will be out of the ordinary or spontaneous.

26 FEBRUARY

Take time out to enjoy a slower pace if possible. You'll enjoying treating yourself or someone special to a little luxury or comfort.

27 FEBRUARY

Developments are likely to go well although you may be easily distracted, so be sure to plan ahead well. Avoid overspending.

28 FEBRUARY

It's a chatty, busy day, so be prepared to think outside the square and embrace new ideas and projects.

March

1 MARCH

You'll feel motivated to get things done but you must avoid rushing, as you will miss key details.

2 MARCH

Today's developments will involve important financial concerns for some Capricorns and for others key talks or a trip. Avoid making mistakes and minor accidents.

3 MARCH

It's a good day for a trip, talks and get-togethers, and if you need advice or help from an expert it will be available. Someone may need your help.

4 MARCH

Someone you admire will have an influence over your day. You'll enjoy fun get-togethers but you may discover you have different priorities.

5 MARCH

Someone close may surprise you, so be prepared to be spontaneous. You may enjoy an impromptu get-together or trip.

6 MARCH

A surprise or unusual development will keep you on your toes. If you're shopping avoid overspending as you'll regret it.

7 MARCH

The full moon in Virgo spotlights a fresh chapter in a shared concern such as joint finances or responsibilities. Consider the long-term ramifications in your decisions.

8 MARCH

You are essentially a practical character, and once you double-check facts and figures you tend to hope for the best, as you will over the coming two days.

9 MARCH

You'll be drawn to looking for balance in particular arrangements involving finances, shared duties and mutual support.

10 MARCH

It's a good day for a get-together with a like-minded person and also to discuss finances and common goals.

11 MARCH

You'll enjoy a change of pace or of place. It's a good weekend for romance and creativity. You'll enjoy music, dance and film but you must avoid forgetfulness.

12 MARCH

Someone close may be feeling sensitive. If it's you, take time out to gain a sense of nurturance. This is a good time to improve your appearance, self-esteem and spirituality.

13 MARCH

The moon at the zenith of your chart may bring your emotions to the surface but you will also feel motivated to excel, so be sure to focus on your goals.

14 MARCH

You may be easily distracted, so be sure to focus at work and on financial matters to avoid making mistakes.

15 MARCH

This is a romantic day, so organise a treat if you haven't already. However, you must avoid misunderstandings, gambling and making mistakes.

16 MARCH

You will gradually feel more practical over the coming days but you must first double-check the details of financial and work plans to avoid making mistakes.

17 MARCH

Key news is on the way. For many this will be to do with finances and for some in your personal life. Be vigilant, as mistakes can still be made.

18 MARCH

This is a super-romantic time that is ideal to deepen romantic relationships; however, you must avoid making rash decisions.

19 MARCH

Take the initiative with plans you'd like to instigate as this is a good time to make changes. Be bold but not impulsive.

20 MARCH

You're a practical person but sometimes you can be seen as stubborn, and currently you risk pushing or rushing an agenda that could put you in a negative light.

21 MARCH

The Aries new moon is a good time to start something new financially or in your personal life. A key get-together or surprise news will add to the excitement.

22 MARCH

Be prepared to initiate talks and work towards the changes you'd like to see in your personal life, as this is a good time to instigate them.

23 MARCH

You'll appreciate the opportunity to turn a corner in your personal life. Be prepared to look outside the box and be brave.

24 MARCH

As you embrace a bolder approach to your own activities you'll inevitably encounter a challenge. Rest assured you can overcome obstacles with a positive attitude.

25 MARCH

You'll enjoy a lovely get-together with someone you admire. Romance could blossom but you must avoid intense topics.

26 MARCH

The Gemini moon will bring out your chatty side and you'll enjoy discussing new options that open up to you.

27 MARCH

A trip, meeting or domestic development may surprise you. There are therapeutic aspects to the day's events. An expert's help will be useful.

28 MARCH

It's a good day for a short trip and for discussions and meetings. Your expertise may be in demand, and if you need expert advice it will be available, especially financially.

29 MARCH

Trust your instincts as your intuition is spot on. However, you may feel super sensitive so avoid taking other people's random comments personally.

30 MARCH

A surprise trip, visit or domestic development is likely. News at work or financially will be constructive. You may experience an ego or financial boost.

31 MARCH

You may need to leave your comfort zone in some discussions and relationships, but rest assured you'll be heard although you must avoid obstinacy.

April

1 APRIL

You'll enjoy a trip or visit somewhere beautiful such as to the coast. It's a romantic day and you'll be drawn to the arts and beauty. Retail therapy will appeal.

2 APRIL

An impromptu get-together, visitor or trip will be enjoyable so be adventurous. Just avoid overspending if you're shopping.

3 APRIL

You have strong beliefs and may encounter opposition to some of your plans if you didn't already. Avoid mix-ups and travel delays.

4 APRIL

Focus on the details, especially financially, to avoid making mistakes. You have an analytical mind but may be prone to overcritical thought, so take things one step at a time.

5 APRIL

It's a good day for discussions and negotiations, especially financially. Your expertise is in demand. If you need help it will be available.

6 APRIL

The full moon in Libra signals a new chapter in a key project, hobby or relationship. For some this will be due to changes in your environment.

7 APRIL

You may experience a surprise. Be spontaneous, as you'll enjoy impromptu get-togethers or a romantic meal or outing. Avoid overspending.

8 APRIL

Meetings, get-togethers and romance will appeal. It's a good day to take the initiative but you must avoid impulsiveness. A trip or change of routine will be enjoyable.

9 APRIL

You'll feel passionate about your guests and activities and will be drawn to improving your status and home life. Just avoid arguments.

10 APRIL

The next two days will involve meetings and developments that require you to be sociable and to improve your communication skills.

11 APRIL

Expect key news, a trip or meeting. This is an excellent time to make long-term changes, especially in your personal life, home or family circumstances.

12 APRIL

The moon in your sign for the next two days will help you to be super practical and put measures in place that help you to accommodate change.

13 APRIL

Be prepared to consider another person's point of view and look for new ways to approach old themes to avoid arguments.

14 APRIL

You will not always agree with everyone, and certain discussions will be productive while others get stuck. Approach financial disagreements carefully.

15 APRIL

Consider looking at disagreements from a fresh perspective. Avoid gambling and be practical.

16 APRIL

You'll enjoy a trip or visit and romance could flourish. It's a good day for a beauty or health boost. Avoid overspending if you're shopping.

17 APRIL

An ideal circumstance may materialise, but if you still disagree over key principles with someone special be inspired to find a fresh way forward.

18 APRIL

The Aries moon will motivate you to be proactive. Your secret to success lies in using tact and diplomacy.

19 APRIL

You'll get a great deal done but you may feel under pressure, so pace yourself to avoid making mistakes that arise from rushing.

20 APRIL

The total solar eclipse in Aries will kick-start a fresh agreement within a relationship or contract, so be bold but avoid a battle of egos.

21 APRIL

You may receive key news. Try to get important paperwork and key talks agreed upon to avoid having to review them at a later date.

22 APRIL

You may be drawn to organising travel or a fresh communication device and to updating or repairing a vehicle.

23 APRIL

The Gemini moon will bring about a chatty day with family, at home and with someone you love. Just avoid tense topics for the best results.

24 APRIL

This is a lovely day for meetings and get-togethers and reviewing some plans, if necessary to fine-tune them. It's a productive time, so be proactive.

25 APRIL

If you are looking for a commitment this could be the day. It's a good day to make personal or financial decisions.

26 APRIL

Trust your instincts, especially with someone close and at work. Don't take random comments personally. Avoid gambling.

27 APRIL

Someone will surprise you and you'll appreciate the opportunity to be a little spontaneous. A domestic, family or creative project can advance.

28 APRIL

Someone may surprise you with their news as they will be more talkative and reveal their feelings. Avoid taking random comments personally.

29 APRIL

A change in your usual routine will take you somewhere new or bring changes at home. You'll enjoy being proactive but you must avoid making rash decisions.

30 APRIL

It's a good day to make plans with someone close, especially in relation to travel and, for some, domestic matters. Avoid erratic drivers and aggression.

May

1 MAY

It's a good time to review your personal life and long-term plans, especially where they concern someone else.

2 MAY

You'll enjoy a reunion or return to an old haunt. You may receive positive financial news, and if you're shopping you must avoid overspending.

3 MAY

Financial and personal matters are best approached from a practical point of view to ensure you're maintaining perspective regarding long-term plans.

4 MAY

You may discover you have over- or underestimated a circumstance, which will provide you with the opportunity to put things right.

5 MAY

The lunar eclipse in Scorpio signals a fresh chapter in your activities and interests. You may be drawn to altering who you spend time with.

6 MAY

A passionate and committed approach to your ventures will pay off but you must avoid appearing overzealous, as conflict may arise.

7 MAY

You'll appreciate the opportunity to do something you love but you must avoid overtiring yourself or overcommitting to work.

8 MAY

You'll enjoy socialising and networking and can achieve a great deal, so be positive.

9 MAY

An unanticipated development could take you somewhere new. You may receive an unexpected guest.

10 MAY

The moon in your sign will bring out your practical side, which will help you to achieve your goals both at home and at work.

11 MAY

The next two days are ideal for setting realistic goals, especially financially and at work. Be prepared to consider new ideas.

12 MAY

This is an excellent time to stride ahead with your projects, especially at work and financially, so be proactive.

13 MAY

You'll enjoy a get-together or return to an old haunt. A trip or meeting will be productive.

14 MAY

Be inspired and trust your instincts with a fun trip or visit. You'll appreciate the chance to develop your interest in the arts and music.

15 MAY

Key news or a get-together will be significant and may even provide good news moving forward. Romance could blossom.

16 MAY

You're about to begin a more abundant phase in your relationships, agreements or financially but you may initially need to overcome a hurdle.

17 MAY

Be prepared to tackle some minor hurdles that will help you improve your communication skills.

18 MAY

This is a good time to reconsider some of your loyalties, personal decisions and investments. Be prepared to step into new territory.

19 MAY

The Taurus new moon signals a fresh chapter at home or with family and someone special. A trip or the opportunity to update a communications device or vehicle will appeal.

20 MAY

A get-together or financial transaction will be significant and could provide a sense of stability, but you must avoid making snap decisions.

21 MAY

You'll appreciate the opportunity to spend more time at home and with someone you love. It's a good day to put change into action but you must avoid feeling pressured or pressuring someone else.

22 MAY

It's a great day for improving relationships and mending bridges, especially if you recently argued. It's also a good day for do-it-yourself projects and improving your environment.

23 MAY

This continues to be a volatile time and past disagreements could resurface, so if you sense tension in the air find ways to collaborate.

24 MAY

It's a good day to bring forward your nurturing side as someone may need your help, and if you need advice it will be available.

25 MAY

You can achieve a great deal but you must avoid stubbornness, especially if existing arguments re-emerge. Someone may appear more boisterous than usual.

26 MAY

You may be surprised by developments, for some at work and for others at home. Be spontaneous, as you'll be glad you were.

27 MAY

Someone who motivates you to be more extroverted will behave true to form and you'll enjoy doing something fun, so take the initiative.

28 MAY

It's an excellent day to focus on clearing a backlog of chores, but you must avoid reigniting old disputes and look for fun ways to get on.

29 MAY

The more precise you are at work the better it will be, as you may be prone to forgetfulness.

30 MAY

Your creative side emerges when the moon is in Libra, and you'll appreciate the opportunity to add a little sparkle to your life both at home and at work.

31 MAY

Look for balance, especially if you're experiencing mid-week tiredness and are feeling vulnerable. Avoid taking other people's random comments personally.

June

1 JUNE

A diligent and careful approach to your plans and projects will pay off. Avoid feeling pressured by others and take breaks when you can.

2 JUNE

A lovely reunion, meeting or trip to an old haunt may be important as it will have long-term significance.

3 JUNE

You'll enjoy being sociable and outgoing and romance could flourish, but you must find ways to relax and avoid pressuring others.

4 JUNE

The full moon in Sagittarius signals a fresh chapter in connection with a group, friend or organisation. Someone has unexpected news. You may enjoy an impromptu trip.

5 JUNE

Intense thoughts, feelings or conversations may bring out strong feelings. A visit or trip will deserve a patient approach.

6 JUNE

The moon in your sign will encourage you to be practical with circumstances, especially where they impact your personal life and goals.

7 JUNE

Be prepared to look outside the square at personal and financial matters to obtain positive results.

8 JUNE

You'll appreciate discussing circumstances with someone whose opinion you trust to gain invaluable perspective.

9 JUNE

It is a good day for get-togethers and, for some, short trips. You may be drawn to a little retail therapy but you must avoid overspending.

10 JUNE

You'll benefit from considering your circumstances from a fresh perspective, especially in relation to your finances and home life. Avoid making assumptions.

11 JUNE

It's a good time to reconsider some of your long-term plans, especially those associated with your home, property or family. You may return to an old haunt.

12 JUNE

The Aries moon will encourage you to be upbeat and outgoing, which is ideal for conversations, but you must avoid appearing bossy.

13 JUNE

Double-check you're on the same page as those you must collaborate with to avoid making mistakes and having unnecessary disputes.

14 JUNE

The earthy Taurus moon encourages you to be practical, which will enable you to overcome difficulties in communications, but you must avoid being stubborn.

15 JUNE

An expense will need paying, and if you're shopping you must avoid overspending. You may discover a difference of opinion with someone close and will need to find a solution.

16 JUNE

A flexible, amenable approach to conversations will bring results. Try to get an agreement on the table if possible.

17 JUNE

Be prepared to review some of your commitments, including financial circumstances. It's a good day for talks and romance.

18 JUNE

Make a wish at the new moon in Gemini, which signals a fresh chapter in a daily routine such as your work or health schedule and, for some, in your personal commitments.

19 JUNE

Be realistic about commitments you make and avoid basing them on assumptions. Double-check details if you're making a long-term financial decision.

20 JUNE

Strong emotions may arise due to tiredness or overwork, so find a way during the day to take breaks and maintain perspective.

21 JUNE

It's the solstice! You'll enjoy being with an upbeat group. Your expertise may be in demand. Aim for your goals and you will overcome obstacles.

22 JUNE

You'll appreciate the chance to be with optimistic people and spend time improving relationships.

23 JUNE

A meeting or trip will be uplifting. There are healing attributes to the day that you'll appreciate.

24 JUNE

A healthy mix of fun and enjoying time with favourite people on the one hand and clearing chores on the other will be satisfying.

25 JUNE

It's an excellent day to dream a little. To avoid misunderstandings and mix-ups, double-check your plans and arrangements.

26 JUNE

Be flexible, as you may experience an unexpected change of pace. Travel and communications may be complex, so be patient.

27 JUNE

If you need advice it will be available. You'll appreciate the opportunity to meet or speak with someone special.

28 JUNE

Being a rational person, sometimes using your intuition seems counter-intuitive yet your instincts are working at full capacity, so be sure to trust them.

29 JUNE

There are healing and therapeutic aspects to the day. It's a good day for meetings and to discuss work and health options.

30 JUNE

It's a good day for discussions to do with work, health and finances, so take the initiative. A commitment could be made.

July

1 JULY

Key news from a partner or colleague is on the way. You may receive a compliment or financial boost. A trip or visit will be fun.

2 JULY

Be prepared to be spontaneous, as a plan or development may come about unexpectedly. You'll enjoy being sociable and outgoing.

3 JULY

The full moon in Capricorn spotlights your personal life if you were born in December and signals a fresh chapter at work or health-wise for January Capricorns.

4 JULY

Consider your true priorities and direct your energy accordingly to avoid feeling a conflict of interest or being torn into different directions.

5 JULY

Consider a fresh approach to an unpredictable domestic or personal circumstance and avoid making rash decisions.

6 JULY

Before you make any decisions, ensure you have adequately researched their likely outcome as communications and developments may cause misunderstandings and delays.

7 JULY

It's a better day for communications, even though you may still be surprised by the news you receive albeit pleasantly.

8 JULY

It's a good day for get-togethers and to enjoy your favourite activities. Romance could blossom, so organise a date!

9 JULY

Be sure to double-check itineraries and plans to avoid making mistakes and assumptions. In this way you could enjoy a therapeutic, relaxing day.

10 JULY

Talks and meetings are likely to be productive and enjoyable. However, you may be seeing the world idealistically so ensure you are practical.

11 JULY

As Mercury enters Leo someone close such as a business or personal partner will be more communicative, although they may initially be a little blunt.

12 JULY

Someone close may need your help, and if you need advice it will be available. Avoid taking the comments of other people personally. Avoid minor bumps and scrapes.

13 JULY

Keep an open mind with talks and developments in areas of your life you share such as your home, duties and communal space at work.

14 JULY

You may be pleasantly surprised by work news and an impromptu guest at home. Be prepared to work a little harder than usual and you will reap the rewards.

15 JULY

You will enjoy spending time looking after yourself and those you love. It's a good weekend for self-development.

16 JULY

Shared finances and duties will benefit from discussion to avoid future misunderstandings. You'll enjoy using pleasant relaxation techniques such as meditation.

17 JULY

The Cancer new moon signals a fresh chapter in a business or personal relationship and, for some mid-January Capricorns, at work. Ensure agreements are clear.

18 JULY

Someone in your environment may be feistier than usual. Be patient, and you may find the love of life is infectious.

19 JULY

Your creative, romantic side is coming out and it's a good time for romance, but you must avoid being easily misled or distracted at work.

20 JULY

This is an excellent day for romance and to indulge in the arts, romance and music. You may be drawn to retail therapy but you must avoid overspending.

21 JULY

I's a good day to reach an agreement financially and make a commitment. Just avoid feeling pressured and do your research first.

22 JULY

An argument that has been brewing may bubble up, so to keep the peace consider looking at your long-term goals. If these overlap you can establish common ground.

23 JULY

There is a healing quality to circumstances. You will enjoy relaxing and a health or beauty treat. Misunderstandings are likely, so double-check you're on the same page as someone else.

24 JULY

Misunderstandings and delays are again possible, so look for balance to avoid feeling tired or vulnerable.

25 JULY

You'll find there is a solution regarding your ultimate goals, and this is a good day to really lean in to your favourite activities and pursue them.

26 JULY

You may need to review some of your decisions to obtain better perspective, and this is an excellent time to research your options.

27 JULY

You may enjoy a reunion and romance could blossom. Key decisions merit careful thought. Avoid making long-term decisions without adequate research.

28 JULY

This is a good day for research, especially with a project or decision you already know will have profound repercussions. Avoid being misled or pressured.

29 JULY

Plans for the weekend may differ from those of someone else, so the more you can work together to enjoy common ground the more you'll enjoy your weekend.

30 JULY

This is a romantic time but you must avoid power struggles. Find ways to relax and enjoy the day.

31 JULY

In the lead-up to the supermoon you may find life a little more intense than usual. Explore ways to relax and be patient.

August

1 AUGUST

The full moon supermoon in Aquarius spells a new chapter in your personal life. It's a good day for meetings and a trip.

2 AUGUST

Key financial or personal commitments can be made; just ensure you're not limiting your options too much.

3 AUGUST

You may be surprised by your own emotions or those of someone close. Avoid rushing, as mistakes could be made.

4 AUGUST

Double-check you're not seeing a relationship or collaboration through rose-coloured glasses. Be inspired but also practical.

5 AUGUST

You'll enjoy spending time with a fun, upbeat character. If you're shopping you must avoid overspending.

6 AUGUST

Take time out to avoid rushing, as you or someone close may be slightly accident prone or feeling under the weather.

7 AUGUST

You are generally a reliable communicator and people find you dependable; however, someone may misconstrue your viewpoints so be super clear.

8 AUGUST

This is a super-productive day for you but mix-ups are possible, so be super clear for the best results.

9 AUGUST

Your expertise and advice will be in demand. However, those who ask for your help may surprise you with their viewpoints.

10 AUGUST

This is a better day for meetings and get-togethers and you'll enjoy a trip or visit.

11 AUGUST

A chattier and more upbeat atmosphere will contribute to a happier mood, and a degree of fun and enjoyment will return.

12 AUGUST

This is a healing day, so if you have recently argued with someone it's an excellent time to mend bridges. It's also a good day for collaboration.

13 AUGUST

You'll enjoy a reunion. Romance and your appreciation of beauty and love will blossom. It's a good day to discuss shared matters, including finances.

14 AUGUST

A work colleague or partner will be more upbeat and more inclined to share their time and feelings with you.

15 AUGUST

Discussions and relationships can develop, so this is a good day for talks and romance could also thrive.

16 AUGUST

The new moon in Leo signals a fresh phase in a business or personal partnership. Someone may even surprise you. Just avoid putting yourself in a weak financial position.

17 AUGUST

Someone who can be unpredictable may behave true to form, so avoid taking their behaviour personally.

18 AUGUST

You are super productive and this is an excellent day to focus on work. It's also a good time to plan ahead for domestic or shared projects.

19 AUGUST

You'll find the relaxation you're looking for and may enjoy making changes at home or in your environment.

20 AUGUST

You enjoy sharing quality time with those you love. Some do-it-yourself projects or home improvement will appeal. Avoid overindulging, as you'll regret it tomorrow.

21 AUGUST

You are in a productive phase. However, your abilities may threaten others so avoid power struggles.

22 AUGUST

A little extra research will go a long way as your efforts may be questioned, so be prepared with answers and avoid power struggles.

23 AUGUST

It's a good time to be super practical with your plans, especially in your collaborations. You may receive key news in a shared venture.

24 AUGUST

An upbeat and outgoing approach will be effective yet you may be slowed down by rules and restrictions, so be patient.

25 AUGUST

It's all full steam ahead, so take the initiative with your carefully laid plans as you'll be efficient and productive.

26 AUGUST

You'll appreciate the opportunity to slow down later on today and during the day to complete chores and socialise.

27 AUGUST

Slow and steady being your mantra for the day will enable you to wind down and enjoy time out. It's a good day to make a commitment.

28 AUGUST

This is another productive day, so take the initiative as your efforts will be appreciated.

29 AUGUST

Be prepared to look outside the box at your various options, especially in your personal life and at home.

30 AUGUST

You'll enjoy dreaming a little, and artistic and creative Capricorns will put clever form to inspired ideas.

31 AUGUST

The Pisces full moon supermoon spotlights a fresh chapter in your finances and, for some, in your personal life. Be prepared to make informed decisions after you research facts.

September

1 SEPTEMBER

Slow and steady wins the race, so avoid rushing as you will attain your goals by being methodical and efficient.

2 SEPTEMBER

Be prepared to take a little extra time to listen to the thoughts of a business or personal partner to avoid mix-ups.

3 SEPTEMBER

It's a good day for a trip somewhere lovely and a reunion. It's also a good time to review domestic plans.

4 SEPTEMBER

You may receive key news from a business or personal partner or collaborator. Meetings or a reunion are likely to go well.

5 SEPTEMBER

This is a good day for get-togethers and also for romance, so take the initiative!

6 SEPTEMBER

A financial matter will catch your attention. You may need to review an agreement or transaction and you'll enjoy a trip or reunion.

7 SEPTEMBER

It's a good day for talks and a financial review and to discuss collaborations.

8 SEPTEMBER

You'll appreciate the company both of work colleagues and people you love, as there is a fun aspect to interactions.

9 SEPTEMBER

Trust your intuition and look for ways to be nurturing of others, and don't forget to feather your own nest.

10 SEPTEMBER

The lead-up to the new moon is an excellent time to make a wish and place intentions, so be sure to formulate your desires.

11 SEPTEMBER

This is a good time to review some of your financial goals and meet experts and advisers who can help you proceed.

12 SEPTEMBER

You're productive and efficient and your colleagues will respond well, so put your energy into your plans as your efforts will succeed.

13 SEPTEMBER

You can add shape and form to your projects, which will lead to positive outcomes, but you must avoid perfectionism and being critical of yourself and others.

14 SEPTEMBER

You are a force to be reckoned with even if you don't realise this. Take the initiative, as your plans will succeed.

15 SEPTEMBER

The new moon in Virgo signals a fresh chapter in a shared circumstance, such as your home life or workspace. Make plans for an inspired weekend.

16 SEPTEMBER

You'll enjoy being spontaneous, especially with someone you love such as a family member. You can make positive changes at home.

17 SEPTEMBER

You are super productive but may be tired or prone to arguments, so ensure you rest up when you can.

18 SEPTEMBER

The Scorpio moon for the next two days will motivate you to enjoy your activities and schedule in fun pastimes to break up work schedules.

19 SEPTEMBER

A financial matter could be ideal but will deserve attention to avoid mistakes. You may receive a compliment or personal boost. Romance can thrive.

20 SEPTEMBER

It's a good time to work towards making the changes in your life you've been planning for a while, but you must avoid appearing overzealous.

21 SEPTEMBER

Long-term changes in your personal life and the way you share duties and/or your home life will take effect, so take the initiative.

22 SEPTEMBER

An adventurous approach to your activities will reap rewards, as your outgoing approach will be infectious.

23 SEPTEMBER

The sun in Libra for the next month will encourage you to be conciliatory in shared circumstances.

24 SEPTEMBER

You may be drawn to retail therapy but you must avoid overspending, as you'll regret it. You may feel super sensitive, so avoid taking random comments personally.

25 SEPTEMBER

Meetings and get-togethers will gain their own momentum. Organise ahead to avoid developments getting the better of you.

26 SEPTEMBER

There is advantage in seeking a fresh perspective from someone else in a shared circumstance if you cannot find common ground yourself.

27 SEPTEMBER

This is a good time to work towards your personal goals by being inspired but also practical and methodical.

28 SEPTEMBER

Arts, music and romance will appeal. Avoid making unnecessary mistakes as you may be easily distracted.

29 SEPTEMBER

The Aries full moon signals a fresh phase in your finances and, for some, in your personal life. Look for balance and avoid making rash decisions.

30 SEPTEMBER

You may be inclined to be uncharacteristically rash and indecisive at the same time, so find ways to slow down and regain your sense of balance. You may enjoy a surprise visit or trip.

October

1 OCTOBER

You'll enjoy company and a change in your usual routine. If you're travelling or organising activities outside your usual sphere be sure to plan ahead.

2 OCTOBER

A lovely trip or meeting will be productive, but you must focus on the details and facts if you're making important decisions or transactions.

3 OCTOBER

It's a good day for putting in motion plans you have already formulated. Collaborations could go well but you must avoid making assumptions.

4 OCTOBER

The Gemini moon will bring out your upbeat and chatty side, and you'll enjoy making long-term plans and organising a fun event.

5 OCTOBER

The more precise you are and the more you keep your eye on your goals the better will be the outcome, as otherwise you may be easily distracted. Rest assured you will overcome obstacles.

6 OCTOBER

You have great ideas and plans, although some of them may require cooperation from others. Just avoid feeling pressured and pressuring others.

7 OCTOBER

Developments at home and in your activities will demand extra energy, but your efforts will be worthwhile.

8 OCTOBER

Focus on favourite activities with favourite people and channel your frustrations into fun events. This will avoid any arguments that may be brewing.

9 OCTOBER

It's a good time for a mini financial review. Avoid arguments, as these are likely to escalate quickly.

10 OCTOBER

This is a good day to make a commitment to someone special and, again, to review personal or financial arrangements.

11 OCTOBER

You'll be drawn to sorting out problems rather than letting them slide. Just avoid being super sensitive and look for solutions.

12 OCTOBER

You'll appreciate the opportunity to pursue your activities but you must avoid feeling your plans can be completed in just one day.

13 OCTOBER

Pursue your passions and invest in yourself and in activities you love. Avoid making rash decisions.

14 OCTOBER

The solar eclipse signals a fresh chapter in communal concerns such as joint finances and shared duties. Avoid taking news personally and look for constructive ways ahead.

15 OCTOBER

Be prepared to be spontaneous and adaptable, as developments will require you to be flexible yet diligent.

16 OCTOBER

The Scorpio moon will encourage you to be proactive, especially with communications and your favourite interests.

17 OCTOBER

Be prepared to focus on your goals, as unexpected developments may easily distract you. Avoid impulsiveness.

18 OCTOBER

You are keen to press ahead with your projects and work, but if someone you collaborate with is less dynamic avoid allowing their mindset to dampen your spirits.

19 OCTOBER

Developments will be more significant than initially meets the eye, so be prepared to show your best side. You may enjoy a reunion or trip.

20 OCTOBER

It's a good day to invest in your favourite activities and projects. Avoid arguments, as they will escalate quickly.

21 OCTOBER

Intense feelings are likely to surface. Aim to channel strong emotions into productive pursuits as you can achieve a great deal, especially at home.

22 OCTOBER

You're communicating well and will enjoy being outgoing. It's a good time for personal development, romance and a trip.

23 OCTOBER

A passionate approach to your activities will be productive but you must avoid appearing overzealous.

24 OCTOBER

It's an excellent day to make a commitment to particular interests, work and activities. You may experience a financial or ego boost.

25 OCTOBER

While you're generally adept at being practical you may feel a little absent-minded, so you will need to focus a little more than usual.

26 OCTOBER

You'll regain a boost in energy levels later today that will enable you to attain your goals. Just avoid taking other people's circumstances personally.

27 OCTOBER

In the lead-up to the lunar eclipse developments can be intense, so aim to find ways to de-stress and especially while you're travelling and involved in complex communications.

28 OCTOBER

The lunar eclipse in Taurus signals a fresh chapter in a relationship or plans such as travel, study or spiritual interests. Avoid making snap decisions.

29 OCTOBER

A trip or conversation will be significant and sports and other interests will appeal. Just avoid rushing and relax.

30 OCTOBER

It's a good time to aim towards building a strong foundation for yourself. It's also a good day to improve domestic dynamics or decor.

31 OCTOBER

Happy Halloween! You'll enjoy decorating your house in a Halloween theme, and welcoming different people into your home and visiting the homes of other people.

November

1 NOVEMBER

You'll enjoy a fun, chatty atmosphere. It's a great time to focus on your projects, especially where you wish to change aspects of what you do.

2 NOVEMBER

A caring approach to yourself and someone close will be rewarding as you invest more time in your own well-being.

3 NOVEMBER

Key talks and meetings will illuminate where you could research a little more into the best way forward. It's a good day for romance.

4 NOVEMBER

You may be surprised by news or a change of circumstance at home or at work, so be adaptable. A trip or visit may be unexpected.

5 NOVEMBER

You have an ability to truly focus on your projects so you may be frustrated by interruptions. A financial or personal matter will require focus.

6 NOVEMBER

You'll appreciate the opportunity to make changes that have long-term repercussions. Romance and collaborations will thrive.

7 NOVEMBER

It's a good day for talks and meetings, especially those at work and to do with finances.

8 NOVEMBER

You'll be drawn to establishing peace and a fair go in negotiations and talks. Aim for your goals and you will achieve them despite challenges arising.

9 NOVEMBER

This is a good day to boost your own status and direction in life. You may feel a little vulnerable, so remind yourself how capable you are.

10 NOVEMBER

Logistics and strategy are two of your strengths, and these qualities will be useful today.

11 NOVEMBER

A sudden or unexpected change of plan is best met with a flexible attitude. Avoid minor bumps and scrapes and erratic drivers.

12 NOVEMBER

This is an excellent time to focus on your goals and personal interests; be prepared to travel or enter fresh territory in the process.

13 NOVEMBER

The Scorpio new moon signals a fresh chapter in a project, career direction and, for some, at home. You may receive unexpected news.

14 NOVEMBER

You'll be truly engrossed in work, chores and busy activities, so remember to take time out to catch your breath.

15 NOVEMBER

It's a good day for socialising and networking and also to discuss joint finances.

16 NOVEMBER

You have a strategic mind and are able to see beyond facts and figures, and you may need to persuade someone close of your abilities.

17 NOVEMBER

You have charm and motivation on your side, making this an excellent day for work projects and interviews. You may experience a financial or ego boost.

18 NOVEMBER

This is a super-productive day and you could boost your status, making this an excellent time to invest in yourself and your abilities. Romance could thrive. Avoid overspending.

19 NOVEMBER

You'll enjoy doing something different with favourite people and could truly improve the feel-good factor in your life.

20 NOVEMBER

You can boost your status and career, so take the initiative as your plans can succeed.

21 NOVEMBER

You like to plan ahead, yet if you give a little leeway with arrangements you'll avoid feeling disappointed by developments.

22 NOVEMBER

An optimistic outlook will reap rewards. However, your sensitivities may arise so take things one step at a time and avoid taking random comments personally.

23 NOVEMBER

This is a super-productive day but you must avoid feeling too frustrated by rules and regulations and find inspiration and relaxation.

24 NOVEMBER

A positive and upbeat approach to your various ventures will reap rewards. Aim to be flexible with shifting goal posts.

25 NOVEMBER

You excel when you work within boundaries yet some boundaries are too strict even for you. Avoid feeling frustrated by making constructive plans.

26 NOVEMBER

An impromptu trip or change in your usual plan will be enjoyable but you may need to first consider someone else's opinions.

27 NOVEMBER

The Gemini full moon signals a fresh phase in your domestic or personal life. Be careful with communications to avoid mix-ups. You'll enjoy a lovely reunion.

28 NOVEMBER

Be prepared to think things through and discuss your plans with those they concern to avoid minor disappointments.

29 NOVEMBER

You may need to persuade someone of the benefits of your ideas, but as you're enthusiastic and well organised you will succeed.

30 NOVEMBER

You'll enjoy meetings and socialising. Just be super clear to avoid mix-ups.

December

1 DECEMBER

Communications will become more manageable over the coming weeks, and the next two days are excellent for making both personal and financial commitments.

2 DECEMBER

You'll enjoy a lovely get-together or reunion. If you're shopping you may find a good deal but you must avoid overspending.

3 DECEMBER

Take your time with discussions and travel to avoid frustrations. You may disagree with someone and must avoid a battle of egos.

4 DECEMBER

You'll feel super passionate about a particular venture or interest, and directing your energy into it will be productive.

5 DECEMBER

This is a good day to make great progress with your activities and finances and in your personal life, so take the initiative!

6 DECEMBER

You'll be looking to establish more balance and clarity within some of your relationships but you must avoid assuming everyone else is too.

7 DECEMBER

Be open to the opinions of others but avoid taking them personally, especially if you disagree. Avoid overspending.

8 DECEMBER

A get-together or trip will be therapeutic on many levels. This is a good time for a reunion or trip to an old haunt.

9 DECEMBER

The Scorpio moon will bring out your deepest feelings and you may be surprised by your reaction to some developments, talks and news.

10 DECEMBER

You'll feel motivated by a favourite activity such as sports. This is a good day for self-development and for get-togethers.

11 DECEMBER

You're communicating well and your projects will advance as a result, so be positive! It's a good day to review your finances.

12 DECEMBER

The Sagittarian new moon may bring a surprise, for some at home and for others socially. Be adventurous, as it's a good time to broaden your mind.

13 DECEMBER

Try to get key paperwork and discussions finalised now, especially regarding your travel, personal and work plans.

14 DECEMBER

The moon in your sign encourages you to formulate fun plans moving forward, especially regarding travel and your favourite hobbies.

15 DECEMBER

There is a therapeutic quality to the day, and you'll find some get-togethers uplifting. You may benefit from a financial or ego boost.

16 DECEMBER

An outgoing approach to your various activities and options this weekend will be productive, as you'll gain the chance to do something different.

17 DECEMBER

It's an excellent day to relax, especially if you overdid some activities yesterday. Avoid forgetfulness and gambling.

18 DECEMBER

Meetings and discussions will be productive and you'll enjoy a reunion or return to an old haunt.

19 DECEMBER

The next two days will be productive if you're working, but you must focus a little more than usual as you may be forgetful.

20 DECEMBER

A social or networking event will be fun and you may meet an upbeat, outgoing crowd.

21 DECEMBER

Be prepared to adapt to circumstances, especially if you're in a different environment. Expect a surprise development or unanticipated delay.

22 DECEMBER

You'll enjoy a reunion or return to an old haunt. It's a good time to transform your environment.

23 DECEMBER

It's a lovely time to enjoy a different environment or company, and travel will take you somewhere you love.

24 DECEMBER

A reunion or nostalgic time will warm your heart. Be prepared to plan for a visit or guests.

25 DECEMBER

Merry Christmas! There is a beautiful and mystical aspect to your Christmas Day that you'll enjoy. Romance will thrive.

26 DECEMBER

You'll enjoy socialising and your favourite activities, indulging in music, art and romance. If you're shopping, avoid overspending.

27 DECEMBER

The Cancer full moon signals the start of a fresh chapter in your daily, work or health routine. You'll enjoy a trip but must factor in the chance of delays and mix-ups.

28 DECEMBER

Meetings will be a focus, and the secret to success lies in planning ahead to avoid delays or disappointments.

29 DECEMBER

This is an excellent time to make changes both in your personal life and at work. You may be drawn to improving your appearance and health.

30 DECEMBER

The Leo moon will bring out your upbeat and dynamic side and you'll enjoy beginning new year festivities early. Just ensure you pace yourself.

31 DECEMBER

Happy New Year! You'll enjoy celebrating with like-minded people and will manage to avoid overindulgence (and a headache) by calling it quits when necessary.

AQUARIUS

20 January - 18 February

FINANCES

The way you earn your money will change in 2023, as will the way you spend, save and invest money. Some Aquarians will be intent on maintaining established ideas about wealth and finances, such as working with cash and savings accounts, while others will be more adaptable to embracing new opportunities. If you find your financial practices are no longer effective in your new circumstances this year be prepared to seek trusted financial advice to ensure you stay on top of your own changing financial situation.

HEALTH

There will be no avoiding certain health matters that you've been unwilling to face over previous years, such as bad habits or addictions. Certain health and well-being circumstances will surface, so it will be nigh-on impossible to ignore niggling health concerns. On the bright side, this makes 2023 the ideal time to bring fresh health practices into being as they're likely to be effective and you'll embrace them. You will be inclined to let old-fashioned ideas go, preferring instead to consider new treatments and health ideologies. A holistic approach to a healthy mind, body and soul will work, so be proactive.

LOVE LIFE

The big news this year is the entry of Pluto into your sign, where it will remain for the next two decades from 2024 onwards. In 2023 you'll gain a glimpse into a new circumstance in your love life that may be due to a fresh relationship that develops during the year or due sadly to the end of an existing one if you feel you've grown apart. The change in your love life will be driven by self-development and a need for excitement, adventure and even something or someone different. If you've been planning a family or an addition to your family be prepared to embrace the new, especially in October.

CAREER

You are likely to be stepping into something new this year that will represent an exciting opportunity to learn a fresh skill set and embrace a different daily routine or work circumstance. Don't be daunted by the fact you'll be entering new territory as it's a case of 'time and tide wait for no man'; an avalanche of change is unavoidable for you now. Luckily, you may gain the opportunity to alter your daily life one step at a time. That being said, some Aquarians will need to embrace an all-or-nothing approach to changes in your work life so you're motivated to leave the past behind.

HOME LIFE

You will undergo considerable changes in your home, family and domestic lives in 2023, which is something you'll need to adapt to initially although it will signal the start of a new chapter moving forward for the next two decades; be sure to plan ahead carefully. If you've been looking for more freedom of movement or a move or are planning renovations or positive change in your family this is something you can attain now, and the key periods for making positive change in this regard will be at the end of March and in April, August and October but you must be prepared to innovate.

January

1 JANUARY

Happy New Year! Strong feelings will arise in connection with the past, work or health matters. Be prepared to pace yourself.

2 JANUARY

It's a lovely day to reconnect with someone special and return to an old haunt. You may be feeling nostalgic or be missing someone, so take things one step at a time.

3 JANUARY

Venus steps into your sign, putting your focus on love and money over the coming weeks. It's a good time to invest in yourself.

4 JANUARY

This is a good time to improve your health, appearance and well-being and for spiritual self-development. You'll enjoy a reunion.

5 JANUARY

An unexpected meeting or get-together will be enjoyable, so be spontaneous.

6 JANUARY

The Cancer full moon brings a fresh chapter in a personal relationship or a creative project. Be prepared to innovate.

7 JANUARY

You'll appreciate the opportunity to go over old ground and review some of your plans for the year. You may also enjoy a reunion.

8 JANUARY

It's a good time to find ways to boost your health and well-being. You may receive unexpected news or bump into an old friend. Romance could blossom, so take the initiative.

9 JANUARY

You'll enjoy get-togethers and the chance to improve both work and domestic relationships.

10 JANUARY

It's a good time to improve your communication skills to ensure you're on the same page as someone special.

11 JANUARY

Be prepared to go over old ground, especially in connection with domestic and financial matters, as you devise a workable plan.

12 JANUARY

Communications, travel and general developments are going to be picking up pace, so be prepared to embrace a busier phase.

13 JANUARY

Friday the 13th! This is a lovely day for self-development and improving your appearance and wardrobe. You'll enjoy socialising or a reunion.

14 JANUARY

Be prepared to make a commitment to a particular plan of action such as a work or health schedule.

15 JANUARY

Be innovative, as this special quality will be useful for avoiding being wrong-footed by a sudden or unexpected change of plan.

16 JANUARY

Someone you share time or space with may seem moody. Avoid contributing to their mood swings and maintain an optimistic outlook.

17 JANUARY

While Mercury prepares to end its retrograde phase there will be mix-ups, and a misunderstanding or travel delays are possible so be patient.

18 JANUARY

Key news from the past or to do with work or health will arrive. The news is likely to be intense and you may wish to research facts.

19 JANUARY

It's an excellent day to get things done, especially in conjunction with friends, groups and organisations, so be proactive.

20 JANUARY

The sun will be in your sign for the next four weeks, bringing a more optimistic and upbeat month your way. Be adventurous.

21 JANUARY

The new moon supermoon in Aquarius signals a fresh chapter in your personal life if it's your birthday today and, for many, at work or health-wise.

22 JANUARY

This is a good time to make a commitment to someone or something you love. You may be surprised by developments.

23 JANUARY

You'll appreciate the opportunity to bring more beauty and love into your life, and the next two days are ideal for romance and making positive changes.

24 JANUARY

You're creative and imaginative, which will add to a romantic atmosphere, but you must avoid overspending.

25 JANUARY

This is a romantic time and you'll be drawn to improving your appearance. A reunion will be enjoyable.

26 JANUARY

The moon in Aries will encourage you to be outgoing but you must avoid appearing bossy, especially at work, and making snap decisions.

27 JANUARY

You may be prone to seeing life through rose-coloured glasses, so be realistic. A social or networking event will require you to focus and to avoid delays and mix-ups.

28 JANUARY

A realistic and practical approach to chores and finances will turn out well for you and clear a backlog of work and/or debt.

29 JANUARY

The Taurus moon will bring out your love of the company of like-minded people. You may be surprised by an impromptu get-together.

30 JANUARY

Adopt an open mind and be proactive about get-togethers and meetings as they will be enjoyable or productive.

31 JANUARY

It's a lovely day to invest in yourself. You may enjoy a shopping spree, compliment or financial or ego boost.

February

1 FEBRUARY

It's a good day for a health treat. You may repay a debt or receive a payment.

2 FEBRUARY

It's a super-productive time for you, especially at home and with creative projects. You'll be drawn to music, romance and the arts.

3 FEBRUARY

Trust your instincts as your intuition is spot on, but avoid taking someone's negative comments personally.

4 FEBRUARY

You may be surprised by a sudden change of plans. Unanticipated delays with travel and computer glitches may arise, so be sure to back up devices.

5 FEBRUARY

The Leo full moon signals a fresh chapter in a personal or business relationship. A fresh daily or health routine may appeal. Avoid making snap decisions.

6 FEBRUARY

Work meetings will be productive. You may be drawn to a beauty or health treat. Avoid overspending if you're shopping.

7 FEBRUARY

If you encounter arguments it may be because you discover you have different values. Consider a fresh perspective.

8 FEBRUARY

You like to be spontaneous and will enjoy an impromptu get-together. You may receive an unexpected financial or ego boost.

9 FEBRUARY

It's a good day for talks at work, in your personal life and to do with finances, as you could come to an important agreement.

10 FEBRUARY

It's a good day for a reunion and a mini financial review. Work discussions are likely to go well.

11 FEBRUARY

It's a good time to make changes to your usual routine, especially those that will improve your health, well-being and appearance.

12 FEBRUARY

You will be drawn to updating your wardrobe or hairstyle and enjoying the arts and romance. Avoid overspending and overindulging, as you'll regret it tomorrow!

13 FEBRUARY

The Scorpio moon will bring your attention to your favourite interests. It's a good day for self-development but you may also be prone to daydreaming.

14 FEBRUARY

Happy St Valentine's Day! The next two days are ideal for romance. You'll appreciate the opportunity to spend time with like-minded people.

15 FEBRUARY

The arts, romance and creativity will appeal. You'll enjoy being positive about your projects at work. A trip or get-together will be healing.

16 FEBRUARY

It's a good day to make a commitment to a particular path, especially if it's your birthday, but you must avoid assuming everyone is on the same page.

17 FEBRUARY

Be practical with your plans as you could organise a lovely social event, but you must keep everyone in the loop to avoid disappointment.

18 FEBRUARY

You'll feel enthusiastic about improving your appearance and environment. Avoid overspending, especially if you're already in debt. You'll enjoy an impromptu get-together or change at home.

19 FEBRUARY

You will enjoy a reunion or return to an old haunt. It's a good day to deepen your relationships.

20 FEBRUARY

The new moon supermoon in Pisces signals a fresh chapter in your personal life and, for some, financially. It's a good day for a health appointment. Avoid gambling.

21 FEBRUARY

You're communicating well but an unexpected development may cause misunderstandings and delays, so be patient. Avoid making financial errors.

22 FEBRUARY

This is an excellent time to plan changes at home or in your environment. News from family or regarding property could be positive.

23 FEBRUARY

The Aries moon will bring out your upbeat, proactive side. However, you may be inclined to make snap decisions.

24 FEBRUARY

This is a lovely day for romance and meeting someone you admire. Singles may meet someone who seems strangely familiar.

25 FEBRUARY

It's a good weekend to relax and establish stable and secure ways ahead both financially and in your personal life.

26 FEBRUARY

A little comfort and time spent alone or with someone special will refuel your energy levels.

27 FEBRUARY

Communications or news could be ideal, but if you've found concentrating difficult recently you must avoid daydreaming, especially at work.

28 FEBRUARY

Upbeat and fun developments at home will improve your mood, and if you've been considering making changes at home it's a good day to discuss these.

March

1 MARCH

Trust your intuition, as it's spot on. It's a good day to self-nurture and treat yourself.

2 MARCH

Key financial and/or personal developments will take your focus. If you're making major decisions ensure you double-check the details.

3 MARCH

You can be super generous and currently risk being taken advantage of, so ensure your loyalties are well placed. Avoid gambling.

4 MARCH

You'll enjoy doing something active this weekend such as get-togethers with friends and sporting or outdoors activities.

5 MARCH

Expect a surprise or spontaneous get-together or trip. Double-check financial transactions to avoid making mistakes.

6 MARCH

An unexpected meeting or trip somewhere you don't normally go will be uplifting, so be spontaneous.

7 MARCH

The full moon in Virgo spotlights a fresh chapter in a business or personal partnership. Be practical but avoid limiting your options.

8 MARCH

Close scrutiny of details, facts and figures is sometimes necessary at work, but you must find ways to relax and unwind when you're at home.

9 MARCH

A balanced and calm approach to personal circumstances will reap rewards.

10 MARCH

It's a good day to discuss personal and financial matters and for meetings and communications, so take the initiative with key topics.

11 MARCH

You may be pleasantly surprised by the outcome of the day's developments. You'll enjoy unwinding at home or with family.

12 MARCH

Take a moment to consider someone else's mood as they may be feeling sensitive. Avoid taking the random comments of other people personally.

13 MARCH

You can be super generous but you must avoid overspending and overly high expectations.

14 MARCH

You will enjoy taking the initiative with personal and domestic matters but you must base your actions on the facts, not assumptions.

15 MARCH

This is a romantic day, so organise a treat if you haven't already. Avoid misunderstandings and mistakes, especially at work and home.

16 MARCH

Double-check that you're not seeing an important personal or domestic matter through rose-coloured glasses. Avoid making snap decisions.

17 MARCH

Important developments are underway that may be fast moving, so ensure they are based on facts and not supposition.

18 MARCH

You may be inclined to be idealistic at the moment and may experience a reality hit, so ensure you do your research to prevent disappointment.

19 MARCH

A strong connection with your past will be beneficial. You'll enjoy a reunion and health treat.

20 MARCH

Meetings and get-togethers could signal further change to come. You may be surprised by some developments and news from someone close.

21 MARCH

The Aries new moon is a good time to start something fresh in your personal life. You'll enjoy a reunion, news from the past or a trip.

22 MARCH

Circumstances demand you be bold and adventurous but don't take risks or engage in impulsive actions.

23 MARCH

As transformative Pluto enters your sign you'll be aware of long-term changes on the way in your personal life or at work if they haven't already arisen.

24 MARCH

Be prepared to embrace something new; you may need to disentangle some commitments to do so. Avoid hanging on to the past.

25 MARCH

Trust your instincts, especially with regard to a personal matter. You'll enjoy a lovely get-together but you must avoid contentious topics.

26 MARCH

The Gemini moon will bring out your chatty side, and you'll enjoy being with like-minded people or taking a trip down memory lane.

27 MARCH

There are healing attributes to the day and you may be surprised by some developments. Your expertise will be in demand and you may need the help of an expert.

28 MARCH

It's a good time to focus on your well-being. A financial or personal matter will take your focus. It's a good day for talks and making financial decisions.

29 MARCH

Be prepared to trust your gut instincts, especially in your personal life. Avoid making snap decisions and both financial and emotional gambling.

30 MARCH

Unexpected developments may catch you by surprise. You may bump into an old friend or discover a financial anomaly.

31 MARCH

You'll muster the energy you need to complete the week and will overcome obstacles even if through sheer willpower alone.

April

1 APRIL

There's an atmosphere of romance and relaxation around you that you'll enjoy. If you're drawn to retail therapy avoid overspending.

2 APRIL

A trip somewhere beautiful will raise your spirits. It's a lovely time for self-development and deepening your spirituality.

3 APRIL

Profound changes in your life will merit a patient approach to avoid frustration. Look at finances from a purely practical point of view.

4 APRIL

You have an analytical mind but may be prone to hypercritical thought, so avoid this by being practical.

5 APRIL

This is a good day for a mini review of your finances as developments will impress on you how important they are. You may feel sensitive, so take breaks.

6 APRIL

The full moon in Libra signals a new chapter in the way you share duties, responsibilities and, for some, joint finances. Look for balance.

7 APRIL

It's a lovely day for romance and a trip somewhere beautiful. You may bump into an old friend or hear unexpected news.

8 APRIL

Music, the arts, romance and creativity will all appeal. Sporty Aquarians will enjoy a match or training. Avoid impulsiveness.

9 APRIL

You tend to be passionate about your hobbies and activities and will immerse yourself thoroughly in these, which will bring a sense of satisfaction.

10 APRIL

Aim for your goals as you are likely to attain them. Be positive.

11 APRIL

You'll gain the confidence to move ahead and make changes, so be optimistic. A financial or personal development will be significant.

12 APRIL

Be proactive at work and plan ahead as your efforts will have clear results. Avoid doubting your own abilities.

13 APRIL

Aim to take your time processing fast-moving events by taking breaks when possible and seeking downtime.

14 APRIL

An expert or adviser will be useful. Your expertise may be in demand. A point of disagreement is best handled one step at a time.

15 APRIL

The moon in your sign will encourage you to seek fresh perspective, especially in matters you are reluctant to change.

16 APRIL

Take time out to indulge your senses and enjoy a treat. Romance can flourish, so organise a date!

17 APRIL

Be inspired but also practical. If anyone can combine inspiration with practicalities it's you, so be positive.

18 APRIL

The Aries moon will motivate you to take a proactive approach to inevitable developments. Be prepared to initiate change yourself.

19 APRIL

You are super productive but may be accident prone if you rush or cut corners.

20 APRIL

The total solar eclipse in Aries will kick-start a fresh agreement with a personal or financial agreement. Be bold, but avoid a battle of egos.

21 APRIL

Try to get important paperwork and communications finalised now to avoid having to review them over the coming weeks and months.

22 APRIL

You may receive key news if you didn't already yesterday. A trip may be particularly poignant.

23 APRIL

The Gemini moon will invoke a chatty day and the chance to connect with your environment, garden and neighbourhood.

24 APRIL

It's a lovely day to enjoy your domestic life and spend time with those you love. If you're shopping, avoid overspending.

25 APRIL

This is a good day to make a financial or personal commitment. Just avoid limiting your options too much.

26 APRIL

You are empathising well with those close to you and could gain a deeper understanding of them. Just avoid taking random comments personally.

27 APRIL

A surprise trip, meeting or domestic development will be pleasant. You may receive an unexpected guest.

28 APRIL

This is a productive day, so be positive about your workload as you can achieve a great deal. You may receive an unexpected invitation.

29 APRIL

You will enjoy being spontaneous and doing something different. A family member may have surprising news for you.

30 APRIL

It's a lovely day to relax but also to get things shipshape at home and in your environment. You'll enjoy daydreaming and being creative.

May

1 MAY

It's a good time to consider your loyalties and main purpose and direction over the coming weeks and months. Today's developments may be poignant in this regard.

2 MAY

A reunion, news or trip may be ideal, but you must avoid overspending or overinvesting if you're considering long-term outgoings.

3 MAY

As a way forward, find balance in your joint finances and shared responsibilities. Delegate if necessary.

4 MAY

You have a romantic outlook that is delightful, but you must ensure you have the facts regarding financial and domestic matters.

5 MAY

The lunar eclipse in Scorpio signals a fresh chapter in the way you share and shoulder responsibilities and joint finances. You'll enjoy a lovely get-together.

6 MAY

A passionate and committed approach to your ventures will pay off but you must avoid appearing overzealous, forgetful or erratic.

7 MAY

You'll be drawn to a more self-nurturing phase, and the need to look after someone else may arise even if they disagree.

8 MAY

A fun and upbeat approach to your work and general direction in life will be productive, which you'll enjoy.

9 MAY

Unexpected news or a surprise development needn't set the cat among the pigeons. Just keep communication channels open for the best results.

10 MAY

Be practical and realistic, especially with matters that are gaining their own momentum.

11 MAY

You may be tempted to see life through rose-coloured glasses and therefore may be disappointed when you experience a reality hit. It's a good time to find the balance between both approaches.

12 MAY

This is an excellent time for negotiations, especially at work, and to make a commitment to a person or financial plan.

13 MAY

It's an excellent weekend for spending time beautifying your domestic life and property. You'll enjoy a musical, artistic or fun event.

14 MAY

You'll appreciate the opportunity to dream a little and thoroughly relax in the company of family and those you love; just avoid thorny topics.

15 MAY

Key financial or personal news will provide you with insight moving forward. Romance could blossom.

16 MAY

You're about to begin a more abundant 12-month phase in your personal life and financially. Some Aquarians may be drawn to travelling.

17 MAY

Be prepared to look at life from a bigger picture concerning your values and principles and how you can achieve your goals peacefully.

18 MAY

Circumstances will demand you be clear about your objectives without making waves or succumbing to outside pressure. Avoid conflict as it will escalate.

19 MAY

The Taurus new moon signals a fresh chapter regarding travel, negotiations, business or finances. You may be drawn to updating a communications device or vehicle.

20 MAY

You'll enjoy the opportunity to be a little more light-hearted with your interactions and will enjoy a sense of freedom.

21 MAY

It's a good day to alter your usual routine and update your environment. However, you must avoid arguments as they will escalate rapidly.

22 MAY

This is a super-productive day and you'll appreciate feeling needed. Just avoid pressuring others and being pressured yourself by being tactful.

23 MAY

You have high expectations and are super energetic but you must avoid arguments and appearing overzealous or pushy.

24 MAY

Your nurturing and mentoring qualities – wishing for the best for others – will arise and enable you to be all the more effective in your projects.

25 MAY

Be prepared to look outside the box at your various commitments, both in your personal life and at work, and take action on common ground.

26 MAY

You may be surprised by news, a meeting or developments. Be positive, as an unexpected development may be just what you want.

27 MAY

It's an excellent day to get chores over and done with early on so you can enjoy quality time with someone special.

28 MAY

It's another good day to clear a backlog of chores, especially paperwork and bills – and then to relax!

29 MAY

A detailed approach to work and responsibilities will pay off. Research facts and figures and follow the trail.

30 MAY

Be prepared to seek the support and collaboration of others where it is needed. Avoid feeling all responsibilities land on your shoulders.

31 MAY

Be prepared to consider messages from another point of view and, equally, ask that others understand your viewpoint. Aim to find common ground.

June

1 JUNE

Avoid taking other people's random comments personally, especially in association with work and projects you can excel at when you focus.

2 JUNE

A key talk, trip or meeting has more significance than meets the eye. Legal matters may be relevant now.

3 JUNE

You'll appreciate the opportunity to enjoy a favourite activity such as sports, self-development and the arts.

4 JUNE

The full moon in Sagittarius signals a fresh chapter in your career, general direction or status or a favourite pastime. You may hear unexpected news or enjoy an impromptu trip.

5 JUNE

A change in your usual routine may bring out strong emotions. It's a good time for a health or beauty appointment.

6 JUNE

The more practical you are the better things will be, especially in relation to your daily life and finances.

7 JUNE

It's a good time to plan and strategise, especially in relation to work and your health and well-being.

8 JUNE

The moon in your sign for the next two days will encourage you to think innovatively and be creative with your forward planning.

9 JUNE

It is a good day for get-togethers and, for some, short trips. You may receive positive financial news and enjoy romance.

10 JUNE

There is a relaxing atmosphere to the weekend that you'll appreciate. However, some chores and financial matters will deserve attention.

11 JUNE

It's a good time to review your health and work routines to ensure they support your needs. It's a good day for a reunion or trip.

12 JUNE

A proactive and positive approach to work and financial matters will reap rewards.

13 JUNE

You may be inclined to get caught up in challenges, but if you put practicalities first you will succeed.

14 JUNE

Double-check facts, as this will enable you to steam ahead with your projects and help you avoid holding plans back because of self-doubt.

15 JUNE

Believe in yourself and your abilities, especially if you're faced with obstacles. Be realistic about delays and be clear with communications to avoid mix-ups.

16 JUNE

Your communication abilities are very good at the moment even if you face obstacles, so be positive. Be patient with delays.

17 JUNE

Be prepared to review some of your commitments, including work and health undertakings. It's a good day for health and beauty appointments.

18 JUNE

Make a wish at the new moon in Gemini, which signals a fresh chapter in your personal life and, for some, at home or with family.

19 JUNE

Your commitment to certain people is clear and it's a good day to make further commitments, but you must ensure you have the full facts. Avoid gambling.

20 JUNE

You have every incentive to work hard and clear a backlog of paperwork. Pay extra attention to financial transactions to avoid making mistakes.

21 JUNE

It's the solstice, a lovely day of celebration. You may experience a therapeutic development financially or in your personal life. Avoid power struggles.

22 JUNE

This is a productive and upbeat day but you must avoid reigniting disagreements, especially at work and with someone special.

23 JUNE

A meeting or personal development will be uplifting. You may receive a compliment or simply feel closer to someone you love.

24 JUNE

A trip or family get-together will feel supportive but you must avoid sensitive topics. You may be forgetful, so keep an eye on your keys.

25 JUNE

A little home improvement or some do-it-yourself projects will add to a sense of security and nurturance. It's a good day to rest, especially if you're feeling forgetful.

26 JUNE

An unexpected change in your usual routine or surprise news from someone close needn't put a spanner in the works. Avoid making rash decisions.

27 JUNE

News or a meeting with someone you admire or who has great influence will be uplifting. It's a good time to make financial decisions.

28 JUNE

Trust your intuition as you are spot on. Just avoid daydreaming, as you may make needless mistakes.

29 JUNE

It's an excellent day to make plans for something special in your personal life. You may receive positive news from a partner, at work or health-wise.

30 JUNE

You'll enjoy a lovely get-together with someone close. It's a good time to make a commitment to a person or project.

July

1 JULY

Expect news from someone special. A trip, commitment or positive financial development will raise your spirits.

2 JULY

An unusual change in your normal routine or environment will benefit from a flexible approach.

3 JULY

The full moon in Capricorn will spotlight a new chapter in your relationship with a friend or organisation. You may be prepared to begin a fresh daily or health routine.

4 JULY

As an innovative thinker your ideas are often way ahead of those of other people, so be prepared to explain some of your thoughts if it's necessary.

5 JULY

You're likely to see someone in a new light, and while this may involve a challenge rest assured you will overcome it.

6 JULY

Be prepared to help someone, and if you need expert advice it will be available. Avoid rushing, minor bumps and scrapes and mix-ups.

7 JULY

News and developments signal a busy day, so be sure to keep up by being spontaneous but at the same time avoid making rash decisions.

8 JULY

This is a good day for a health or beauty appointment. If you're working you'll be busy. Romance could flourish, so organise a date!

9 JULY

You may feel under pressure and that someone close misunderstands you, so take extra time to relax and deepen their understanding of you.

10 JULY

The day's events will certainly gather their own momentum. It's a good time to be creative but ensure you also focus on facts and details to avoid making mistakes.

11 JULY

As Mercury enters Leo you'll feel more expressive and motivated to achieve your goals. Just avoid rushing and pressuring others.

12 JULY

It's a good day to look after yourself and avoid rushing and to gain a sense of purpose, especially in relation to your creative abilities. It's also a good day for a health appointment.

13 JULY

You may be inclined to gamble financially or emotionally but are better to avoid risk-taking by carefully researching your choices.

14 JULY

A pleasant surprise, visit or trip will raise your spirits. Some work or health matters may put you under pressure but rest assured: you will attain your goals.

15 JULY

You'll enjoy the benefits of domestic bliss at your home or someone else's. Take time out to self-nurture.

16 JULY

Your ideas, beliefs and wishes may differ slightly from those of someone close. Be clear about your intentions to avoid friction.

17 JULY

The Cancer new moon signals a fresh chapter in your daily routine regarding either health or work. Avoid making snap decisions and assumptions.

18 JULY

The Leo moon for the next two days will motivate you to be busy at work and accomplish your many tasks.

19 JULY

This is a busy, productive time for you; just avoid taking on more than you can handle and delegate if necessary.

20 JULY

You're thinking creatively and imaginatively and musical and artistic projects will thrive. However, you must avoid daydreaming and forgetfulness.

21 JULY

You will not always agree with everyone and someone else's opinions may seem complex, so aim to find common ground and you will.

22 JULY

It's a good day for work meetings even if you feel nervous or challenged. Show your best side, and you may be pleasantly surprised by news. Avoid arguments, as they will become long term.

23 JULY

Someone close may have a change of mind, so be adaptable within reason. Find ways to discuss common aims. Avoid misunderstandings and travel delays by planning ahead.

24 JULY

A conciliatory approach to someone may be needed and an apology accepted. Someone unpredictable will behave true to form.

25 JULY

It's a good time to reconsider some of your goals, especially regarding work and areas you share.

26 JULY

Your feelings and those of someone close will be strong, making this a good time to find out exactly where you stand.

27 JULY

This is a lovely day for romance and getting closer to someone you love or admire. However, you must avoid making assumptions.

28 JULY

Double-check you're still on the path you wish to follow, and if not make tracks to choose a more suitable way ahead.

29 JULY

It's an excellent day to clear a backlog of chores at home and in the garden, and also to do a mini financial review. You'll enjoy a fun, active day.

30 JULY

Be prepared to be honest about your feelings and the feelings of someone close to avoid labouring under a delusion.

31 JULY

You may experience a slight case of Mondayitis but rest assured: you will manage to complete chores and put a smile on your face.

August

1 AUGUST

The full moon supermoon in Aquarius spells a new chapter in January Aquarians' personal life and in February Aquarians' work or health routine. It's a good day for meetings and talks.

2 AUGUST

It's a good day to discuss important commitments, including personal and financial matters.

3 AUGUST

Be prepared to focus on the details of your various agreements and arrangements but avoid overanalysing them, as variables may change moving forward.

4 AUGUST

The Pisces moon will bring out your inspired ideas and imagination, which is ideal for creative work, but others may find you absent-minded and forgetful.

5 AUGUST

This is a lovely time for romance, the arts and personal development, but if someone needs your full attention – at work, for example – you may disappoint them unless you focus extra hard.

6 AUGUST

You're communicating more proactively and will find interactions more immediate and upbeat as a result.

7 AUGUST

You have high hopes and you'll need to take on board someone else's opinions to avoid arguments or disappointment.

8 AUGUST

Be realistic with travel, communications and negotiations and avoid being stubborn; work towards a bigger-picture outcome.

9 AUGUST

Some of your ideas may seem slightly left field or unpredictable to others or their ideas may seem absurd to you, so to gain an even playing field consider other people's viewpoints and work towards collaboration.

10 AUGUST

It's a good day for making commitments and agreements and for negotiating. A trip or get-together will be enjoyable.

11 AUGUST

You'll enjoy a reunion and the chance to relax at the end of this week. There is a therapeutic feeling to the day.

12 AUGUST

You'll appreciate a health or beauty treat. Someone close has good news, and you may experience an ego or financial boost.

13 AUGUST

It's a romantic day and you may enjoy an impromptu get-together as someone close surprises you. Mid-February Aquarians will enjoy a change of routine or beauty treat.

14 AUGUST

You have extra energy to burn and will be productive as a result, and may benefit from working off excess energy at the gym or outside.

15 AUGUST

It's a good day for meetings and get-togethers and for taking action with your various projects. A health matter will progress.

16 AUGUST

The new moon in Leo signals a fresh phase in a business or personal partnership; someone may even surprise you. Some Aquarians will be starting a new work or health schedule.

17 AUGUST

While making new agreements and plans, ensure you're on the same page as the person or people you're making arrangements with. Avoid making assumptions.

18 AUGUST

This is a good day for research and finding out exactly where you stand, especially in relation to a collaboration or a work or health matter.

19 AUGUST

You'll be drawn to finding peace of mind and a sense of fair play. Someone close will prove helpful.

20 AUGUST

It's a good time to double-check you're on the same page as someone you admire and who admires you to avoid future disagreements and power struggles.

21 AUGUST

A little tension and pressure can be motivating, but if you feel constantly under stress this can be super tiring. Find ways to unwind.

22 AUGUST

A disagreement may arise simply through having made assumptions. Avoid turning plain disagreements into a power struggle and find common ground.

23 AUGUST

Aim to get important paperwork and joint decisions finalised to avoid having to review them further down the line.

24 AUGUST

The moon at the zenith of your chart may put your heart on your sleeve, so if you feel vulnerable take time out. Be practical and reasonable for the best results.

25 AUGUST

Developments at work and in collaborative efforts will progress under their own steam. This can be a super-productive time. You may enjoy a reunion.

26 AUGUST

An earthy, relaxing and enjoyable day will get you back in touch with your priorities and the people you truly love.

27 AUGUST

It's a good day for negotiations and making a commitment to a person or plan of action.

28 AUGUST

A dedicated approach to your work and collaborations will succeed. Just take things one step at a time and avoid rushing.

29 AUGUST

The Aquarian moon will encourage you to look positively at your circumstances and boost your health and well-being.

30 AUGUST

A lovely relaxing time is on the way for you later in the day. First, though, chores will be completed and you'll manage to overcome obstacles.

31 AUGUST

The Pisces full moon supermoon spotlights a fresh chapter in your personal and business relationships. Double-check you're on the same page and research the facts.

September

1 SEPTEMBER

This is a good day to be practical above all else and avoid making rash decisions and rushing projects.

2 SEPTEMBER

You will enjoy looking after yourself and your health and someone special. If you're tempted by retail therapy, avoid overspending.

3 SEPTEMBER

Focus on practicalities, especially where joint responsibilities and finances are concerned. You'll enjoy a reunion or return to an old haunt.

4 SEPTEMBER

A business or personal partner has news for you. It's a good day for a health or beauty treat and for meetings and a change of environment.

5 SEPTEMBER

A change of routine will be enjoyable. It's a good day for romance and the arts.

6 SEPTEMBER

You may be drawn to reviewing previous agreements with someone close. You'll enjoy a reunion; just avoid sensitive topics.

7 SEPTEMBER

You'll be drawn to a beauty or health treat. It's a good day to discuss your options at work and with someone close.

8 SEPTEMBER

Collaborations are likely to go well, so take the initiative and delegate chores if possible. You may enjoy a fun event but you must plan ahead.

9 SEPTEMBER

This is a lovely day to focus on domestic matters and family. You may be drawn to reorganising your diet and paying more attention to cooking and nutrition.

10 SEPTEMBER

An active and upbeat pastime will prove to be a drawcard. You may enjoy organising a reunion, and finding favourite pastimes you all have in common will work well.

11 SEPTEMBER

It's a good day to take the initiative with various talks both at work and regarding finances, as you're likely to reach agreements.

12 SEPTEMBER

A colleague or personal partner is likely to feel more upbeat about their projects, and their enthusiasm will be catching.

13 SEPTEMBER

A work or personal project will deserve focus so you don't make mistakes. Just avoid overanalysing details as this will be counterproductive.

14 SEPTEMBER

Be prepared to see your collaborations and relationships from someone else's point of view and be practical with arrangements.

15 SEPTEMBER

The new moon in Virgo signals a fresh chapter in a personal or business relationship. Be practical with plans for the weekend and they will succeed.

16 SEPTEMBER

You'll enjoy an impromptu get-together, and a trip somewhere different will be fun.

17 SEPTEMBER

A last-minute change of plan needn't put a spanner in the works if you're spontaneous and adaptable. Avoid taking circumstances personally.

18 SEPTEMBER

You'll feel passionate about your activities and beliefs but others may not feel the same way, so be prepared to find common ground.

19 SEPTEMBER

It's an excellent day for romance, but you must ensure you're on the same page and avoid misunderstandings. Keep an eye on financial transactions to avoid making mistakes.

20 SEPTEMBER

You'll enjoy physical activities such as sports and working off excess energy in constructive ways.

21 SEPTEMBER

This is a good day to discuss long-term changes you'd like to make, especially at work and health-wise and regarding joint responsibilities.

22 SEPTEMBER

You'll be drawn to socialising and networking with an upbeat crowd. Avoid overindulging and overspending, which you'll regret.

23 SEPTEMBER

The sun in Libra for the next month will encourage you to look for peace and harmony in your personal life, beginning today.

24 SEPTEMBER

Your expertise may be in demand as someone will ask for your help. If you need help it will be available. Avoid overspending.

25 SEPTEMBER

It's an excellent day for meetings and get-togethers, as they will be productive. Just avoid allowing some disagreements to railroad constructive projects.

26 SEPTEMBER

You'll find it easier to express your perspective and others will understand you better, so take the initiative and discuss your plans.

27 SEPTEMBER

You like to dream a little and be creative. You could make great progress with personal projects but you must focus on work to avoid absent-mindedness.

28 SEPTEMBER

Arts, music and romance will appeal. You may be easily distracted, so avoid making unnecessary mistakes.

29 SEPTEMBER

The Aries full moon signals a new phase in your personal life. You'll be ready to make a fresh work commitment. Look for balance and avoid making rash decisions.

30 SEPTEMBER

Be spontaneous, as you'll enjoy socialising and networking. You may bump into an old friend. Avoid making rash decisions.

October

1 OCTOBER

It's a lovely day for a get-together and romance could thrive. Just avoid forcing your hand with agreements that are already set in stone.

2 OCTOBER

You'll appreciate the opportunity to improve your appearance and deepen your understanding of someone you love. Romance could thrive; just avoid misunderstandings.

3 OCTOBER

It's a good day for putting plans in motion, particularly in connection with work, collaborations and travel. Just be sure to double-check the details to avoid making mistakes.

4 OCTOBER

The Gemini moon will encourage you to be more outspoken at home and about family matters you feel need attention.

5 OCTOBER

The more precise you are in communications and especially stating your intentions clearly the better it will be for you.

6 OCTOBER

You have great ideas and plans, although someone whose cooperation you require may not agree. Healthy discussion will be productive.

7 OCTOBER

Brush up on your communication skills, as you may need to persuade someone of your ideas and plans.

8 OCTOBER

Tact and diplomacy will go a long way to greasing the wheels of good communications, especially concerning health matters and plans for the day.

9 OCTOBER

You may need to undergo a tough conversation that requires you to commit to certain ideas. Be prepared to discuss things but avoid arguments, as they will escalate.

10 OCTOBER

Discussions needn't turn into arguments as long as you are willing to find common ground and balanced fair play.

11 OCTOBER

There are therapeutic aspects to the day but someone – perhaps even you – may be feeling sensitive, so take things one step at a time.

12 OCTOBER

This is a productive day, especially with activities you love, as you'll feel positively engaged. However, some communications will require extra tact.

13 OCTOBER

It's an excellent day to truly put your back into your work and projects as your efforts will be successful.

14 OCTOBER

The solar eclipse signals a fresh chapter in a key relationship. Be prepared to discuss sensitive matters, including finances and health.

15 OCTOBER

It is impossible to second guess people yet your gut instinct will give you a good idea of where you stand with someone else. This may arise in a surprising way.

16 OCTOBER

Be prepared to work towards your goals diligently, as you will attain them.

17 OCTOBER

News and conversations may require you to look outside the box at their significance and relevance to you personally. Be open-minded.

18 OCTOBER

You're keen to press ahead with your favourite activities, interests and pastimes, which you'll enjoy as you'll gain the chance to let off steam.

19 OCTOBER

A key get-together or talk will highlight the dynamics of a relationship. If you find you've been idealistic you will gain the opportunity to reset your sights.

20 OCTOBER

It's another good day for talks, and you're likely to gain a deeper appreciation of someone else's feelings. Avoid second guessing and get the full information you need.

21 OCTOBER

Your feelings and those of someone else may differ. Avoid taking intense circumstances personally but find ways to be productive regardless of disagreements.

22 OCTOBER

You'll enjoy improved interpersonal dynamics but must again avoid sensitive topics, as an intense dynamic still surrounds communications.

23 OCTOBER

A trip, get-together or the chance to pursue your favourite hobbies will feel uplifting, so take the initiative!

24 OCTOBER

It's an excellent day to discuss and commit to shared ventures such as work projects and joint financial and personal arrangements.

25 OCTOBER

Be prepared to dream a little and use your imagination to foster an enjoyable atmosphere, as you'll enjoy spending time with someone you love.

26 OCTOBER

This is still an excellent time to build a solid base with someone special. Discussions and plans are likely to take root.

27 OCTOBER

Your expertise and help will be in demand, and if you need support or expert advice be sure to reach out as it is available.

28 OCTOBER

The lunar eclipse in Taurus signals a fresh chapter in a shared situation such as joint finances, duties or space at home. Avoid impulsiveness; do your research first.

29 OCTOBER

An active and outgoing day will appeal. Someone close may feel particularly passionate about certain matters and these will benefit from discussion. Avoid making snap decisions.

30 OCTOBER

You'll appreciate the opportunity to be a little more outspoken yet light-hearted, which will add to your ability to be productive.

31 OCTOBER

Happy Halloween! You'll enjoy the sociable vibe of the day and a change in environment, but you must avoid being rash.

November

1 NOVEMBER

This is a good time to make changes in your daily life so you create more time for yourself and those you love.

2 NOVEMBER

Be prepared to look at the nurturing aspects of your life and how to deepen relationships and increase the time available for favourite activities.

3 NOVEMBER

Key talks and meetings will illuminate the best way forward both financially and romantically.

4 NOVEMBER

You may be surprised by developments. Plan well ahead, as travel and communications may be delayed or erratic.

5 NOVEMBER

Be prepared to pace yourself as you may otherwise tend to overdo things. If you're tempted by retail therapy avoid overspending, as you'll regret it.

6 NOVEMBER

This will be a productive day that is perfect for taking the initiative, especially at work and with beauty and health appointments.

7 NOVEMBER

It's a good day for talks and meetings, especially regarding your favourite activities including the arts, travel, study and sports.

8 NOVEMBER

A balanced and peaceful approach to areas you share such as joint finances and space in the office or at home will be productive.

9 NOVEMBER

Be prepared to shine and, to do so, put in the extra hard work and avoid succumbing to low self-esteem and a lack of confidence.

10 NOVEMBER

You'll feel more outspoken and may tend to speak before you think things out, so avoid putting someone offside.

11 NOVEMBER

A surprise development will mean a change in your usual routine. Be adaptable but avoid making snap decisions. A change of environment may appeal.

12 NOVEMBER

The lead-up to the new moon is an excellent time to make a wish, in your case regarding shared areas and relationships.

13 NOVEMBER

The Scorpio new moon signals a fresh chapter in the way you share various concerns, including joint finances and duties. A relationship may be a focus and you may receive unexpected news.

14 NOVEMBER

An outgoing and upbeat attitude will be productive. Just be sure to choose your words carefully to avoid an unintentional offence.

15 NOVEMBER

It's a good day for get-togethers and romance, so organise a date if you haven't already!

16 NOVEMBER

You have strong skill sets and may need to persuade someone close of your abilities. You will overcome obstacles but will need to be tactful.

17 NOVEMBER

Dream big, as you can make positive inroads towards your desired goals. Romance, the arts and music will all appeal.

18 NOVEMBER

A get-together will be memorable. A passionate time is on the cards, so choose your activities wisely and invest deeply.

19 NOVEMBER

It's a good time for self-development, so look for ways to deepen your understanding of yourself and others.

20 NOVEMBER

This is a lovely day for socialising and networking. You're at your charming best and will be influential.

21 NOVEMBER

A generally romantic vibe will be inspiring, but if you have serious facts and figures to deal with you will need to focus a little harder.

22 NOVEMBER

A romantic outlook comes with a sensitive disposition and you may feel super vulnerable, so pace yourself. Avoid taking random comments personally.

23 NOVEMBER

It's a good day for a mini financial review. Work hard, as you'll achieve your goals. Avoid arguments as they will turn into a Mexican stand-off.

24 NOVEMBER

You have surplus energy to burn, so be sure to channel it into constructive activities such as sports as otherwise you may tend to feel restless and at a loose end.

25 NOVEMBER

It's an excellent weekend to review your strategy and plans, especially regarding long-term goals including study, travel and hobbies.

26 NOVEMBER

An abrupt change of circumstance will merit a practical and careful approach. Consider looking at circumstances from another person's point of view.

27 NOVEMBER

The Gemini full moon signals a fresh chapter in a personal circumstance and, for some, regarding travel, work and relationships. Be extra clear to avoid misunderstandings.

28 NOVEMBER

You may be drawn to updating a communications device or vehicle. Be prepared to strategise with long-term travel plans.

29 NOVEMBER

You are generally optimistic and outgoing and may be inclined to be overgenerous or have unrealistic expectations, so maintain perspective.

30 NOVEMBER

You'll enjoy meetings and socialising; just be super clear with communications to avoid mix-ups.

December

1 DECEMBER

Communications will become less feisty and more grounded over the coming weeks, which will enable you to plan ahead better starting today!

2 DECEMBER

It's an excellent day for making practical plans, especially socially and regarding long-term commitments.

3 DECEMBER

Although you're looking for a peaceful atmosphere disagreements may arise, which will create an intense day. Make arrangements carefully but be prepared to be spontaneous.

4 DECEMBER

You'll feel increasingly motivated to express yourself more passionately, especially in a close relationship. Just avoid appearing super intense for the best results.

5 DECEMBER

This is a good day for collaborations and deepening your understanding of someone special. Romance could thrive.

6 DECEMBER

Be prepared to consider the details of your long-term plans with someone special such as a business or personal partner.

7 DECEMBER

You're thinking creatively at the moment and will appreciate discussing your ideas with similarly imaginative thinkers.

8 DECEMBER

There are therapeutic aspects to the day. You may enjoy a career or ego or financial boost. News or a meeting will be enjoyable.

9 DECEMBER

Take the initiative with your projects and plans as you're communicating well. Just avoid sensitive topics and implementing change too quickly.

10 DECEMBER

Financial matters will deserve careful appraisal. You may need to make changes to your budget. Romance can flourish.

11 DECEMBER

Meetings and talks will be productive. It's a good day for collaboration. A financial transaction will be a focus.

12 DECEMBER

The Sagittarian new moon signals a fresh chapter in your direction, status or career. Be prepared to be on your toes as you may experience a surprise.

13 DECEMBER

Try to get key paperwork and discussions completed now, especially regarding a group, friend or organisation, to avoid having to review agreements over the coming weeks.

14 DECEMBER

You're communicating effectively and meetings with organisations and groups will go well. Believe in yourself.

15 DECEMBER

This is an excellent time to demonstrate just what you have. You may feel vulnerable or sensitive but you will succeed.

16 DECEMBER

The moon in your sign for the weekend will encourage you to look outside the square at circumstances, which will enable you to stay on top of developments.

17 DECEMBER

A nurturing approach to yourself and others will be productive, especially if you're feeling sensitive.

18 DECEMBER

Words will flow, and if you have important financial, travel or legal matters to review this is an excellent day to do so.

19 DECEMBER

Be prepared to double-check whether you're looking at life through rose-coloured glasses and to make a course adjustment if you discover you are.

20 DECEMBER

An upbeat and outgoing development will be enjoyable but you must avoid rushing and having unrealistic expectations.

21 DECEMBER

You'll enjoy a reunion or return to an old haunt. However, you may experience unexpected delays or misunderstandings so be patient.

22 DECEMBER

You'll enjoy socialising or a return to an old haunt. You may receive good news from a friend or organisation.

23 DECEMBER

You'll enjoy indulging in all the seasonal delights, including good food and good company. You'll indulge in last-minute Christmas shopping but must avoid overspending.

24 DECEMBER

You'll appreciate the opportunity to socialise and slow down the general pace of your life. A meeting with an authority or father figure will be significant.

25 DECEMBER

Merry Christmas! You'll enjoy relaxing and music, romance and the arts and simply enjoying a beautiful day.

26 DECEMBER

A favourite hobby or activity will appeal and you'll enjoy picking up where you left off.

27 DECEMBER

The Cancer full moon signals the start of a fresh chapter in your personal or family life. You'll enjoy socialising but must factor in the chance of delays and mix-ups.

28 DECEMBER

A return to a circumstance will take you back somewhere familiar. However, there may be delays and misunderstandings so plan ahead.

29 DECEMBER

A change in your daily routine will be enjoyable. You may appreciate a trip or venturing into new territory.

30 DECEMBER

You'll enjoy being with upbeat and outgoing people so seek good company, as you'll be glad you did.

31 DECEMBER

Happy New Year! The celebratory aspect of the day's developments will appeal to you and you'll enjoy actively ringing in the new year.

FINANCES

It's an excellent year to review your financial plans as you'll gain the opportunity to put in place new ideas during the year, ideas that could provide you with longer-term security and stability. However, some aspects of these plans may involve risk-taking and these are best avoided. It's more than likely that you will change your work circumstances and, at the least, you'll be reviewing the groups and organisations you associate with such as your employers and collaborators. This will naturally have an impact on your finances.

HEALTH

Saturn in your health sector for the first quarter will enable you to put in place a strong health and fitness routine that you're best to stick with for the rest of the year. Plan ahead early on to create by mid-March a sustainable fitness schedule for the remainder of 2023. This is an excellent year if you're hoping to lose weight, but you need to avoid resuming bad health habits from mid-June onwards to maintain positive health advantages you gained earlier in the year. If you have suffered from slight anxiety or depression in the past this is an excellent year to consider looking at your health from a holistic point of view, that your body, mind and spirit are inseparable and that each area impacts the other.

LOVE LIFE

Neptune in your sign until March 2025 brings romance to front and centre stage, making this a wonderful year to enjoy your love life. Peak times for romance include the end of January, from mid- to the end of February, mid-March and mid-September. Just ensure in 2023 that you're not seeing life through rose-coloured glasses and provide yourself with regular reality checks, because you'll enjoy the benefits of romance so much more and will not fall prey to disappointment.

CAREER

You'll contemplate associating with new groups and organisations in 2023, which will invariably mean that you'll consider changing the organisations you work with. You're ready for change in your career, and not only with whom you collaborate but also potentially in expanding your skill set and entering brand new territory. You're ready to take the initiative, as change will not be as daunting as it was in previous years. Key months when new career options will appeal will be June, July and December.

HOME LIFE

Mars travelling through your fourth house of home and property for the first quarter will bring considerable change and, at the very least, the feeling that you would like to make alterations at home if possible. The second quarter will provide the opportunity to embellish your home via some do-it-yourself projects or home improvements. If relationships have become strained at home, the second quarter is an excellent time to devise clever ways to bring more love into this important area of your life. If you're considering major changes at home the new moons in mid-June and mid-July will be positive times to put plans in motion.

January

1 JANUARY

Happy New Year! You may experience an intense start to the year as a connection with your past or a particular group of people takes your focus.

2 JANUARY

You'll enjoy a lovely to get-together and romance could blossom. Be prepared to look after yourself, and if someone else needs help it will be available.

3 JANUARY

Venus steps into Aquarius, bringing the chance to indulge a little in your senses and favourite activities. You'll enjoy a change of pace.

4 JANUARY

You'll appreciate the opportunity to boost your health and appearance and may enjoy a reunion or return to an old haunt.

5 JANUARY

An unexpected meeting or get-together will be enjoyable, so be prepared to accept invitations and try something new.

6 JANUARY

The Cancer full moon brings a fresh chapter in a domestic or personal circumstance. Be prepared to self-nurture and nurture others.

7 JANUARY

You'll enjoy a lovely reunion and doing something different. It's a good day to double-check paperwork, especially financial statements.

8 JANUARY

Be spontaneous, as an unexpected social event or get-together will be enjoyable. You may be surprised by news.

9 JANUARY

This is a productive day and you'll manage to get on top of chores and paperwork. It's also a good day to improve your health and appearance.

10 JANUARY

This is still a sociable time for you, so enjoy the opportunity to connect with people whose company you enjoy.

11 JANUARY

Be prepared to review certain work and health schedules. You may need to reorient some of your focus.

12 JANUARY

Projects, communications and financial matters that have been on the back burner are about to take centre stage, so be prepared to move forward with your projects.

13 JANUARY

Friday the 13th! There's a romantic aspect to the day that you'll enjoy. A social or networking event is likely to appeal.

14 JANUARY

It's a good day to complete chores and fulfil obligations. Arrangements are likely to fall into place.

15 JANUARY

Be prepared to be flexible, as you may experience an unexpected change of plan or a change in your usual schedule.

16 JANUARY

It's a good time to review and complete outstanding paperwork. An unavoidable situation is best tackled patiently and innovatively.

17 JANUARY

You're keen to stride ahead with your projects and plans, however, you may experience travel or communication delays so plan ahead.

18 JANUARY

You may experience an intense circumstance as news from a friend or organisation must be attended to. Mix-ups and a misunderstanding are possible, so be patient.

19 JANUARY

An outgoing and upbeat attitude will be productive; however, you'll also need to adapt to prevailing circumstances.

20 JANUARY

The next four weeks will be ideal for being innovative in your daily life and work and health practices. It's an ideal time for self-development.

21 JANUARY

The new moon supermoon in Aquarius signals a fresh chapter in your work or health schedule. This is a good day for a beauty or health treat but you must be clear in your communications.

22 JANUARY

A commitment to a work, health or beauty program is on the cards. However, you may receive unexpected news that requires your attention.

23 JANUARY

Be inspired by new ideas and a fresh appreciation of your own abilities but also be prepared to be practical.

24 JANUARY

The moon in your own sign will motivate you to use your intuition, especially with regard to collaborations and someone close in your life.

25 JANUARY

This is a lovely day to reconnect with someone you admire and work developments are likely to progress. Romance could thrive.

26 JANUARY

You'll feel motivated to be productive but may need to persuade someone else of your bright ideas. Be proactive but also patient.

27 JANUARY

You're a fundamentally sensitive person and may need to be strong to avoid taking circumstances personally. Your expertise will be in demand.

28 JANUARY

Be practical with circumstances that are outside your control as you have the capability to rise above obstacles and enjoy a fun and varied day.

29 JANUARY

The Taurus moon will encourage you to treat yourself and a loved one but you must avoid overspending and overindulging, which you'll regret.

30 JANUARY

You are effective and capable and communicating well, so be prepared to move a project forward in innovative and clever ways.

31 JANUARY

This is a good day for a health or beauty appointment and for a lovely reunion. Work meetings are likely to go well.

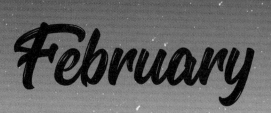

February

1 FEBRUARY

It's a good day for a health or beauty appointment. There are healing attributes to the day that are perfect for self-development and spiritual activities.

2 FEBRUARY

Trust your instincts with regard to the best way forward in a personal or domestic circumstance. Avoid taking any adverse matters personally.

3 FEBRUARY

Your sensitivity may be coming to the surface, making this a good time to improve your abilities to gain a sense of personal calm and stability through meditation, for example.

4 FEBRUARY

An unanticipated change of routine or sudden change of circumstance will merit a versatile approach.

5 FEBRUARY

The Leo full moon signals a fresh chapter in your daily or health routine. Be prepared to discuss your circumstances with someone close, especially if disagreements arise.

6 FEBRUARY

You'll enjoy socialising, the arts, romance and spiritual development. Work meetings could go well but you will need to focus extra hard.

7 FEBRUARY

The Virgo moon will enable you to focus and get things done both at work and in your personal life, but you must avoid indecision and, inversely, making snap decisions.

8 FEBRUARY

An unexpected development will be a pleasant surprise and may even improve your self-confidence or bank balance.

9 FEBRUARY

It's a good day to get on top of work chores, and also for improving health and well-being.

10 FEBRUARY

Significant news or a get-together may be intense, so avoid knee-jerk reactions and take your time to process developments.

11 FEBRUARY

Someone close will have a calming and reassuring approach and presence. Avoid ignoring red flags in a circumstance and look for solutions.

12 FEBRUARY

This is a lovely day to cocoon and treat yourself to a little self-indulgence such as enjoying good food, music and the arts. Romance will also appeal and thrive.

13 FEBRUARY

Trust your intuition, especially in relation to someone you must share duties or even finances with.

14 FEBRUARY

Happy St Valentine's Day! The next two days are ideal for romance, especially if your birthday is in mid-March. Avoid rushing and minor bumps and scrapes.

15 FEBRUARY

You'll be drawn wholeheartedly to romance, and if a secret romance is underway you must avoid being caught!

16 FEBRUARY

A work or personal commitment will be a focus. Double-check that you're on the same path and, if not, review your commitment.

17 FEBRUARY

It will be a productive day at work, and if you're not working you'll enjoy doing something different for a change.

18 FEBRUARY

A reunion or return to an old haunt will be enjoyable. Be prepared to go outside your comfort zone but avoid being distracted if you're travelling.

19 FEBRUARY

This is an excellent time to deepen your connection with a friend or group and romance can flourish, so take the initiative. It's also a good time to change your appearance.

20 FEBRUARY

The new moon supermoon in Pisces signals a fresh chapter in your daily routine or health schedule, and if it's your birthday you'll begin a fresh chapter in your personal life.

21 FEBRUARY

Be prepared to leave your comfort zone at work and regarding your commitments both in your personal life and financially, but avoid making rash decisions.

22 FEBRUARY

You'll gain confirmation that your recent decisions are correct. You will enjoy news from the past regarding health or work, or will enjoy a trip.

23 FEBRUARY

You will appreciate feeling positive and outgoing about your abilities and decisions. Avoid pandering to doubts or anxiety.

24 FEBRUARY

A strong connection with someone you admire will raise your spirits. This is a lovely day for a reunion and meetings at work.

25 FEBRUARY

It's a good weekend to indulge in the senses and enjoy quality time with someone you love.

26 FEBRUARY

Be prepared to see matters from someone else's perspective and the value of creating stability and security in your life.

27 FEBRUARY

It's a good day for meetings at work and to discuss your ideas, and also for health and beauty appointments.

28 FEBRUARY

An innovative, imaginative approach to chores and work projects will be productive; just avoid forgetfulness and idealism.

March

1 MARCH

You'll appreciate the opportunity to spend time at home and to catch up with work chores. A reunion may appeal.

2 MARCH

This is an excellent time to focus on your personal life and values to discover where you wish to place your full attention over the coming days and weeks. Your expertise will be in demand.

3 MARCH

A personal or health matter will deserve careful attention. You may be drawn to investing or double-checking your financial circumstances. An expert will help.

4 MARCH

You will enjoy being active and making headway with a health or work matter. This is a good time to boost your self-esteem and physical health.

5 MARCH

Be spontaneous and prepared to look outside the box at your various options, both in your personal life and financially.

6 MARCH

A surprise will open your eyes to new opportunities and possibilities both in your personal life and financially.

7 MARCH

The Virgo full moon spotlights a fresh chapter in a relationship if it's your birthday today or before and a fresh chapter at work or health-wise if it's your birthday after today.

8 MARCH

Now that Saturn is in your sign you'll gain the opportunity to be more practical about your plans, which will enable you to build more stability and security.

9 MARCH

Look for a balanced approach to a collaboration or relationship that brings out your sensitive side.

10 MARCH

This is a good day to discuss finances and personal matters. You'll enjoy a lovely get-together or reunion.

11 MARCH

You'll enjoy being spontaneous, and a lovely surprise visit or development will raise your spirits. You may receive a financial or ego boost.

12 MARCH

This is a good day to look after yourself and those you love. Avoid minor bumps and scrapes. It's a good day for spiritual development.

13 MARCH

You can be super generous but must avoid overspending and having overly high expectations.

14 MARCH

You are keen to be productive, however, others may have their own plans so you must be sure you're on the same page. Avoid forgetfulness and impulsiveness.

15 MARCH

This is a romantic day, especially if it's your birthday. Take some time out and avoid making assumptions about arrangements.

16 MARCH

You are imaginative and sometimes can be an idealist. Double-check that your plans align with those of others to avoid disappointment over arrangements and plans.

17 MARCH

Key talks and meetings could be ideal but you must plan ahead to avoid travel delays. Keep communications clear to avoid misunderstandings and delays.

18 MARCH

You will appreciate the opportunity to alter your usual routine and spend time with people whose company you truly love. It's a good time to improve your appearance and well-being.

19 MARCH

You'll enjoy a reunion and deepening your connection with friends.

20 MARCH

You're communicating well and will feel more expressive over the coming weeks so you must avoid appearing a little overzealous.

21 MARCH

The Aries new moon is a good time to start something new in your personal life. Just avoid making snap decisions and be prepared for a slow transformation.

22 MARCH

You may tend to feel impatient when the moon is in Aries, so take a moment to gather your wits to avoid impulsiveness.

23 MARCH

Your instincts, intuition and ability to make long-term change in your daily routine will kick in over the coming weeks and months, so be prepared to put your plans in motion.

24 MARCH

You may be quietly re-evaluating your loyalties and even some relationships. Avoid making snap decisions and be prepared for a long game.

25 MARCH

Someone whose company you truly value will prove to be a positive influence. You'll enjoy investing in your home. Avoid taking the opinions of other people personally.

26 MARCH

This is an excellent day to invest in yourself, your home and close relationships as you will gain a sense of nurturance.

27 MARCH

A health matter will be in the spotlight; it's a good day for a health appointment. Your expertise will be in demand.

28 MARCH

Conversations and meetings may be super significant but you must avoid exaggerated expectations. Be practical and plan for positive outcomes.

29 MARCH

You'll be drawn to looking after your domestic circumstances and being practical with health and personal arrangements.

30 MARCH

Surprising developments may involve an unexpected financial or work improvement.

31 MARCH

Take the initiative with your projects, meetings and relationships as you may be pleasantly surprised by the outcome.

April

1 APRIL

It's a lovely weekend to enjoy the company of someone you love and treat yourself to something special.

2 APRIL

Romance can blossom and you'll enjoy good food and company. If you're shopping just avoid overspending, as you'll regret it.

3 APRIL

This is a good time for a mini financial review and to double-check that you're on track with your work projects to reach certain targets or goals.

4 APRIL

You'll be looking for balance in your relationships and must avoid needless arguments that stem purely from someone's stubbornness.

5 APRIL

Your focus on health and well-being will be productive. If you have undergone a loss this is a good time to work constructively towards more abundance.

6 APRIL

The full moon in Libra signals a new chapter in a relationship. Avoid taking developments personally and look for balance.

7 APRIL

Romance will thrive, so organise a date if you haven't already. You may be pleasantly surprised by news or an event.

8 APRIL

You'll enjoy being productive at home and finding ways to feather your nest such as through improving home decor or domestic dynamics.

9 APRIL

A partner or friend will prove particularly helpful with your various plans and projects. You may be drawn to investing in your home or health.

10 APRIL

You'll enjoy finding the time to focus on your favourite activities and pastimes such as sports and self-development.

11 APRIL

This is a productive day and you could make inroads into improving your financial and work circumstance, so take the initiative.

12 APRIL

Be practical about your projects and things will fall into place; don't doubt your abilities.

13 APRIL

You have high expectations and your goals can be reached but you must avoid rushing. Be methodical instead.

14 APRIL

It's a good day for a financial review, especially if you've gone into debt. A meeting with an authority figure will be productive.

15 APRIL

Think outside the box at your various options and activities and be prepared to enter new territory.

16 APRIL

This is a lovely day for relaxation, the arts, film and romance. Just avoid overspending and overindulging, which you'll regret tomorrow.

17 APRIL

The moon in your sign will bring out your philosophical side. You may have a light-bulb moment, especially in connection with work and finances.

18 APRIL

The Aries moon will motivate you to be productive and outgoing, especially in connection with long-term changes you'd like to make.

19 APRIL

A positive approach to your chores and work will be effective, but you must avoid believing that Rome was built in a day.

20 APRIL

The total solar eclipse in Aries will kick-start a fresh agreement. Be bold but avoid a battle of egos.

21 APRIL

Try to get important paperwork and communications finalised now in relation to finances and your personal life, which will avoid you having to review them over the coming weeks.

22 APRIL

You can make practical and worthwhile decisions and enjoy life at the same time! Just avoid overindulging, which you'll regret.

23 APRIL

The Gemini moon will deliver a chatty day and the chance to connect with people you love. A short trip or visit will be enjoyable.

24 APRIL

Talks, meetings and communications in general will bring a busy atmosphere your way; just avoid misunderstandings.

25 APRIL

This is a good day to make a financial or personal commitment, so take the initiative with discussions and negotiations.

26 APRIL

A caring and nurturing approach to someone in your family, a friend or someone at home will be welcome and productive.

27 APRIL

You may be surprised by news, an impromptu visit or trip. Some Pisces will receive an unexpected compliment or financial boost.

28 APRIL

This will be an active and health-oriented day ideal for improving your well-being, appearance and diet.

29 APRIL

You'll discover unexpected benefits in some of your relationships but you must avoid making assumptions about other people.

30 APRIL

A busy, productive day at work will be rewarding. Someone close has good news for you.

May

1 MAY

It's a good time to consider your loyalties, both socially and at work. Think about where you derive the most fulfilment and pursue those activities.

2 MAY

Key financial or personal news is on the way. You'll gain the opportunity to improve your financial and personal circumstances.

3 MAY

Ensure you have all the details necessary to make informed decisions that could affect your work and financial lives.

4 MAY

You may discover whether you've over- or underestimated your circumstances, especially in your personal life and domestically.

5 MAY

The lunar eclipse in Scorpio signals a fresh chapter in shared areas such as finances and personal commitments to others. A domestic or personal development will be delightful.

6 MAY

You enjoy the luxuries in life and may be prone to going to excess. Avoid forgetfulness.

7 MAY

Your attention will go increasingly on finding more comfort and love at home and in your environment. You will find balance even if, at first, you must make an effort to establish calm.

8 MAY

You are super productive but will also benefit from being sensitive to the feelings of other people, especially if they are suffering from a touch of Mondayitis.

9 MAY

Be prepared for a surprise that will require you to be adaptable and spontaneous. Avoid appearing erratic yourself.

10 MAY

Be practical and realistic, especially with matters that gain their own momentum.

11 MAY

There is merit in looking at circumstances from outside the box to regain perspective, especially if you feel some things have lost traction.

12 MAY

This is a good time for a mini financial review and to go over work and health plans to ensure everyone is on the same page.

13 MAY

Be practical with changes at home and in your usual routine and you'll enjoy some lovely reunions, get-togethers and developments.

14 MAY

The moon in Pisces will encourage you to be intuitive about important decisions but also to double-check facts and be diligent with your decision-making.

15 MAY

This is a good time to put plans in motion, especially to do with family and creative projects. Communications are likely to improve after key news arrives.

16 MAY

You're about to begin a more abundant 12-month phase financially, and you may need to first devise a clever budget. A personal matter will deserve attention to avoid arguments.

17 MAY

A proactive approach to your work and activities will be productive, however, you must avoid appearing bossy.

18 MAY

You're on the way to achieving major goals and in the process you may encounter challenges, so be prepared to negotiate.

19 MAY

The Taurus new moon signals a fresh chapter financially and regarding your personal investments. Be positive and practical.

20 MAY

A chatty, light-hearted approach to socialising and friendships, groups and organisations will bring an enjoyable, fun day.

21 MAY

This is an excellent day to make changes in your environment and meet new people. However, you may tend to rush developments or appear intense so avoid arguments.

22 MAY

Creative projects and investing in yourself and those you love will be productive. Just avoid arguments as it's still an intense time.

23 MAY

You have your own opinions about matters and may feel challenged by others to leave your comfort zone. A little flexibility will work wonders; avoid stubbornness.

24 MAY

You're communicating well and will find this a busy or chatty time. Trust your instincts, especially with important communications, as your intuition is spot on.

25 MAY

You are known for your philosophical outlook, and this quality will be useful to break a stalemate in communications that risk upsetting the status quo.

26 MAY

Pleasantly surprising news will boost your feel-good factor, especially in a personal context and financially.

27 MAY

An active, outgoing approach to clearing a backlog of chores will be productive. Be prepared to discuss a thorny topic but avoid being drawn into arguments.

28 MAY

It's a good day for chores and a lovely day to socialise and develop a sense of stability and security through pleasant pastimes.

29 MAY

You'll appreciate the sense of stability and security that certain people and your work offer you and will regain a sense of being grounded.

30 MAY

Be prepared to discuss your ideas and plans with those they concern in a light-hearted and constructive way for the best results.

31 MAY

Look for balance in communications and plan to relax this evening. Someone in your environment may feel sensitive, so avoid taking their moods personally.

June

1 JUNE

You prefer to be more certain of your decisions yet you may feel under pressure to make rash ones, so weigh your options carefully.

2 JUNE

A personal or financial development will be significant and will help you decide longer-term choices.

3 JUNE

You'll feel passionate about your activities. Romance, music and the arts will thrive, so be sure to organise something special.

4 JUNE

The full moon in Sagittarius signals a fresh chapter in your interests and general direction. Research options and turn a corner in a key relationship or with travel. You may experience a surprise.

5 JUNE

It's a good day for a beauty or health treat. Changes in your usual routine are best approached with a calm attitude.

6 JUNE

This is an intense time, so find ways to move ahead in the most practical way possible for the best results.

7 JUNE

An innovative approach to work and your health and well-being will be effective and will help you move on from a stuck situation.

8 JUNE

Someone from your past will prove to be supportive, insightful and helpful, so be sure to touch base.

9 JUNE

A financial matter could move forward but you must avoid overestimating potential outcomes. You'll enjoy a get-together.

10 JUNE

The moon in your sign for the weekend will be a blessing and will provide the opportunity to relax and recoup energy. You'll also enjoy a lovely reunion.

11 JUNE

You'll enjoy reconnecting with someone special and may return to an old haunt. You may need to review your finances.

12 JUNE

A get up and go approach will be productive, so take the initiative. Just avoid assuming everyone is on the same page as you.

13 JUNE

Some delays or uncertainties may inadvertently help you reach your goals, so be sure to work within guidelines and parameters.

14 JUNE

The Taurus moon will bring your values and principles front and centre, helping you be productive, but you must avoid butting heads with someone important.

15 JUNE

You are communicating well so may just need to double-check you're on the same page as someone at work. Avoid overspending.

16 JUNE

An adaptable approach to work, finances and socialising will bring your charming side to the surface and you'll enjoy get-togethers.

17 JUNE

A lovely family get-together or romantic day will raise your spirits. You may plan a return to an old haunt or will need to review your finances.

18 JUNE

Make a wish at the new moon in Gemini, which signals a fresh chapter in your domestic life and, for some, regarding travel and personal arrangements.

19 JUNE

You may be drawn to updating a communications device or vehicle. Consider your budget carefully and avoid making assumptions in your personal life.

20 JUNE

Be prepared to self-nurture and also look after someone who may need a helping hand. If you need advice it will be available.

21 JUNE

It's the solstice, a lovely day of celebration. You may need to choose between commitments, but if you prepare well ahead you may be able to accommodate both social and personal commitments.

22 JUNE

It's a super-productive day; just avoid rushing and cutting corners. It's a good day for a health appointment.

23 JUNE

You'll appreciate a domestic or financial improvement and may enjoy updating decor. It's a good day to boost health and well-being. A meeting or news will be significant.

24 JUNE

This is an excellent day to get on top of chores at home and in your environment. Someone special may wish to help. Just avoid forgetfulness.

25 JUNE

It's a lovely day to dream and enjoy your domestic life. A trip somewhere beautiful will be relaxing but may entail delays. Avoid misunderstandings.

26 JUNE

An unexpected change in your usual routine or surprise news at work or regarding health is best navigated one step at a time. Avoid having knee-jerk reactions.

27 JUNE

You'll appreciate the input of someone special, especially with regard to finances, your home life and/or a planned trip.

28 JUNE

Someone close may feel more emotional than usual. You'll find that a nurturing and supportive approach will work wonders.

29 JUNE

Plan ahead with work and domestic matters as you'll enjoy seeing progress in both these areas. It's a good day for health and beauty appointments.

30 JUNE

There is a therapeutic aspect to the day and you'll enjoy a visit or short trip. It's also a good time to discuss both work and domestic plans.

July

1 JULY

You'll appreciate feeling close to someone you admire and will be drawn to investing in your home and environment. You will enjoy a fun day but you must avoid making rash decisions.

2 JULY

A change of routine is best planned ahead to avoid unwelcome surprises. An investment or personal matter may deserve a review.

3 JULY

The full moon in Capricorn spotlights a fresh chapter regarding your loyalties, either to a friend or organisation. Look for the most secure way ahead.

4 JULY

Consider a fresh perspective at work and towards someone you collaborate with to avoid disagreements.

5 JULY

Trust your intuition and appraisal of current personal and work circumstances and be prepared to alter your approach to someone if necessary.

6 JULY

You're a sensitive character and must avoid taking the random comments of other people personally unless, of course, criticism is merited.

7 JULY

It's a good day to discuss matters and be prepared to listen to someone else's opinion. You will enjoy being creative and a fun get-together.

8 JULY

This is a good day for a health or beauty appointment and for romance and fun activities, so organise something special.

9 JULY

Favourite weekend activities such as sports, self-development and socialising will be attractive but you may also need to relax.

10 JULY

Creative and artistic Pisces will love current circumstances as you'll feel inspired. However, you may also be easily distracted. Romance could blossom.

11 JULY

As Mercury enters Leo you'll feel more expressive and motivated, especially in your personal life and with creative projects.

12 JULY

Your expertise will be in demand as you are seen as someone who always helps out. It's a good day to improve your own energy levels.

13 JULY

You may be tempted to throw caution to the wind, especially in important areas such as work and health. Be prepared to halt that process if necessary.

14 JULY

It may be a hard-working day, so pace yourself. You'll enjoy being spontaneous and will appreciate the company of someone you love.

15 JULY

This is an excellent weekend to put yourself and your needs first and to self-nurture and take time out.

16 JULY

You may be tempted to resume a bad habit but must focus on health and well-being as your priorities.

17 JULY

The Cancer new moon signals a fresh chapter in your personal life or regarding a creative project. Be careful with communications to avoid mix-ups.

18 JULY

The Leo moon for the next two days will produce a busy and upbeat daily routine, so be prepared to focus and avoid rushing.

19 JULY

This is a busy, productive time for you. You'll be seen as efficient and will excel if you also demonstrate your collaborative skills.

20 JULY

You're thinking creatively and imaginatively, which will help you thrive in your creative endeavours. Romance will blossom. Avoid daydreaming and forgetfulness.

21 JULY

You may experience a sense of being under pressure more than usual, so ensure you take breaks.

22 JULY

You'll enjoy a change in your usual routine and may consider deepening some relationships and releasing others. It's a good day for a health or beauty treat.

23 JULY

This will be an active and intense day, so ensure communications are steady and avoid arguments.

24 JULY

Be prepared to review a particular schedule such as a health, work or fitness routine you have outgrown.

25 JULY

Someone close may express their emotions, which will enable you to understand them a little better. It's a good time to review shared duties or finances.

26 JULY

Find ways to channel your energy into productive pursuits as you can achieve a great deal.

27 JULY

You'll receive important news at work or regarding health and well-being. It's a good day for a reunion and to discuss important topics; just ensure you have all the facts.

28 JULY

Developments may make you question some of your loyalties and activities. Avoid perfectionism and being overly analytical.

29 JULY

While you may wish to relax and let the past week go you'll have certain commitments to fulfil, but after those are done you'll enjoy a fun event.

30 JULY

You'll appreciate the uplifting effect of music and the arts and daydreaming a little, so clear space for yourself if possible.

31 JULY

You're seen as being practical, realistic and dedicated, even if this is not how you feel yourself! Be inspired and you will attain your goals.

August

1 AUGUST

The full moon supermoon in Aquarius spells a new chapter in your work or daily health schedule. It's a good day for meetings and talks.

2 AUGUST

Discussions concerning finances, work or shared duties are on the table. Be practical about agreements you make.

3 AUGUST

You may be looking at life with unrealistic expectations or, contrarily, pessimistically, so ensure the commitments you make are realistic.

4 AUGUST

This is an inspired, creative time for you but you may be prone to daydreaming. It's a good day for a health or beauty appointment.

5 AUGUST

You'll be drawn to active and outdoors activities and to engaging with those you love to share fun times with.

6 AUGUST

You have extravagant tastes sometimes, so if you're considering an investment ensure it is realistic and manageable.

7 AUGUST

This is a productive day at work but you must avoid rekindling disagreements. Find ways to collaborate.

8 AUGUST

Although you're known as a dreamer you can be very methodical, and today's stars will encourage you to achieve your goals in practical ways.

9 AUGUST

You may be surprised by an abrupt change of plan or of schedule, so be prepared to be flexible.

10 AUGUST

It's a good day for meetings both at work and socially. You may receive good news, financial in nature for some. A trip may be on the cards.

11 AUGUST

Trust your gut instinct and your communication skills as you can make great progress with your various projects and enjoy fun get-togethers.

12 AUGUST

This is a good day to focus on your health and well-being and for self-development. You may need to help someone, and if you need help it will be available.

13 AUGUST

Romance is in the stars, so organise a date if you haven't already. It's a good day for talks and for beauty and health treats.

14 AUGUST

You'll enjoy a slightly more playful and upbeat approach to life that will enable you to be super productive in many areas.

15 AUGUST

Be prepared to take the initiative at work and with your health and well-being. A business or personal partner has good news.

16 AUGUST

The new moon in Leo signals a fresh phase in your work or health circumstances. News may surprise you. Be prepared to put in extra work to achieve your goals.

17 AUGUST

Talks with an authority figure will prove helpful as they will encourage you to be practical in the way you organise your time and schedule.

18 AUGUST

A business or personal partner's advice, help and collaboration will be invaluable, so be sure to seek collaboration.

19 AUGUST

Clear your schedule so you can find time to relax with someone special. Chores may accumulate but other activities are calling.

20 AUGUST

You'll be drawn to engaging in your favourite pastimes such as the arts and music but will need to attend to certain commitments first.

21 AUGUST

You have obligations to a friend or organisation that may put you under pressure, but rest assured you will succeed.

22 AUGUST

Your values differ to those of someone else, so aim to find common ground if possible. If arguments arise, check you're not seeing life purely idealistically.

23 AUGUST

Key news or developments will provide increased direction, especially regarding a close relationship.

24 AUGUST

Over the coming weeks you'll begin to feel more practical about your responsibilities, especially at work.

25 AUGUST

This is a good time to make changes within a personal or professional relationship, and the help of a friend or organisation will be invaluable.

26 AUGUST

It's a good day to reorganise your daily routine and environment so they suit you better.

27 AUGUST

It's a good day for negotiations and making a commitment to someone close, a financial review or a work and health routine.

28 AUGUST

Be prepared to think outside the square and collaborate with people on exciting projects. A friend or organisation may be particularly helpful.

29 AUGUST

The Aquarian moon will encourage you to gain fresh perspective in a personal or work relationship and to find more balance as a result.

30 AUGUST

The lead-up to the Pisces supermoon may be intense, so take a little extra time for yourself to avoid impulsiveness.

31 AUGUST

The Pisces full moon supermoon spotlights a fresh chapter in your personal life for February Pisces and in your work or health schedule for March Fish.

September

1 SEPTEMBER

Someone close may need a little support and understanding, and if you do be sure to reach out.

2 SEPTEMBER

The Aries moon will bring a sense of pressure and feelings will rush to the surface, so avoid needless bumps and scrapes and find time to relax.

3 SEPTEMBER

Your compassionate, supportive side will be appreciated, especially by a partner or colleague.

4 SEPTEMBER

You may be drawn to reviewing your health, beauty and work schedules so they suit you better. You'll enjoy a reunion and, for some, a financial boost.

5 SEPTEMBER

You may receive positive news from a partner and enjoy a boost at work. It's a good day for self-development and improving your appearance.

6 SEPTEMBER

News from a personal or business partner will be significant. It's a good day to review finances and work schedules.

7 SEPTEMBER

Talks and discussions will be productive, especially in relation to work, health and finances. Romance could blossom.

8 SEPTEMBER

This is a good day for talks, so why not initiate discussions over important topics such as finances?

9 SEPTEMBER

You may experience a compliment or boost in self-esteem. It's a good time to invest in yourself and your home and personal life.

10 SEPTEMBER

An active and upbeat activity will appeal. You'll enjoy socialising but must avoid sensitive topics.

11 SEPTEMBER

A partner, colleague or someone you must collaborate with has important news for you. Avoid impulsiveness.

12 SEPTEMBER

You'll appreciate the feeling that you can steam through your projects and chores and make great headway. You will be drawn to being physically active.

13 SEPTEMBER

This is another productive day although you may tend to be a stickler for details. News regarding a review will catch your attention.

14 SEPTEMBER

This is a good day to consider how you would prefer your daily life and routine to proceed and to begin putting a clever schedule in place.

15 SEPTEMBER

The new moon in Virgo signals a fresh chapter in a personal commitment and at work for some Pisces. Be practical and your plans will succeed.

16 SEPTEMBER

A business or personal partner will have exciting news. This is a good time to put in motion changes you'd like to see in your personal life.

17 SEPTEMBER

Be prepared to look at finances from a new perspective. The same applies to a personal circumstance or area of disagreement.

18 SEPTEMBER

Your dedication to your commitments is appreciated; just avoid becoming overzealous.

19 SEPTEMBER

You'll appreciate someone's attention, but if you find it distracting aim to focus a little harder at work. Avoid making investments without adequate research.

20 SEPTEMBER

Sports, favourite activities and self-development will help calm your mind, especially if you have recently been easily distracted or influenced.

21 SEPTEMBER

This is a good day for romance and for collaborations, so take the initiative and make changes you'd like to see in your life.

22 SEPTEMBER

You will attract attention as you are optimistic and efficient, which will help you reach your goals. It's a good day for a health or beauty boost.

23 SEPTEMBER

The sun in Libra for the next month will encourage you and someone close to actively look for more peace and calmness in your relationship.

24 SEPTEMBER

You are a super-sensitive person and can take other people's rash comments personally. Your support and help may be in demand.

25 SEPTEMBER

It's a good day for constructive talks, especially at work and financially. Just aim to find common ground to avoid arguments.

26 SEPTEMBER

An upbeat approach to collaborations and finding solutions to problems will be effective.

27 SEPTEMBER

The Pisces moon for the next two days will encourage you to be resourceful and work towards ideal outcomes as opposed to looking for problems.

28 SEPTEMBER

The arts, music and romance will appeal. You may be easily distracted, so avoid making unnecessary mistakes.

29 SEPTEMBER

The Aries full moon signals you're ready to turn a corner in a personal relationship or financial commitment, but you must avoid impulsiveness.

30 SEPTEMBER

You may be surprised by news and developments. Be prepared to be spontaneous but avoid making rash decisions.

October

1 OCTOBER

You'll enjoy several get-togethers but you may also feel slightly under pressure, so ensure you leave plenty of time for travel and avoid rushing.

2 OCTOBER

It's an excellent day for honest discussions, especially in your personal life and, for some, at work. You may be drawn to updating your wardrobe.

3 OCTOBER

Double-check your schedule and plans to avoid making mistakes. That aside, this is a good day to make long overdue long-term changes.

4 OCTOBER

The Gemini moon will bring out your chatty, inquisitive self, making this a good time for get-togethers and research.

5 OCTOBER

Be prepared to organise your day because, as a result, things will go much more smoothly. Some communications may be challenging but rest assured: you will attain your goals.

6 OCTOBER

Certain groups and organisations have their set rules, and while you prefer to go about your projects in your own way you may need to stick with their schedule.

7 OCTOBER

You have your set principles, yet if someone challenges these you'll need to maintain an open mind and avoid being stuck in your ways.

8 OCTOBER

This will be a productive day for clearing a backlog of chores and enjoying some relaxation.

9 OCTOBER

You or someone close may be a stickler for rules yet sometimes some give and take is necessary. Avoid conflict, as it will quickly escalate.

10 OCTOBER

This is a good day to come to a new arrangement or review existing agreements, especially at work and regarding your health.

11 OCTOBER

Focus on your health, well-being and peace of mind to gather a sense of purpose within discussions. Avoid taking the opinions of others personally.

12 OCTOBER

There are therapeutic aspects to conversations so you must avoid allowing intense feelings to cloud your judgement.

13 OCTOBER

A practical and reasonable approach towards collaborations will be productive, so take the initiative with specific goals in mind.

14 OCTOBER

The solar eclipse signals you're turning a corner in a shared circumstance. Be prepared to discuss sensitive matters, including finances and health.

15 OCTOBER

Be prepared to look at someone else's viewpoint from a fresh perspective as this may encourage you both to establish common ground.

16 OCTOBER

Strong feelings in you or someone close are likely, but if you channel emotions into constructive pursuits this will be a productive day.

17 OCTOBER

You may be surprised by an unanticipated turn of events or hear from someone from your past unexpectedly.

18 OCTOBER

An adventurous, optimistic approach to your ventures will be successful but you must avoid bruising someone else's ego.

19 OCTOBER

Someone close has news for you. You may enjoy a reunion but you must avoid making assumptions.

20 OCTOBER

It's a good day for discussions, particularly to do with joint efforts and finances. Tension may arise and arguments will be counterproductive.

21 OCTOBER

Some communications will be intense, so take things one step at a time. A social event will merit a tactful approach.

22 OCTOBER

You'll feel motivated to express your deeper feelings, as will someone close. This is a lovely day to make a commitment. Romance will thrive and a change of routine will be enjoyable.

23 OCTOBER

The sun in Scorpio for the next four weeks will bring your passions to the surface, which is ideal for romance although you must avoid arguments.

24 OCTOBER

A work or health circumstance will progress. It's a good day to make a commitment to a person or plan.

25 OCTOBER

The moon in your sign will bring out your artistic, creative, romantic side. Just avoid absentmindedness.

26 OCTOBER

You have your own ideas about the best way forward in your personal life and so does someone close. Look for common ground.

27 OCTOBER

You're methodical, energetic and focused, so even if you feel there's a big day ahead of you rest assured you will attain your goals.

28 OCTOBER

The lunar eclipse in Taurus points to a fresh chapter in your personal life and with an agreement and, for some, financially. Agreements can be made but you must avoid making rash decisions.

29 OCTOBER

Consider news carefully, as you may be inclined to make snap decisions. Fully research large investments.

30 OCTOBER

An upbeat, chatty day may take you outside your usual environment but you'll enjoy entering fresh territory.

31 OCTOBER

Happy Halloween! You'll enjoy the quirky, upbeat atmosphere of the day and may even be surprised or will surprise someone else with your plans.

November

1 NOVEMBER

You'll be drawn to discussing some of your commitments with those they concern and to looking for more nurturance in your daily life.

2 NOVEMBER

Your family, a friend or domestic situation will catch your eye. You may look for ways to invest more in your home or family.

3 NOVEMBER

This is potentially a romantic day. You'll certainly appreciate the arts, music and dance; however, a personal or financial matter will need your focus.

4 NOVEMBER

You may be surprised by developments and will need an adaptable attitude to the day's plans. Avoid impulse buys.

5 NOVEMBER

This is a passionate, romantic time. A little tension will deepen ties, but major stress is a passion killer. Avoid taking other people's behaviour personally.

6 NOVEMBER

You'll enjoy socialising and networking, and if you'd like to deepen your relationship with someone this is the day to do it!

7 NOVEMBER

You're communicating intuitively at the moment, which is different from most people's approach so avoid making assumptions. It's a good day for romance.

8 NOVEMBER

A business or personal partner will be looking for more balance and fair play in your relationship. This is a good day to make agreements, even if they are challenging.

9 NOVEMBER

A social or networking event will be transformative. Avoid taking other people's comments personally. If you need expert advice it will be available.

10 NOVEMBER

Certain communications will require you to be brave. Avoid doubting your abilities, as you can attain your goals.

11 NOVEMBER

Be spontaneous, as an unexpected invitation or development will require you to be on your toes. If you're shopping, avoid impulse buys.

12 NOVEMBER

It's a good time to plan ahead and find out your partner's or family's agenda and set the ball rolling.

13 NOVEMBER

The Scorpio new moon signals a fresh chapter in shared concerns such as joint finances and duties. You may be surprised by news and a trip will take you somewhere different.

14 NOVEMBER

Travel plans and favourite hobbies and pastimes will attract your attention. It's a good time to plan ahead for holidays.

15 NOVEMBER

Work meetings are likely to be successful. It's a good time to discuss shared finances and for a trip.

16 NOVEMBER

You have wonderful plans you'd like to engage in, however, you must be realistic, especially financially. Where there's a will there's a way.

17 NOVEMBER

You love to share your good fortune with others and will gain the opportunity to do so. The arts and music will appeal. Romance can truly blossom, so organise a date.

18 NOVEMBER

You'll appreciate spending quality time with someone you love; just avoid sensitive topics. If you're making a large investment ensure you research it first.

19 NOVEMBER

You'll appreciate the opportunity to improve your personal relationships and will also enjoy socialising.

20 NOVEMBER

Work and social get-togethers will gain their own momentum. It's a good time to deepen your friendships.

21 NOVEMBER

The moon in Pisces will bring out your sensitivity, so maintain a positive outlook. There are therapeutic qualities to your activities such as sports.

22 NOVEMBER

Someone close has news, and you may need to discuss sensitive topics with them.

23 NOVEMBER

It's a good day to get chores done but you must avoid cutting corners and arguments as they will become a Mexican stand-off.

24 NOVEMBER

You're a determined and diligent character, and when you set your sights on goals nothing will deter you. Ensure you keep people in the loop.

25 NOVEMBER

Lovely activities such as sports or self-development will appeal. There will be rules to follow that may be frustrating but they will provide a solid platform.

26 NOVEMBER

Someone may alter their plans at a moment's notice and you may be surprised by their opinions. Be adaptable but stick to your values.

27 NOVEMBER

The Gemini full moon suggests you're turning a corner in your values, principles and finances. Be extra clear to avoid misunderstandings.

28 NOVEMBER

It's a great day to discuss your travel and personal plans with those they concern. You'll enjoy a chat or get-together.

29 NOVEMBER

You have set yourself a high benchmark but rest assured you can reach it despite some obstacles.

30 NOVEMBER

Meetings are likely to go well. It's a lovely day for sports, your favourite activities, travel and socialising so take the initiative.

December

1 DECEMBER

Good communication skills are key to your success, so be brave and outgoing but stick with the facts and figures.

2 DECEMBER

You may receive beneficial news at work. It's a good weekend to plan travel and for get-togethers.

3 DECEMBER

Double-check you're on the same page as someone close and be prepared to re-establish common ground if you're not.

4 DECEMBER

You'll feel increasingly passionate about your opinions and values so you must avoid conflict and look for healthy ways to collaborate.

5 DECEMBER

Work meetings will be productive. You may enjoy a reunion or return to an old haunt. It's a good day to make a commitment.

6 DECEMBER

You'll see the other side of the coin a little more clearly in an ongoing disagreement with someone.

7 DECEMBER

You may need to be a mediator for someone else's arguments, so brush up on your relationship skills to show what you're capable of.

8 DECEMBER

You'll enjoy the therapeutic aspects of the day. A trip or get-together will have a healing quality, and you may hear positive news at work or financially.

9 DECEMBER

An enjoyable pastime will be motivational. If you're planning an emotional or financial investment ensure you have all the facts.

10 DECEMBER

Financial or personal matters will deserve careful appraisal. You may need to review your budget. Romance can flourish.

11 DECEMBER

This is a good time to boost your career and status, so be prepared to reach out to collaborators and employers to improve your circumstances.

12 DECEMBER

The Sagittarian new moon signals a fresh chapter in a favourite activity. You may be drawn to travelling or study. Ensure you do your research to avoid an unnecessary surprise.

13 DECEMBER

Try to get key paperwork and discussions completed now, especially regarding work and your status, to avoid having to review agreements over the coming weeks.

14 DECEMBER

A practical yet adventurous approach to your career and activities will reap rewards.

15 DECEMBER

There are therapeutic aspects to your activities. You'll appreciate the opportunity to indulge in favourite activities such as sports and self-development.

16 DECEMBER

The moon in Aquarius will encourage you to leave your comfort zone socially and you may meet an interesting circle of people.

17 DECEMBER

Be prepared to see things from another person's point of view but avoid taking their opinions personally. You may be forgetful, so avoid making major decisions if possible.

18 DECEMBER

It's a good day for a return to an old haunt and for reunions and meetings.

19 DECEMBER

Trust your instincts and avoid being easily misled. You are creative and imaginative, so artistic work will flourish.

20 DECEMBER

Be positive about your projects and plans as you'll enjoy feeling freer and more spontaneous. A trip will be enjoyable.

21 DECEMBER

A change in your usual routine or at work will be productive. You may receive unexpected news or bump into an old friend. Avoid feeling frustrated by delays and be patient.

22 DECEMBER

A reunion and social event will be enjoyable. You may need to review a work plan. A trip to an old haunt will be enjoyable even if there are delays.

23 DECEMBER

A change of plan or the need to accommodate someone else's plans needn't dampen your spirits. You'll enjoy the chance to slow down.

24 DECEMBER

A lovely reunion will boost your feel-good factor and status and you'll appreciate a sense of security and stability.

25 DECEMBER

Merry Christmas! You'll appreciate all the romance and trimmings of this celebratory day, including music and festive treats.

26 DECEMBER

A trip or get-together will be enjoyable; you'll appreciate spending time together.

27 DECEMBER

The Cancer full moon signals a fresh chapter in your domestic or family life. You may turn a corner with a creative project and some activities such as travel may be delayed. Avoid mix-ups.

28 DECEMBER

You'll be drawn to a familiar place or to reuniting with someone from the past. Avoid misunderstandings and making assumptions.

29 DECEMBER

You'll appreciate the opportunity to dream a little and indulge in romance, the arts and music. You will deepen certain relationships.

30 DECEMBER

You'll appreciate the generally festive feeling that builds towards New Year's Eve and will enjoy being outgoing.

31 DECEMBER

Happy New Year! This New Year's Eve has a momentum of its own, although you'll also enjoy planning special events.